Praise for Collaborative Product Design

"Collaboration is the key to successful product design work. Good collaboration makes it possible to succeed against long odds. Bad collaboration will break any method, tool, or technique. Austin gets that, and has created a practical and non-dogmatic guide that will help you understand the elements of collaboration, and hopefully, design great collaborations of your own."

JOSH SEIDEN, COAUTHOR OF *LEAN UX*

"Austin has a knack for simplifying the most complex concepts and practices. His book is a welcome addition to my product design canon."

**JEFF PATTON, PRODUCT DESIGN COACH
AND AUTHOR OF *USER STORY MAPPING***

Collaborative Product Design

Help Any Team Build a Better Experience

Austin Govella

Beijing · Boston · Farnham · Sebastopol · Tokyo

Collaborative Product Design
by Austin Govella

Published by O'Reilly Media, Inc., 1005 Gravenstein Highway North, Sebastopol, CA 95472.

O'Reilly books may be purchased for educational, business, or sales promotional use. Online editions are also available for most titles (*http://oreilly.com*). For more information, contact our corporate/institutional sales department: (800) 998-9938 or *corporate@oreilly.com*.

Acquisitions Editor: Jennifer Pollock
Developmental Editor: Angela Rufino
Production Editor: Kristen Brown
Copyeditor: Jasmine Kwityn
Proofreader: Rachel Monaghan
Indexer: Lucie Haskins

Cover Designer: Karen Montgomery
Interior Designers: Ron Bilodeau and Monica Kamsvaag
Illustrators: Jose Marzan and Rebecca Demarest
Compositor: Kristen Brown

May 2019: First Edition.

Revision History for the First Edition:

2019-04-29   First release

See *http://oreilly.com/catalog/errata.csp?isbn=0636920057895* for release details.

978-1-491-97503-9

[TI]

[*contents*]

[*Preface*]

THIS IS THE LAST book you'll ever need only if something tragic happens to you in the next 24 hours.

This book probably isn't for you. Your coworkers recognize brilliance. They follow your recommendations without any fuss, give you plenty of time to think about...*whatever*. You never rush to complete anything. You never start over or change direction, and your boss never changes their mind or asks for anything crazy.

I wish I had a gig like that.

I work on cross-functional teams where people from business, technology, and design mill about and barely speak the same language with less and less time to do more and more. It doesn't matter how close we get because the direction always changes, and the deadline never moves.

FIGURE P-1

Some poor schlubs work across silos, or—even worse—on cross-functional teams where business, technology, and design have to work together

I wrote this book for poor schlubs who schlep ideas across silos to get things built with ridiculous deadlines (Figure P-1). This isn't a process book. It's a get things done book. For people who work on teams. Teams get things done when they work better together.

This book isn't full of new things. It's full of boring, old things. No new process to guarantee good results. No secrets to success. You don't need new. Don't change *what* you do. Change *how* you do it. This book collects tools that seed a new way to work that helps teams communicate, collaborate, and prioritize their work. Your team will build better products, and you'll help them do it.

Tried, Tested, and Reviewed by the Real World

These tools evolved over 20 years where I led cross-functional teams on all kinds of projects for all kinds of industries.

Many of these tools began their genesis at Comcast, where I developed new products and redesigned flagship consumer products for Livia Labate. After Comcast, these tools continued to evolve at Avanade, where Matt Hulbert and Jamie Hunt let me test and refine them with scores of clients for B2B and B2C products across different industries and around the world.

To ensure these tools passed muster, we asked Andrew Hinton, Christian Crumlish, and James Kalbach to review everything for accuracy and clarity. To make sure everything made sense for beginners, we reached out to Kat King and Eden Robbins, both in the early stages of their careers. Dan Klyn, Adam Polansky, and Dan Brown provided invaluable early feedback. Finally, we asked Jessica Harllee to review everything because she doesn't put up with anyone's nonsense, and we didn't want you to either.

Organized So You Learn How You Learn Best

This book has five main parts—none of which include buzzwords like empathy, agile, lean, or AnythingOps. Instead, Part I lays the foundation for everything else with how to think about products and improve team collaboration. Then, we grouped everything else around the types of questions and problems that face product teams:

- Goals and vision—How do you get everyone to agree on and align around project strategy and what you're trying to do?

- Users—How do you define what your users need you to build now versus later?

- Interactions—How do you improve how users move into, out of, and through your systems?

- Interfaces—How do you explore ideas and prototype interfaces, so you test ideas the fastest, easiest way possible?

Each part begins with a foundation chapter with basic information. Then each tool has its own chapter that describes how to use it and offers tips and tricks (Figure P-2).

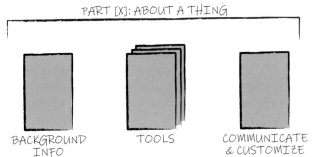

PART [X]: ABOUT A THING

BACKGROUND INFO   TOOLS   COMMUNICATE & CUSTOMIZE

FIGURE P-2
Each part includes chapters with background info, instructions for each tool, and a guide on how to customize the tool for the job

Organized this way, choose how you read the book to learn how you learn best (Table P-1). Read the book from start to finish, all 21 chapters, or start with the basics and read only the nine foundation chapters. You can also start with a specific topic based on your current interests or needs.

TABLE P-1. Read the book the way you learn best

THE HERO'S QUEST 21 CHAPTERS, 380 PAGES	FOUNDATIONS FIRST 9 CHAPTERS, 110 PAGES	TOPIC FIRST ~5 CHAPTERS, 60 PAGES
Read from start to finish and learn how to work better at every step of the product design process.	Read the foundation material in Part I and then each of the following chapters. Part I: Design and Collaboration (all four chapters) Chapter 5: The Strategic Landscape Chapter 9: Elements of Users and User Research Chapter 14: Elements of Interactions Chapter 17: The Visible and Invisible Parts of an Interface Chapter 21: Checks (and Balances)	Consume a specific topic based on your current needs or interests. Part I: Design and Collaboration, four chapters Part II: Project Strategy, four chapters Part III: Users, five chapters Part IV: Interactions, three chapters Part V: Interfaces, five chapters
Takes more time	Takes less time	Takes the least time

That flexibility is kind of the theme of this book. Things are different for different teams on different projects in different organizations, so the real skill is knowing how to adjust what you do, so it works better for you in your current circumstances.

Designed as an Easy-to-Use Reference

After the main ideas have sunk in, the real usefulness comes when you reference the book later, so we've tried to make it as easy as possible to find things. Whether you're looking for a tool, checklist, or specific how-to information.

Headings are explicit and banal, so you can scan the table of contents and find very specific parts of the book (Figure P-3).

FIGURE P-3
Clear headings make it easy to find specific information in the table of
contents

Once you've chosen a tool, we've made it easy to grab and use. Each tool
includes a link to templates, worksheets, and even presentation slides
you can download and print or even edit and customize. And if you collaborate remotely, we've included direct links to online templates you
can grab and use.

Find further reading and resources on the website:

http://pxd.gd/index/methods

Linked to the Broader Community

Imagine if zombies rise and civilization falls. There'd be no internet for
reading Medium articles. Even though we want this book to survive on
its own, it really isn't the last book you'll ever need.

In each part, you'll find links to the companion website where we've
collected books and articles for further reading. And because it's on the
web, we can update recommendations as new material appears or ages.

And if you need help, post a question to the Twitter handle, @austingovella,
and we can continue the conversation.

Better Organizations Build Better Products

Organizations—not designers—design and build everything. To build better products, you have to work better together. You need better teams and better organizations. This means you need to improve the skills of everyone in the group. The secret is: what you do doesn't change. How you do it changes. Change how you work, so you focus on helping your team build better products.

Although this book covers an array of tools just waiting for you to take advantage of, collaboration holds teams back the most. Better collaboration lays the foundation for everything else you do with your team, and that's where Part I starts. How can we help teams work better, together?

[*I*]

Design and Collaboration

YOUR ORGANIZATION CREATES PRODUCTS and services, but it can make better products and services, and you're going to help them. In this book, you won't find a new way to design. This book isn't about changing what you do. It's about taking what you already do and changing how you do it, about working better together with your team, your stakeholders, and your clients.

Think of your organization as an experience machine (Figure I-1). Ideas go in, everyone does their part, and an experience comes out. Imagine you work for a coffee company. Someone has the idea to sell coffee in stores across the country. So, everyone does their part, and in cities and towns across the country, customers can walk into coffee shops. That coffee company is a machine for making coffee-related experiences.

FIGURE I-1

Your organization is a user experience factory. Ideas go in, everybody does their part, and a user experience comes out the end.

Every experience made by every organization is made up of countless products and services. Although you can help your organization build different products and services, it's easier to improve what your organization already builds.

To improve these experiences, you need a set of tools you can use to tweak different parts of the experience machine, and that's what you'll find here. Each part of the book focuses on tools for different parts of the machine. Each part begins with a short introduction—like this one—that explains what that part focuses on and what you'll learn from each chapter. In addition to these tools, you also learn how and why the tools work.

This part describes an improved way to think about design and collaboration, so you can help your organization build better experiences. Instead of changing what you do, change how you do it.

The Elements of Design: Think-Make-Check and the Four Models

To HELP YOUR TEAM build better products, they have to design better. Often, when we think about better design, we focus on the things we design. Do they work better, look better, feel better? Unfortunately, those design outcomes aren't what designers *do*.

In this chapter, we'll look at two foundation concepts:

- What you do when you design: Think-Make-Check

- What you do it to: users, interfaces, interactions, and systems—design's four models

These two concepts form the foundation for everything else in this book and help your team communicate and collaborate better when they build new products.

Think, Make, Check: What Designers Do

Let's say you design a fancy coffee mug with a new kind of handle,[1] and want to know if the new handle is easy to use. Is it better to ask people if it's easy to use? Or is it better to watch and see if they have any trouble?

---

1 3D coffee cup design by Bernat Cuni (*http://cunicode.com*)

3

Of course, it's better to watch what people do than it is to ask them. When you watch people, you see what they do. When you ask them, you hear what they hope to do. Watching people reveals their behavior. Behavior is what you want to affect.

If you *ask* a designer what they do, they talk about user experience or being user-centered or representing the user or empathy or whatever. That's what they *say* they do, what they aspire to. If you watch a designer, what do they really do? Designers think about things, make things, and show things to other people.

If you want to improve as a designer, improve how you think about things, make things, and show things to other people.

LEAN UX AND THINK-MAKE-CHECK

Sometime around 2010, Janice Fraser wanted to bring better user experience to startups that didn't have the budget or the time to do traditional design. Janice sketched a stripped-down, "lean" user experience process with three steps. First you think, then you make, then you check (Figure 1-1). After you check, you start over and think, make, check again. And again. Think-Make-Check.

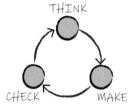

FIGURE 1-1

Janice Fraser's lean UX process has three steps: first you think, then you make, and then you check

Think-Make-Check isn't *lean user experience*. Think-Make-Check is just *user experience*.[2] Janice learned Think-Make-Check from one of her partners at Adaptive Path[3] in early 2001. By Janice's recollection, Think-Make-Check actually originated sometime in the late 1990s in HotWired's[4] user research lab.

---

2   If you're interested in Lean UX, grab Jeff Gothelf and Josh Seiden's book, *Lean UX*.

3   Adaptive Path, one of the first user experience consultancies, was co-founded by Lane Becker, Janice Fraser, Jesse James Garrett, Mike Kuniavsky, Peter Merholz, Jeffrey Veen, and Indi Young.

4   *HotWired*, the first commercial web magazine, launched on October 27, 1994.

Think-Make-Check frames design as a process of analysis and testing. You don't need to do "lean UX" to Think-Make-Check. All designers Think-Make-Check whether they know it or not. Even you.

THINK-MAKE-CHECK IN PRACTICE

Imagine you create a persona. You can divide the work into three steps (Figure 1-2):

1. Analyze existing user research.

2. Draft a persona document.

3. Share the persona with your client.

First you *think* about the users, then you *make* a persona, and then you *check* it with your client. Think-Make-Check.

ANALYZE USER RESEARCH
THINK

DRAFT PERSONA DOCUMENT
MAKE

SHARE WITH CLIENT
CHECK

FIGURE 1-2
You use the Think-Make-Check process when you create personas

Every design activity fits the Think-Make-Check model. Making wireframes? Think about the user's context and what they need to do, draft a wireframe, and show it to the developer. Developing strategy? Think about the landscape, draft goals and vision, check it with the client. It's Think-Make-Check all the way through (Figure 1-3).

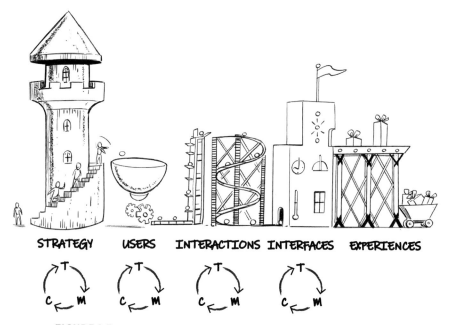

STRATEGY   USERS   INTERACTIONS   INTERFACES   EXPERIENCES

FIGURE 1-3

Think-Make-Check runs all the way through the experience machine

If designers think, make, check all the time, you might ask: what do designers think, make, and check?

Design's Four Concerns: Users, Interfaces, Interactions, and Systems

You can divide what designers Think-Make-Check into four topics:

- The User
- The Interface
- The Interaction
- The System

Every design activity you do and every deliverable you make combines and communicates users, interfaces, interactions, or systems. Every time you Think-Make-Check, you think, make, and check one or more of these four *models*. To create more effective personas, journeys, and wireframes, you need to understand what we mean by users, interfaces, interactions, and systems.

THE USER

USER

Every product has users. You might call them customers, end users, actors, influencers, stakeholders, whatever. Design creates things people will experience, use, or get annoyed with. It's not just designers that think about users. When you start a new project, everyone on the team pictures the user in their head.

Personas represent a *model* of your user. They are not real users. Real users click around and curse and search and do things. A persona gives your brain a model of a user to think about while you build the experience. Whether or not you actually create a persona, user models pop up in every wireframe or prototype you make.

Every wireframe and prototype assumes a certain type of person will use it. Whether or not you describe a persona or talk about a user, your team imagines who the user is when they see the design. Your team imagines a model of the user even when you don't specify one.

The user is the most critical thing that you Think-Make-Check. When you think about the user wrong, you build products for the wrong user.

THE INTERFACE

INTERFACE

How many times has someone asked you to make a wireframe? When most people think about design, they think about what it looks like. They think about the interface.[5] When you Think-Make-Check designs, you probably review a picture of some kind of interface.

As a designer, you spend a good portion of your time thinking about and making *models* of interfaces. Architects draft blueprints. Graphic designers create mockups. Interaction designers code prototypes. Most tutorials and how-tos you see on the web focus on how you can better Think-Make-Check models of interfaces. Interface models are the easiest way for people to talk about a design because they're so concrete.

THE INTERACTION

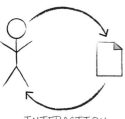

INTERACTION

The interaction refers to how users *interact* with an interface over time. Like users, interactions are always there. When you talk about a wireframe, you imagine how a user will see it, then click on something, then see something else. A wireframe seems like it captures a single screen at a single moment in time, but, in your head, you imagine a series of interactions between the user and several screens.

You think in scenes, not screens. Even though we spend much of our time on interfaces, interactions do a better job of describing the entire experience. Keeping the interaction in mind makes it easier to Think-Make-Check interfaces.

---

5   Of course, we should all memorize Steve Jobs: "Design is not just what it looks like and feels like. Design is how it works."

THE SYSTEM

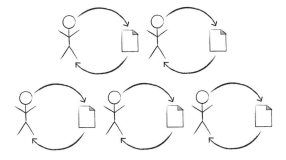

SYSTEM

When a *user* engages with an *interface*, we call that an *interaction*. When you connect several interactions together, you create a *system*. Sitemaps, journey maps, and service blueprints illustrate *systems*. Although you don't always work at the system level, when you create a visual mockup or design a slick check-out process, you have an idea of the system in your head.

Though we don't often think about the system, the system creates constraints and opportunities around our products. Architect Eliel Saarinen said: "Always design a thing by considering it in its next larger context—a chair in a room, a room in a house, a house in an environment."[6] Truthfully, you will find it impossible to ever design without thinking about the broader context. Whenever you Think-Make-Check any design, you have a picture of the system in your head.

THE FOUR MODELS IN PRACTICE

As an example, let's say you create a customer journey map. The journey map illustrates how a user moves into, through, and out of your system. The journey map documents models you and your team have made about the user and their interactions with some interfaces (Figure 1-4):

- The journey map assumes a specific type of user (i.e., your customer)

---

6   Hepler, Donald and Paul Wallach. Architecture Drafting and Design. New York: McGraw-Hill Inc, 1965, pg. 418.

- The journey map assumes specific types of interfaces (i.e., your website, Google search results, confirmation emails, etc.)

- The journey map assumes specific processes (i.e., how a user searches for and compares products, how a user completes the check-out process, etc.)

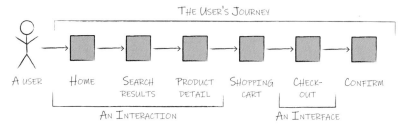

FIGURE 1-4

The journey illustrates assumptions you've made about the user, the interfaces, and the user's interactions with those interfaces

When you share the journey map with your team, you check that everyone has the same picture in their head for how the user will move through the system. You check that everyone has the same model. When you Think-Make-Check your model of the system, everyone on the team imagines who the user is, what the interfaces look like, and how many screens and clicks are involved in each of the interactions.

In product design, you spend your days Thinking, Making, and Checking models of users, interfaces, interactions, and systems. To build better products, you have to get better at two things:

- How you think, make, and check

- Knowing what model to think, make, or check

Each part of this book focuses on a different kind of model, and the tools help you improve how you think, make, and check by yourself or with your team.

Think-Make-Check should be easy, but I'm not sure you noticed: there are a million ways to make the different models. What makes the right persona? Should you make wireframes or prototypes or neither? What elements should appear in a journey map?

This reveals the fundamental question: How do we know what information should go into our models? What information should we include in our personas, wireframes, or journey maps, so we can check them with the right people?

When we talk about what information to include in a model, we're talking about fidelity.

[2]

Fidelity: Check the Right Things with the Right People

NOT EVERY PERSONA OR wireframe or prototype or journey map looks the same. Why is that? Turns out, you can describe differences between one deliverable and the next with *fidelity*.

When your model looks *more like the real thing*, we say it has *more fidelity*. Things with more fidelity take more time to make. Things with less fidelity are more difficult for your teammates to check.

Four factors affect how much fidelity appears in your models:

- Audience—Who will check your model?

- Distance—Are you co-located or remote?

- Time—Are you communicating same-time or staggered?

- Reach—How much will the model be shared with others?

To make and check the right things, you adjust their fidelity.

Fidelity Changes What's Included in the Model

Imagine you take a photo of yourself in the mirror. The photo looks just like you. It's a high-fidelity *model* of you. Now, imagine you draw yourself as a stick figure. That stick figure is a low-fidelity model of what you look like (Figure 2-1).

FIGURE 2-1

When your model looks more like the real thing, we say it has more fidelity.[1]

When you Make a model, you choose how much information to include. How you Think about the model limits the information you have available. The feedback you want from a Check requires different kinds of fidelity. A model is like a signal fire. The bigger the fire, the farther away you can see it, but you're limited by how much wood you have to burn (Figure 2-2).

FIGURE 2-2

Fidelity is limited by how much you know about the thing. At the same time, you need more fidelity to share things with people.

---

1   Illustration by Christina Wodtke after Scott McCloud

When you understand how to control fidelity, you focus effort where it's most effective. Don't add color to a wireframe if you only need to discuss layout. Focus on the important information. Ignore the unimportant information. Since you Make things so you can Check them, optimize fidelity for the audience who will do the checking.

AUDIENCE DETERMINES FIDELITY

Design is always a hypothesis. Your team's vision is your shared hypothesis. When you Think-Make-Check something, you check your hypothesis. The question is: Who evaluates the hypothesis? When you Think-Make-Check, who does the Check?

Four possible audiences can Check your models (Figure 2-3):

- You, yourself

- Your team

- Your organization and partners

- Your users

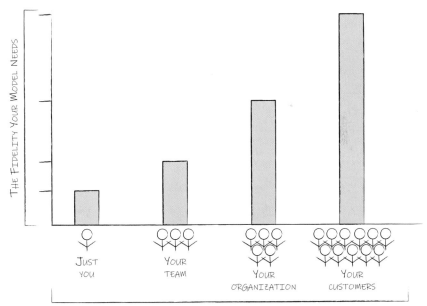

FIGURE 2-3

Four audiences can Check your models: yourself, your team, your organization, and your users, and each audience needs more fidelity as they get farther away from you.

Do you ever jot something down, lean back, tilt your head, and think about your idea? That's you Thinking about something, Making something by writing it down, and Checking it with yourself. You know yourself pretty well, so you can keep the fidelity pretty low. A few scribbles and you still know what you meant.

Your team is the second audience who can Check a hypothesis. After your team, other people in your organization and end users represent the third and fourth audiences who can Check your hypothesis.

Imagine each audience as being farther and farther away from you, and the farther away, the less you speak with them, so the less the audience knows. When you Check something with yourself, you can include a lot less information since you know where you're coming from. In the same way, you and your team speak a lot and share a lot of assumptions about your users, the interfaces they'll use, and their interactions over time.

However, when it comes to other people in your company, they're even farther away from the project. They won't have the same assumptions about the users, interfaces, and interactions. In general, the farther away the audience, the less vision they share, and the more context they need before they can Check your hypothesis. The farther away the audience, the more fidelity you need in your model.

Imagine you and your team wireframe a homepage for an international coffee company with a carousel at the top.

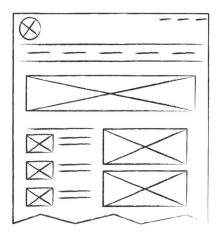

On paper, the carousel looks like an image. You and your team understand the image represents a slide show and that different slides can appear. If you seal the wireframe in an envelope and mail it to your CEO, though, will they understand the image is a carousel? When you and your team combine the wireframe with your shared understanding, you understand the image is a carousel. Your CEO, who is farther away from the project, may not share that same understanding. The wireframe does not have enough information, or fidelity, for the CEO to Check your hypothesis about the carousel.

Fidelity is tied to how far away your audience is from the project. Based on your audience and the hypothesis you want to test, you share models at higher or lower fidelity. Although distance from the audience and amount of vision you share affects fidelity, other aspects about your audience also have an impact. Specifically, what communication channel will you use? How will you share with the audience?

COMMUNICATION CHANNEL AFFECTS FIDELITY

It's easy to understand you need different fidelity based on what the audience knows. However, whenever we Check something with an audience, we communicate in a *channel*, and the channel also affects fidelity. Is this a conversation, an email, a delivered document? Three elements affect fidelity in the communication channel:

- Distance
- Time
- Reach

Distance—co-located or remote

When you Check something with someone, are you talking to someone next to you? Or, are you communicating with someone far away? The farther apart, the harder it is to communicate and collaborate. If you're co-located, you can stick sketches on a wall. If everyone is remote, you have to take pictures and upload them somewhere. If you're remote, quick questions have to come through IM, email, or phone calls. If you're co-located, you can pop your head over the cube wall and ask a quick question. With tone of voice, body language, and gestures, in-person conversations have more fidelity than remote conversations.

Time—synchronous or asynchronous

Are you communicating in real time, synchronously, like a back-and-forth conversation, or are you communicating asynchronously, like an email correspondence? Or, is it a combination, like an IM conversation you both leave and come back to?

When you speak synchronously, you share and discuss large volumes of information as part of the back-and-forth of normal conversation. Any gaps between your understanding and your audience's—any gaps in the vision you share—can be managed through conversation. If you don't understand something, you ask a question. If someone misunderstands you, you can explain it again.

When you communicate asynchronously, it takes longer to fix the understanding gap. Just like with physical distance, the farther apart you are in time, the more difficult it is to get answers to follow-up questions or work through misunderstandings. Synchronous conversations have more fidelity than asynchronous conversations (Figure 2-4).

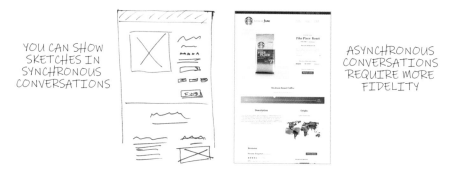

YOU CAN SHOW SKETCHES IN SYNCHRONOUS CONVERSATIONS

ASYNCHRONOUS CONVERSATIONS REQUIRE MORE FIDELITY

FIGURE 2-4
Asynchronous conversations need more fidelity than synchronous conversations.

It's important to note that asynchronous communication doesn't just happen when you talk with other people. We often Make things so the team can remember their decisions. Three months from now, you might not remember whether a link goes to a new page or opens a lightbox. A documented design allows you to have a time-shifted conversation with yourself.

Reach—shared or not shared

The communication channel's third facet is reach: how far will your audience share whatever it is you're Checking? This is the CEO effect.

Several years ago, a sales manager and I spent a good bit of time designing a Facebook application. We had a shared understanding. After I shared mockups with the sales manager, he forwarded the mockups to the CEO to review. With almost no information about the Facebook application, the CEO rejected many elements in the design.

Luckily, the sales manager replied with our rationale, and the CEO could check the design with the right information. Imagine if that conversation hadn't gone well? What if the CEO had already made up their mind? We would have wasted all of that time.

When your boss asks for that whiteboard sketch and sends it to their boss, who shows it to someone else, who doesn't understand what they see and complains to the CEO, who emails to veto the design, that whiteboard sketch had a lot of *reach*.

As with distance and time, if you won't be around to explain your model to whoever sees it, you need to add your explanation into the model itself. If the Facebook application mockups had included some explanation, the CEO may not have freaked out. If you can't be present to provide context, your model will need the additional fidelity of further information, so it can speak for you (Figure 2-5).

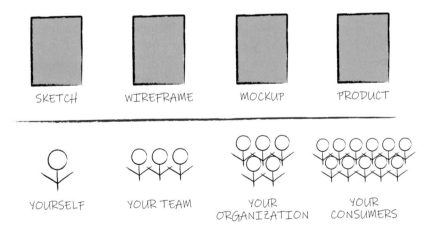

FIGURE 2-5
Based on how far your model may travel, you may need additional fidelity.

FIDELITY, AUDIENCE, AND CHANNEL IN PRACTICE

When you Make something, you need enough fidelity to Check your hypothesis. And the fidelity must be appropriate for the audience and adjusted for the communication channel.

Let's compare common communication channels to see how fidelity, audience, and channel work in practice. In each of the following examples, I assign a number from 1 to 3 to represent how much fidelity your model needs (1 for low fidelity and 3 for more fidelity). Then, for each example, we'll adjust that fidelity based on the audience and channel.

Example 1: A sketch you check with yourself

Let's start with an easy example: a rough wireframe you want to check with yourself. Since you are checking with yourself right now, you don't need to adjust the fidelity at all. You can Check low fidelity models with yourself. Just sketch it, lean back, and review (Table 2-1).

TABLE 2-1. A quick sketch you check with yourself can have a low fidelity

HYPOTHESIS	Is the layout OK?	
AUDIENCE	Only you	1 – low
DISTANCE	Co-located, not remote	1 – low
TIME	Synchronous	1 – low
REACH	Won't be shared	1 – low

Example 2: A sketch you check with a teammate

Imagine you bump into a teammate in the hallway and show them the same sketch. Since you're checking the wireframe with a teammate, the sketch by itself probably won't be enough, so you add some verbal explanation. But you don't need much, since you're both on the same team, and they have some idea about what you're working on. You need a little more fidelity to Check a model with someone else (Table 2-2).

TABLE 2-2. To Check the same sketch with someone on your team, you need a little more fidelity

HYPOTHESIS	Is the layout OK?	
AUDIENCE	Someone on your team	2 – medium
DISTANCE	Co-located, not remote	1 – low
TIME	Synchronous	1 – low
REACH	Shared with your team member	2 – medium

Example 3: A screen you share with a future developer

Let's imagine you show the same screen six months from now to a new developer, and you won't be around to explain in person. Because it's being developed, a sketch isn't enough. You need some explanation about what happens when you click things and what things look like, so the developer can write the HTML and CSS (Table 2-3).

TABLE 2-3. A detailed wireframe you share with the developer has a really high fidelity

HYPOTHESIS	Is the content, functionality, layout, and design OK?	
AUDIENCE	Someone on your team	2 – medium
DISTANCE	Co-located, not remote	1 – low
TIME	Asynchronous	3 – high
REACH	Can be shared with anyone	3 – high

Even though we used fake numbers to illustrate fidelity, you can see how different situations require models to include more or less information. Next time you hear someone talk about wireframes versus sketches or prototypes versus specs, ask yourself what the team is trying to do:

- Who is the audience?

- What is the channel?

- What information does the audience need to answer the question?

The Model's Fidelity Affects Iteration

At the right fidelity, you include the right information, so your audience can Check your hypothesis. Every time you Check something, you learn something and use those learnings to improve the next version. Each turn through the Think-Make-Check loop refines your idea. Each turn is another iteration (Figure 2-6).

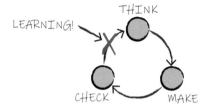

FIGURE 2-6

Think-Make-Check is a learning process.

Design is not a process for creating interfaces or products. Design is a learning process. As a designer, run through the Think-Make-Check loop over and over again to learn how to improve the experience.

THINK-MAKE-CHECK THE THINGS YOU WANT TO LEARN

When your model has the right fidelity, you Think-Make-Check the right thing with the right audience to learn the right thing. You collaborate on more valuable conversations and spend less time on less valuable conversations. If you Think-Make-Check the wrong thing, you waste the iteration.

Usually, the faster you learn, the faster you improve the experience. The more fidelity in your model, the more time it takes to Make. More time to Make reduces how fast you learn. When you Make things with just enough fidelity, and no more, you optimize your learning. Both agile development and lean startups use quick iterations to accelerate learning. Agile teams check their work after short sprints. Lean startups build minimum viable products (MVPs) to check with customers and iterate as quickly as possible.

You also want to learn the *right* things. While lower fidelity allows faster iteration, it limits what you can learn. Higher fidelity models provide the opportunity for higher fidelity, higher quality, more accurate learning. Nothing teaches more than real customers using a real product (Figure 2-7).

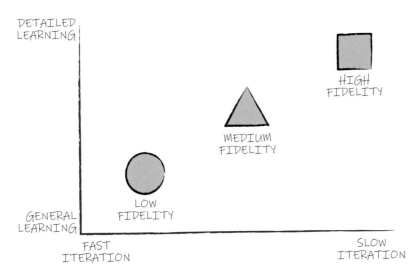

FIGURE 2-7
Different types of fidelity afford different iteration speeds and provide different quality learnings.

For each of the four models—users, interfaces, interactions, and systems—you can adjust the fidelity, so you can have the right conversations with the right audience to learn the right things.

Think-Make-Check Means Design Requires Collaboration

Back in the day, designers thought they created designs. Many designers consider themselves responsible for the user experience, that they represent the user and others represent the business and the implementation.

Funny thing, though: the experience isn't a stack of wireframes, a persona, and a sitemap. The user experience is what happens after *everyone* works together and ships something. The designer does not design the user experience. The organization designs the user experience. The organization ensures the user's needs are represented. Everyone in the organization impacts the user experience.

So, if you want to improve the user experience, you have to improve how the *organization* designs. You have to help the experience machine build better experiences. All your skill, insight, and talent are worthless if your organization builds bad things.

Help your organization learn more and faster. Think-Make-Check users, journeys, interfaces, and systems at the right fidelity to improve how fast and how well you can iterate. Keep the audience and channel in mind, so you have the right fidelity for the right conversations and learn the right things. Later on, each model has its own part of the book and its own set of tools to help you Think-Make-Check at the right fidelity.

Think-Make-Check, the four models, and fidelity are the things that help you choose the right tool, use it best, and optimize it to make it better. However, you can't do this alone. If the entire organization creates the experience, better products require that you work better together with everyone on your team. That's what we cover next.

The Elements of Collaboration: Shared Understanding, Inclusion, and Trust

IN HIS CLASSIC, *The 7 Habits of Highly Effective People*, Stephen Covey offers one of the best pieces of advice: Begin with the end in mind. Covey writes, "Begin with the End in Mind means to begin each day, task, or project with a clear vision of your desired direction and destination, and then continue by flexing your proactive muscles to make things happen."

Successful collaboration requires you to begin with the end in mind. If you work with your team to Think-Make-Check a model, what does successful collaboration look like when you're done?

Teams who collaborate well do three things (Figure 3-1):

- They share an understanding and vision
- They include everyone
- They trust each other

SHARED UNDERSTANDING   INCLUSION   TRUST

FIGURE 3-1
Successful collaborative teams exhibit three behaviors: shared understanding, inclusion, and trust.

Together, these three behaviors reinforce each other and help teams collaborate better. Because these are things you do, you don't have to believe them, just do them. And you don't have to be good at them. Practice makes you better. Keep flexing your collaboration muscles to make collaboration better.

Share Understanding, the First Principle of Collaboration

SHARED UNDERSTANDING

To *collaborate* means to *work together* on some thing, the same thing, a shared thing. To work together on some thing, you must share an understanding about the thing. In research on successful teams, UIE founder Jared Spool discovered that teams with a shared understanding are "far more likely to get a great design."[1]

It's not a matter of whether or not your team has a shared understanding. It's a matter of degrees. Shared understanding works on a scale from "total" to "none" (Figure 3-2). Teams who share less understanding won't work as well together. Miscommunication means people work on the wrong things. Misunderstandings mean people make the wrong changes.

FIGURE 3-2
Shared understanding isn't a yes or no proposition. The amount of understanding you share with someone goes from "none" to "total."

---

1 Spool, Jared. "Attaining a Collaborative Shared Understanding." UX Articles by UIE. User Interface Engineering, 18 Jan. 2012. Web. 04 Dec. 2016.

The more understanding you share, the better. The amount of shared understanding that's possible depends on who you want to share understanding with. In Chapter 2, we noted four possible audiences:

- Yourself

- Your team

- Your organization and partners

- Your customers

Each audience shares a different amount of understanding. You are the only person you share total understanding with. The more and more people with whom you collaborate, the less and less understanding you share (Figure 3-3). The amount of understanding you share with different audiences explains why your models need more or less fidelity.

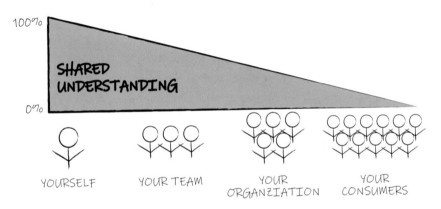

FIGURE 3-3
The more people you collaborate with, the less understanding you share. You share total understanding with yourself and less and less understanding as you collaborate with people farther away from the project.

SHARED UNDERSTANDING MEANS
SHARED LANGUAGE AND VISION

I love hole-in-the-wall Mexican joints. In Houston, the staff who run my favorite one only speak Spanish. When I slide into a red vinyl booth, I know just enough Spanish to order my favorite dish, *carne guisada*, with my preferred beans, *frijoles refritos*, and my preferred tortilla, *mais*.

I can collaborate with my server because we share enough Spanish to get my order right. We share enough of the same language to collaborate and fill my stomach with hearty, Mexican beef stew.

In contrast, if I wanted to collaborate with a Spanish-speaking web developer, we would have a hard time. We don't speak the same language. She may not know the English word for "wireframe" or "call to action." Regardless of how loudly and slowly I say, "el-call-to-action" and "wireframo," that's not Spanish. If we want to work together, we need to communicate in a way that respects and includes both of us.

In design, when you show a wireframe, you share your understanding of the screen with everyone who sees the screen. Everyone on the team can use the same language to talk about the screen and Check your thinking.

Shared understanding works for more than just interfaces. In "Attaining a Collaborative Shared Understanding," Jared Spool notes successful teams develop a "common perception of the project's goals and outcome." You've heard the vision President John F. Kennedy described to the U.S. Congress about the moon: "I believe that this nation should commit itself to achieving the goal, before this decade is out, of landing a man on the moon and returning him safely to the earth." Kennedy's clear, concrete vision, shared by Congress, NASA, and the nation, helped America do just that.

When you define user profiles and personas, you share your understanding of your users, so everyone on the team can design for the same person. When you document user journeys and flows, you share an understanding of how the user moves through your system.

Whether you share understanding to work together as a team, or you share your understanding to Check with others, shared language and vision let you collaborate and communicate more effectively.

SHARED UNDERSTANDING DRIVES FIDELITY

For wireframes, experience tells you what information to include based on similar problems and similar kinds of projects. People who work in software and websites know they need content, functionality, and layout. Everyone just knows. That's what a wireframe *is*. We share that understanding about what goes into a wireframe.

Shared understanding about wireframes helps when we collaborate with each other in hallways or conference rooms. This same understanding helps us collaborate even when we're apart.

Shared understanding creates the rules you use when you collaborate, and the rules explain how to adjust the fidelity. The easiest way to talk about an interface is a simple list of content and features. What will it do? What do you see? A shared understanding of screens helps you understand how to increase the fidelity. To improve the fidelity of a list of content and functionality, you add layout and transform your list into a wireframe. To improve the fidelity of a wireframe, you add interactivity and transform it into a prototype.

Shared vision creates the common language that helps you work together. To collaborate means to work together on something. A shared understanding is just as important as who you collaborate with.

Include Everyone, the Second Principle of Collaboration

INCLUSION

To include everyone means the entire team works together. When teams collaborate well, everyone contributes to the work. Especially when you work across silos, you can't create a shared understanding unless you bring different disciplines together.

Just like with shared understanding, including everyone isn't an all or nothing proposition. Any time your team collaborates, different members participate in different amounts (Figure 3-4). Especially on larger teams where you can't have everyone on every decision, different people will collaborate on different parts of the whole. They key is that everyone who needs to contribute has the opportunity to.

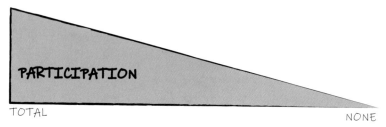

FIGURE 3-4
Including everyone isn't a yes or no proposition. How much your team members participate will vary from totally to not at all.

INCLUDING EVERYONE SHOWS RESPECT

To include everyone, you have to listen to everyone. Including everyone requires you respect everyone's perspective. To include everyone, you have to value everyone else's perspective as much as you value your own. You have to let go of your ego.

To include everyone, you have to realize you don't own anything. As a designer, you stop owning the design. Instead, you start helping the team create better products.

Naturally, when you approach a problem, you focus on issues important to you. When you include everyone, you have to understand issues important to others and go further to treat those issues as important as your own. If you're a visual designer and you feel like the brand experience is super important, that's OK. You also have to consider the developer's thoughts about feasibility as just as important as the brand experience.

When you include everyone, you collect the team's perspectives, wisdoms, and insights and fold them into the team's shared understanding. You harness the value of the entire team's years of experience. When you reach out to pull in someone who isn't participating, you tell them that you respect their insight, that you value them as a team member.

When you include everyone, you work as a team. You collaborate.

REACH OUT TO INCLUDE EVERYONE

To include everyone means you have to actively reach out to your team-mates, coworkers, and end users. In the lean startup world, they talk about getting out of the building to talk with customers.[2] Getting out of the building means reaching out to your customers to include their perspectives in your product vision.

Think of your head as a building. How do you get out of your head to talk to everyone else on your team? You always Think-Make-Check with yourself. Including everyone else means you Think, Make, and Check with your team as well.

For any collaboration—really, any conversation—include everyone who needs to be or wants to be included. When you look at the people in the room, on the conference call, or on the screenshare, rate how well each person has participated. Who hasn't contributed? That's who you pull into the conversation.

I customized each of the tools in the following parts of the book to pull your team into the conversation, so you can include everyone.

INCLUSION ALSO MEANS WAITING

Including everyone also means waiting. Sometimes a team member isn't ready to collaborate. Maybe they're occupied by something more pressing. Maybe they're not in a collaborative frame of mind. Maybe they don't like you. When you reach out to people who don't want to collaborate, you show them you want their input and welcome their participation. But don't push. Including everyone means you let everyone know they have an open door and a welcome place. Reach out, and they will participate when they're ready.

---

2   Lean startup calls this "customer development." For an introduction to customer development, check out *The Entrepreneur's Guide to Customer Development*, by Brant Cooper and Patrick Vlaskovits.

Trust Everyone, the Most Important Principle of Collaboration

TRUST

To work together on a shared vision, everyone on the team must respect everyone else.

When your team shares an understanding, everyone knows what they're working on, why it's important, and what the outcome will look like. When you include everyone, you demonstrate you value everyone's input and that the entire team will work together. However, regardless of how much understanding you share and how many people you include, respect limits how well you work together.

Like shared vision and working together, respect isn't an all-or-nothing affair. Imagine your team's mutual respect on a scale from "total" to "none" (Figure 3-5).

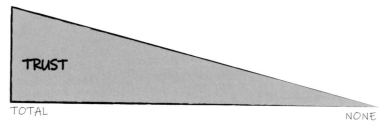

TOTAL   NONE

FIGURE 3-5

The amount of trust your team possesses can be measured on a scale from none to total.

When you respect your team members, you respect their decisions, their feedback, and what they do.

TRUST EVERYONE'S DECISIONS

Most collaboration happens with questions and conversation. When you collaborate, you ask people what they think. When your teammate answers a question, they share a decision they've made. On any good team with diverse experience, backgrounds, and viewpoints, these decisions will conflict. Collaboration unfolds as the team works through these conflicts to reach a consensus, a decision everyone agrees on.

TRUST EVERYONE'S RESPONSIBILITIES

Back in the early 2000s, I worked as a frontend developer, writing valid, semantic, accessible HTML and CSS and JavaScript from scratch. I know how valid, semantic markup creates more accessible interfaces, reduces bugs, and makes websites easier to maintain. As far as I'm concerned, valid, semantic code is a no-brainer.

A developer delivered some terrible, horrible, no good, very bad spaghetti code. Why would he deliver bad code? Was he lazy? Ignorant?

It didn't matter.

First, the poor quality of his code was my opinion, my ego at play. To work together, you have to let go of your ego. Second, it wasn't my responsibility. My job was wireframes. The frontend was his job. Whether you think you could do a better job than someone else, it doesn't matter. It's their job. They will do it the way they think is best.

Believe it or not, you're not the greatest mind in the world. You don't have all the answers. People on your team will have different and better ideas about the user experience than you do. Just like you want the team to trust you when you make a decision, you have to trust the decisions your team members make.

This includes decisions they make based on personal limitations. These limitations could apply to skill or experience or understanding. It doesn't matter. Everyone on the team, including you, has limitations. With collaboration, there is no right decision. There is only the team's decision, the best decision for the team. You run the experience machine together. You have to trust the person next to you will do their part.

TRUST EVERYONE'S DREAMS

On an ecommerce site, I wanted the server to query the database and send results to the browser, so users could see search results without JavaScript. The developers wanted to use Angular. This meant the server sent nothing to the browser. Instead, Angular used the browser to get the search results.

Most users have the same experience. The user loads the page and sees a list of search results. For me, the screen no longer worked without JavaScript. The page didn't work as designed, but for the developers, this was about their dream of implementing Angular.

Have you ever wanted to do something cool and different just because you saw it somewhere else? You get excited and put a new widget into your wireframe or used a new prototyping tool. In *Becoming Steve Jobs*, Brent Schlender and Rick Tetzeli capture the importance of dreams in a quote from Jony Ive:

> There are a number of things that you have achieved at the end of a project. There's...the actual product itself, and then there's all that you learned. What you learned is as tangible as the product itself, but much more valuable because that's your future. You can see where that goes and demand more of yourself...it yields these even more amazing results, not just in the product but in what you learned.[3]

Maybe a team member's decision feels less than practical. Maybe it's based on a dream of something new they can learn. You may not understand the importance of that dream, but you must respect their decision. It may be about more than your current project. It may be a dream about what the team can learn, so they can grow in the future.

TRUST EVERYONE'S FEEDBACK

Does everyone on your team have veto power? Can anyone unilaterally reject an idea? In *The Toyota Way*, Alex Warren, a former Toyota executive, describes how they gave every worker the power to unilaterally stop the assembly line.

> We give them the power to push buttons or pull cords—called "andon cords"—which can bring our entire assembly line to a halt. Every team member has the responsibility to stop the line every time they see something that is not standard. That's how we put the responsibility for quality in the hands of our team members. They feel the responsibility—they feel the power. They know they count.[4]

---

3   Schlender, Brent, and Rick Tetzeli. *Becoming Steve Jobs: The Evolution of a Reckless Upstart into a Visionary Leader.* New York: Crown Business, 2015.

4   Liker, Jeffrey K. *The Toyota Way.* New York: McGraw-Hill, 2004.

The worst thing about collaboration is when you work hard, show something, and receive critical feedback. Just like you respect your team's decisions, you respect their feedback. As you and your team Think, Make, and Check things, your team will provide a lot of early feedback. You need their feedback. They need your feedback. The feedback you give each other helps the team build a better experience.

Though you need to include everyone and respect their feedback, that doesn't mean all feedback is accurate. Feedback is up for discussion.

If you share the same vision and include everyone, then you respect that their feedback comes from a good place. That doesn't mean the feedback isn't up for discussion, that you can't try and sell your idea. If something is important to you, leverage your passion and experience and explain the decisions you made. Have the team explain their feedback. Discuss the feedback and arrive at the best decision for the team.

Sometimes, the team will agree with you. Sometimes, you'll agree with the team. Good teams never agree on everything, and you won't always like what the team decides. That's OK. Collaboration is about what the team decides, not what you think is best.

MEASURE PSYCHOLOGICAL SAFETY WITH THE SCARF MODEL

Respect is an emotional need. It makes your team members feel at ease, so they trust they can provide input and feedback free from judgment. David Rock of the NeuroLeadership Institute developed the SCARF model to describe five emotional needs that help people feel safe and respected. SCARF stands for Status, Certainty, Autonomy, Relatedness, and Fairness (Figure 3-6).

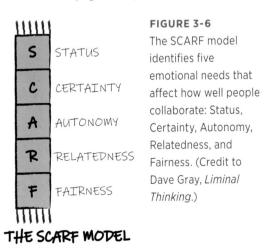

FIGURE 3-6

The SCARF model identifies five emotional needs that affect how well people collaborate: Status, Certainty, Autonomy, Relatedness, and Fairness. (Credit to Dave Gray, *Liminal Thinking*.)

THE SCARF MODEL

An emotional need might seem like an optional warm fuzzy. Humans like to think of themselves as logical, rational beings in control of weaker emotional impulses. However, as Rock notes, emotional needs control your behavior as much as physical needs. For collaboration, your emotional needs govern whether you approach the group and participate or view the group as a threat and back away.[5]

The "andon cords" Toyota placed on assembly lines show the SCARF model at work. Management empowered line workers to build great vehicle experiences. As Warren explained: "They feel the responsibility—they feel the power. They know they count."

In *Liminal Thinking*, Dave Gray shares a checklist of questions that reveal how much trust you share with members of your team.[6]

TABLE 3-1. David Gray's SCARF checklist for evaluating trust among team members

STATUS	Does this person feel important, recognized, needed by others?
CERTAINTY	Does this person feel confident that they know what's ahead, that they can predict the future with reasonable certainty?
AUTONOMY	Does this person feel like they have control of their life, their work, their destiny?
RELATEDNESS	Does this person feel like they belong? Do they feel a sense of relatedness; do they trust the group to look after them?
FAIRNESS	Does this person feel like they are being treated fairly? Do they feel that the "rules of the game" give them a fair chance?

If collaboration feels rough with any of your team members, ask yourself this list of questions to look for missing emotional needs. Good collaboration requires that all team members feel like they belong, and are needed and respected by the team. Collaboration requires that everyone feel like they are equal participants, listened to and treated fairly.

---

5   Rock, David, "SCARF: A brain-based model for collaborating with and influencing others," *NeuroLeadership Journal*, No. 1, 2008.

6   Gray, David. *Liminal Thinking: Create the Change You Want by Changing the Way You Think*. Brooklyn, NY: Two Waves, 2016. *http://www.liminalthinking.com*.

Collaboration Is the Key to Better Products

If you don't own the product experience—if your team and your company own that experience—then you have to stop trying to control the experience and start improving the experience machine.

When you help the team share understanding, everyone works toward the same goal and makes decisions with the same criteria. When you include everyone, you build trust and help the team work together toward the best possible experience. It also builds continuity between every part of the experience that the team touches.

When you work better with team members and clients, you expand your influence on the quality of the product experience. You can improve the experience machine at every step. Collaboration helps the entire organization create better experiences. Collaboration is the toolset you use to hack the experience machine and build better experiences.

[4]

Collaboration in Practice: Frame, Facilitate, and Finish

OFTEN WHEN WE THINK of collaboration, we think about working directly with others, the facilitation of conversations and discussions. Yet facilitation is probably the least important part of collaboration.

Collaboration includes three parts:

- The frame: what and how you will collaborate
- The facilitation
- The finish: the final outcome of the collaboration

In this chapter, we'll look at how Frame-Facilitate-Finish helps you put better collaboration into practice.

Every tool in this book follows this same roadmap: frame, facilitate, finish. Whether hallway conversations or CEO presentations, the same roadmap applies. Once you learn and follow this roadmap, you improve how you collaborate with anyone about anything.

Collaboration Is Its Own Problem

When someone asks you a question, you reach into your years of experience, your education, and your own bank of knowledge. A design expert answers questions from a design perspective. A developer answers questions from a development perspective. This happens when you visit the doctor. You tell the doctor, "it hurts when I do this." Immediately, the doctor shifts into medical expert mode to offer a diagnosis and treatment.

Edgar Schein, a prominent thinker in organizational development, has a term for when you respond to situations as an expert. Schein calls this "process consulting."[1] When you react as an expert, you work through your expert process to find the expert's answer. You revert to expert mode out of habit before you wonder if your default expert mode is the right way to approach the problem.

When you approach a project and look for ways to collaborate, set aside your usual expertise. Nothing you know about wireframes or personas or research will help you collaborate. Collaboration isn't a design problem. It's a collaboration problem. Use the Frame-Facilitate-Finish roadmap to see how to fix the collaboration problem.

Collaboration Has a Repeatable Structure

Collaboration has a structure. First you frame the question, then you explore and discuss, then you decide on a collective answer. Think of this as frame, facilitate, and finish (Figure 4-1).

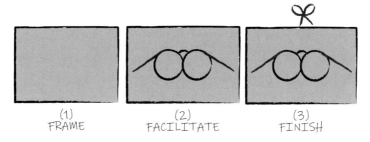

(1) FRAME   (2) FACILITATE   (3) FINISH

FIGURE 4-1
To collaborate, you first frame the question, then facilitate exploration and discussion, and finish by making a collective decision

Collaboration is a conversation. Like any conversation, when you start, you tell everyone what you're talking about. Then, you talk about it. Finally, you end the conversation. In good conversations, you frame the topic, facilitate the discussion, and then finish the conversation.

---

1   Schein, Edgar H. *Humble Consulting: How to Provide Real Help Faster.* Berrett-Koehler Publishers, 2016.

When people think about collaboration, they get stuck on the middle, on facilitation, where people ask questions and sticky notes and sketching happen. However, the important part of collaboration isn't facilitation. The part that ensures you create something valuable, that's the beginning and the end, the frame and the finish. So, let's start with a look at the frame and the finish before we dive into facilitation.

Collaboration Starts with a Frame

(1)
FRAME

The first step in the roadmap to collaboration is the frame. When you start with a frame, you tell everyone what to expect. You tell them what you will talk about. If it's more than conversation, you explain what everyone will do, and you describe why this conversation is important.

The frame leverages our three collaboration principles at a micro scale. When you share what you will talk about, what to expect, and why it's important, you seed the shared understanding necessary for a productive conversation. The frame also provides an opportunity to explicitly include everyone and reinforce that you welcome and respect their contributions.

That seems like a lot, but four simple questions reveal everything you need to create the frame:

- What will you do?
- What will you end up with when you're done?
- How will you do it?
- Why is it important?

If you want to collaborate with a couple team members to sketch an interface, you might answer those questions this way:

WHAT WILL YOU DO?	We will sketch this screen.
WHAT WILL YOU END UP WITH WHEN YOU'RE DONE?	When we're done, we'll have a wireframe we've all agreed on.
HOW WILL YOU DO IT?	We will sketch the screen together.
WHY IS IT IMPORTANT? (WHAT WILL YOU USE THIS FOR?)	Sketching the screen together will make sure we all agree on what we're building and why.

A FRAME CREATES A COLLABORATIVE MINDSET

To tell everyone *what you will do* is a lot of build-up to sketch a screen, but it's important build-up. When everyone knows what the collaboration will look like, you set three important expectations.

First, you plant the seed that they will participate. This shifts their thinking from observer to collaborator. When you tell them what they will do, they imagine themselves contributing to the discussion and taking the marker into their own hands.

Second, when you tell them *what they'll end up with* and *why it's important*, they understand why they should care. This encourages them to invest in the discussion and participate.

Lastly, when you explain *how you will do it*, they know what to expect. For example, if they expect questions before you sketch, they won't get impatient when you ask about the user and the task instead of sketching. When the team knows what will happen, they know to trust you while you work toward the end goal of walking out with a wireframe that everyone agrees on.

Well-framed discussions activate the principles of collaboration. When you tell your team what you're doing (as well as why and how you're doing it), you create a shared vision for the conversation. When you explain how you will do it and specify that everyone participates, you include everyone and imply that everyone's input will be trusted.

ABBREVIATE FRAMES WITH MORE EXPERIENCED TEAMS

If you and your team have previously collaborated, it's still good to run through what you're doing and why. This makes sure everyone stays on track and doesn't forget any important steps. However, with teams that work together often, you can shorten the frame.

Using the sketching example, you could say: "We will sketch this screen, so we agree on what we're building and why. Let's start with the user and context and then sketch the screen."

There's no requirement to answer the four questions in succession as we did here. Communicate naturally. Use the four questions as a checklist to make sure you include all necessary information in the frame. Once you've set the frame, you can facilitate the conversation. But first, and more important than facilitation, you have to know how you will finish.

Finish Collaboration with a Captured Outcome

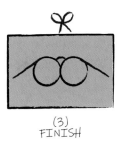

(3)
FINISH

The last step in the collaboration roadmap is the finish. Good collaboration ends when the team comes to a consensus. Working together, the team makes a collective decision. And if you do not explicitly capture this outcome, then no one can be sure you made a decision. In this example, the outcome is a sketch of a screen. All conversations and collaborations have an outcome. Making sure you capture this outcome is critical to a good finish.

Whether you collaborate on goals and vision, users, journeys, or interfaces, the end of every discussion can produce one of two types of outcomes:

- A single thing
- Several things

In this example, when we've finished, we have a single sketch on a single screen. We end up with a single sketch because we wanted to align on a single sketch. In contrast, if we wanted to sketch five different ways to lay out a screen, we could end up with an outcome of several sketches.

Of course, a sketch isn't the only way to capture an outcome. You can capture outcomes in four different formats:

- Words
- Diagrams
- Sketches
- Worksheets or canvases

In each of the following sections, each of the customized tools shows you how to arrive at specific, concrete, actionable, and documented outcomes in different formats. This captured outcome is how you know the team has finished collaborating.

But you can't just walk out of the room. No one will know what happened. Once you've captured the outcome, you have to explicitly let everyone know you're done. You can do this by rephrasing your frame in the past tense:

- What did you do?
- What did you end up with?
- How did you do it?
- Why is it important?

Using our example, you might describe the finish like this:

WHAT DID YOU DO?	We sketched this screen.
WHAT DID YOU END UP WITH?	We now have a wireframe we've all agreed on.
HOW DID YOU DO IT?	We sketched the screen together.
WHY IS IT IMPORTANT?	Sketching the screen together makes sure we agree on what we're building and why.

When you finish in this way, it's like you close the frame. You reiterate what you did and why you did it and remind everyone why it was important and how it will help going forward. Critically, a good finish reminds the team that they collaborated, were successful, and have something to show for their time.

WHEN YOU PLAN, START WITH THE FINISH

Do you remember how Stephen Covey advised to start with the end in mind? You collaborate successfully when you end up with what you wanted to end up with. That means, before you start, identify what you want to end up with. And be specific.

Will you walk out with a single thing? Or several things? Will they be words, diagrams, sketches, or a worksheet or canvas?

This finish, this outcome, is the one thing that drives everything else. It drives the frame, it signals the finish, and in the middle, it guides the facilitation.

Facilitate Collaboration Through Four Steps

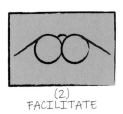

(2)
FACILITATE

Whenever someone asks for help with workshops or some other collaborative session, they want help with facilitation. Will people participate? Will they follow instructions? What if someone talks too much or not enough? What if participants can't agree?

Facilitation seems like the most important collaboration skill, but it's not. Even though facilitate is the second step in Frame-Facilitate-Finish, we cover it last for a couple of reasons. First, to collaborate, you start with the finish and identify the outcome. Second, in the frame, you explain the outcome and how you'll get there. Only after you've identified the finish and set the frame do you even start to think about facilitation. In that sense, facilitation represents the least important part of the collaboration roadmap.

Another reason we cover it last: facilitation is a lot easier than it looks. As you'll see throughout the customized tools in later sections, facilitation moves through the same four stages. Regardless of whether you collaborate on users, journeys, or interfaces, facilitation only has four types of activities (Figure 4-2):

- Open

- Analyze

- Synthesize

- Close

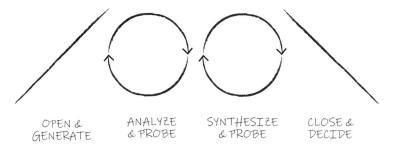

OPEN &
GENERATE

ANALYZE
& PROBE

SYNTHESIZE
& PROBE

CLOSE &
DECIDE

FIGURE 4-2

Good facilitation moves through four stages: open, analyze, synthesize, and close

Open is where you start from nothing and generate some ideas and starting points. In analyze, you break those ideas down to learn more about them. Next, you synthesize the ideas into something new, and finally, you close by coming to a stopping point.

For the cynical, slicing every collaborative session, workshop, and group activity into four steps seems terribly convenient. But stick with me. Each of the tools in later sections demonstrates how effectively these four steps focus and improve facilitation.

You can find similar structures in other books on facilitation. Dave Gray, Sunni Brown, and James Macanufo suggest a related set of steps in their fantastic book, *Gamestorming*,[2] and David Sibbet's *Visual Meetings*[3] offers a similar structure, although the steps are in a different order.

---

2 Gray, David, Sunni Brown, and James Macanufo. *Gamestorming: A Playbook for Innovators, Rulebreakers, and Changemakers.* Sebastopol, CA: O'Reilly, 2010.

3 Sibbet, David. *Visual Meetings: How Graphics, Sticky Notes, & Idea Mapping Can Transform Group Productivity.* Hoboken, NJ: John Wiley & Sons, 2010.

As we saw with both the frame and the finish, four questions make sure you plan your collaboration well. Similarly, facilitation's four steps act like a checklist, so you can make your collaboration as successful as possible. And, if you're nervous, the structure lets you focus more on the collaboration and less on the mechanics.

MAGIC, FACILITATION GLASSES

I have two kids, seven and twelve, so Harry Potter is big at my house. When the seven-year-old saw the facilitation steps, she shouted, "Harry Potter glasses!"

Sure enough, it does look like Harry Potter glasses. I'd like you to remember the facilitation stages as a pair of glasses. You put the glasses on to collaborate with your team. Analyze and synthesize are *lenses* you use to look at a problem space, ways to perceive that world. The open and close are ear pieces that attach the lenses to your head.

Whenever you start to collaborate, put on your magic facilitation glasses to remember how to get a good view of the problem.

STEP 1: OPEN

If you want to collaborate on some topic, you need something to collaborate on. That's why facilitation starts with the open step. In open, the team generates a bunch of options and ideas. When you open, you "get people thinking and spark their imaginations."[4] The Design Council calls the open "a 'phase of divergent thought,' where...team members keep their perspectives wide to allow for a broad range of ideas and influences."[5]

Open stages start with open-ended questions:

- What different kinds of users might use this app?
- What kinds of content can we include in this interface?

During the open stage, anything goes. You want to create lots of inputs. Ideas generated during open fuel the later stages. In following stages, the team will analyze and synthesize these inputs. The more options the team generates, the better the outcomes.

Sometimes, you don't need to generate a list of options. Sometimes, you already have a list of things you start with. For example, instead of brainstorming a list of users, maybe you already have a list of users. In these situations, instead of generating options, you can start by reminding everyone of what the options are. In either case, use the open stage to identify the options that fuel analyze, synthesize, and close.

During open, you facilitate activities like brainstorming.

---

4   Gray, David, Sunni Brown, and James Macanufo. *Gamestorming: A Playbook for Innovators, Rulebreakers, and Changemakers.* Sebastopol, CA: O'Reilly, 2010.

5   A Study of the Design Process. The Design Council, 2005. Web. 5 Jan. 2017.

STEP 2: ANALYZE

In analyze, take every input in turn, and learn more about each of them. Once your team has lots of inputs, you start to sift through and make sense of things. In the analyze stage, you want to learn more about the various options, break them down into smaller parts, and learn what they're made of.

During analyze, you ask questions that explore options in more detail:

- What is this made of?

- How does this work?

- Where does this come from?

- Can you provide an example?

Analyze is like looking through a lens to better understand the inputs your team generated in the open stage. Analyze isn't the only lens. After analyze, you look at the options through a synthesizing lens, but you can't synthesize until you have a good understanding of the available options. Understanding reveals ways options are similar and different. This learning fuels the next stage when we synthesize what we've learned.

Analyze also helps verify

When you ask a question to learn more about an input, you provide an opportunity for clarification. You invite people in the room to discover whether they understand something different. In a session, a site's user was named the "decision maker." I thought this meant they wrote the check. In reality, the decision maker was an engineer who made sure purchases met technical specifications. Asking questions about the decision maker helped the team verify what that meant.

STEP 3: SYNTHESIZE

In the analyze stage, you learn more about each generated option. In the synthesize stage, you learn how various options relate to one another.

During synthesize, you ask questions that compare and contrast:

- How are these options similar?
- How are they different?
- How are they related?

Synthesize is the second lens you use to understand the inputs from the open stage. You use what you learned in analyze to explore how the inputs are related to one another. During synthesize, you often create affinity maps, placing sticky notes into groups based on commonalities. You also create maps and diagrams. Are the inputs related by time? Does one evolve to become another? Are they different parts of a single process?

For example, let's say you work with clients and identify three types of users for a coffee site:

- Casual coffee drinker
- Regular coffee drinker
- Coffee connoisseur

During analyze, you might generate all the tasks and contexts and needs specific to each type of user. You would learn how to identify each of these users. What makes a user a "casual coffee drinker"? In synthesize, you might reveal that all three represent a single user, at different stages in their coffee evolution.

ALWAYS PROBE FOR MORE

At both analyze and synthesize, you often have the opportunity to go beyond initial discussion and probe for more information. When you probe, you push the team to think differently. In probe you ask questions that trigger the team to think of new possibilities:

1. What have we missed?

2. Are there different ways we could think about this?

3. Are there similar things from a different context we can apply here?

In analyze, you can probe the team to think of additional inputs or additional ways to understand the inputs you have. In synthesize, you can probe the team to think of ways to compare each input or new ways to relate them.

Like the open stage, probes let you inject divergent thinking back into the process to capture any ideas you may have missed. Probes improve the team's understanding of the problem space.

STEP 4: CLOSE

In finish, you need a concrete, captured outcome. Close is the last stage of facilitation, right before you move from facilitate to finish, so now's the time to bring the collaboration to a close. Close is the opposite of open. Instead of generating options, you home in and identify the final choices. The team makes decisions about the outcome. When you finish the collaboration, these decisions let you document the final outcome for the finish. You move from working with inputs to choosing the outputs.

During the close stage, you ask deciding questions:

- What ideas are more important?

- What ideas are more feasible?

- What ideas do we like the most?

During close you facilitate activities like prioritization and voting. The close step creates the team's shared vision about what is important, what was decided, and what to carry forward. And once it's decided, you're ready to move to the finish, document the outcome, and tie the collaboration up with a little bow.

Formal and Informal Collaboration

All this structure makes collaboration feel very formal. It can be. In formal collaboration sessions like workshops, this structure makes a lot of sense.

A structured approach is just as valuable for informal collaboration. When you bump into your favorite developer in the hall or run a wireframe review, the structure works like a checklist. The structure keeps conversations on track and makes sure you end a conversation with a valuable, concrete decision. No wasted meetings!

Some people like structure. They live for it.

Other people don't like structure. They like to wing it. They trust their experience and instincts to guide them through the design process and collaborating with their team. If you are uncomfortable with structure, these stages and steps can feel artificial and limiting.

I get it. I'm one of those people. I don't like structure. I like to run free.

Don't think of this structure like prison bars that hold you back. This structure is more like monkey bars, a playground you can climb on and jump off of. This structure lets you run free and collaborate in a safe, productive space.

Design and Collaboration, All Together Now

The experience machine feels like a massive, gargantuan complex that resists change. Yet you can make it better. With little more influence or authority than working on your next project, the tools in this book help the experience machine build better products.

The key to better projects is better collaboration. The collaboration roadmap to Frame-Facilitate-Finish works as a checklist to help you structure team work together with the collaboration glasses to help you structure collaboration for the best outcomes.

Think-Make-Check and fidelity provide a frame for managing what you are doing as you design experiences, but design is meaningless if you can't work with your organization to build something. The collaboration roadmap explains why the tools work. Frame-Facilitate-Finish tells you how to use them.

Your organization will build better experiences, and you're going to help.

[*II*]

Project Strategy

STRATEGY

A WORKMAN LAYING BRICKS took such extra care with his craft that anyone could notice. A priest walking by asked what he was building. "We're building a grand cathedral," said the workman.

"Your craftsmanship is a testament to your faith," said the priest.

The next week, when the priest walked by, he saw a new workman. When he asked what had happened to the wondrous craftsman from the week before, he learned the careful craftsman had been fired. "Why did you fire a wonderful craftsman when building a grand cathedral?"

"Because we're building a factory."

At the beginning of the experience machine lives the why behind what you do, the strategy. The project's goals and the product vision should guide everything you and your team do. But... You and your team have to share the same goals and vision.

Your team can work better together, and you're going to help them do it. In the chapters that follow we'll examine the basic elements of strategy and then explore two collaborative activities that help project teams create and align around shared goals and future visions.

[5]

The Strategic Landscape

FOR A STRATEGY WORKSHOP, service-line managers, the IT team, and one lonely marketer packed themselves into a conference room. It was a savvy group. Each manager delivered high-performing services across channels including mobile, web, and in stores. They had a vision of where they wanted to be, goals to get them there, and an understanding of problems they faced.

IT wanted to minimize services. Marketing wanted to push the technology envelope. Retail wanted to reduce wait time with simpler stores, and Merchandising wanted to pack stores with trinkets. They had vision, but they had different visions. They didn't have a single, clear vision that everyone shared.

That's strategy: the single, bright line everyone in the organization can see, understand, and follow *together*. When everyone shares the same goals and vision, then each part of the experience machine works in harmony with the others. And, although they may not be building the right things, at least they're building the same things.

Shared vision and goals help teams stay aligned, so they work better together. Shared vision and goals help your team work with the broader organization. This chapter disassembles strategy into its component parts, so you can identify where your team may be misaligned and get everyone working together again.

Strategy breaks into three parts:

- Goals, drivers, and barriers: three parts of the strategic landscape

- Four types of barriers: technology, culture, process, and people

- Three types of goals: project, department, and organizational

At the end of this chapter, you'll be able to diagnose and apply the tools in this section to help your team identify goals and align around vision.

Strategy Is About Change

Strategy explains how you evolve from your current state to a future state (Figure 5-1).

FIGURE 5-1

Strategy defines how the organization evolves from its current state to a future state.

Of course, there's more than one possible future. Your goals describe how you want to evolve from your current state to a single, preferred future state out of the set of all possible future states (Figure 5-2).

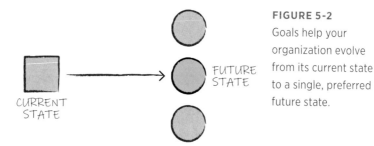

FIGURE 5-2

Goals help your organization evolve from its current state to a single, preferred future state.

In this way, strategy represents the choices the experience machine plans to make in the future. Goals guide these choices. Of course, goals do not exist in a vacuum. The organization's environment affects its strategy. Three questions can reveal your strategy's context:

- Why should you change? What's driving the change?

- Why haven't you changed? What barriers prevent change?

- What will change? What concrete actions signal that change is a success?

Drivers Explain Why to Change

Strategy focuses on the change from the current state to a future state. Looking forward, it's easy to focus on how you will get there (goals), the barriers in your way, and what success will look like (vision). However, before leaping toward the future, understand your organization's past and present.

Many projects do fine without understanding the "why." However, understanding why aligns the team to a higher purpose. The why is part of the rallying cry. An organization won't spend resources to change to a future state without good reason. Organizational drivers explain why you want to move from your current state to a future state (Figure 5-3). What forces push the organization to change?

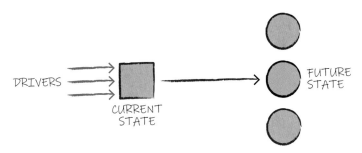

FIGURE 5-3
Drivers represent the forces pushing your organization to change.

Another way to identify drivers is to ask: what happens if we don't change? One manufacturer felt if they didn't launch an ecommerce site and grow it to 25% of total revenue within five years, their market share would be captured by competitors. For the manufacturer, not going out of business drove the change from being a manufacturer and distributor to a sales and distribution platform.

All projects have drivers. A vehicle manufacturer felt they had maximized their customer's lifetime value, optimized as much as possible, and maximized their revenues. They envisioned a future state where customers purchased more over their lifetime. Increased revenue drove the organization to change from a current state of maximized revenues to a future state with higher customer value. Something always drives organizations to change.

Drivers explain the scope and scale of the organization's change. People look silly running around screaming unless they're being chased by a monster.

Barriers Explain What Blocks Change

While drivers represent forces that push your organization to change, barriers represent opposing forces that prevent change (Figure 5-4). A barrier answers the question: why hasn't your organization already changed?

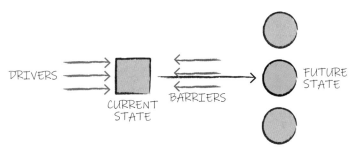

FIGURE 5-4

Barriers represent an opposing force that prevent change.

Four types of barriers prevent organizations from reaching future states:

- Technology barriers

- Cultural barriers

- Process barriers

- People barriers

TECHNOLOGY BARRIERS

A financial services firm wanted employees to stop storing sensitive, confidential files on their laptops. This wasn't your typical "confidential" data. In financial services, if confidential data leaks, people go to jail. To fix this, the firm decided to force employees to store files in a secure cloud. Unfortunately, the firm didn't have a secure cloud. Not having a secure cloud is an example of a technology barrier. That barrier prevented the firm from reaching the future state.

CULTURAL BARRIERS

In addition to not having a secure cloud, the financial services firm faced a cultural barrier. Employees didn't believe any system could be as secure as their laptops. With this belief embedded in the firm's culture, employees would never move sensitive files to the cloud. Even if a secure cloud overcame the technology barrier, employees believed the files would be less secure, so they wouldn't move them. The firm's culture created a barrier to change.

PROCESS BARRIERS

One thing that contributed to employees' lack of trust was that the firm had no process for managing security. When employees kept sensitive files on personal laptops, they used personal, ad hoc processes to provide access to clients and teammates. Without a shared process to determine, assign, and understand security, the firm could not manage the move to a secure cloud.

PEOPLE BARRIERS

The last type of barrier has to do with people themselves. Like technology barriers, without the right people, organizations can't change. A large software company wanted to move from selling to CIOs to selling to consumers. However, only one member of their team had online marketing experience. The company needed people with digital strategy skills. They had a people barrier. Although you can hire or train to overcome people barriers, organizations can't change to preferred future states until they have the right people and skills.

Goals and Getting to the Future State

When projects start, even though everyone believes they know the goals, three problems can arise:

- People can't articulate their goals, so they can't make decisions with them, or
- They've articulated their goals, but haven't shared them, so they don't know if the team shares the same goals, or
- They've articulated and shared their goals, and not everyone understands or agrees with the goals.

The current state, future state, drivers, and barriers represent the context that frames your strategy. Goals explain how you believe you will navigate the context to arrive at the future state (Figure 5-5).

James Kalbach defines goals as an "interlocking set of choices that aligns activity and shows causality: if we do this, then we expect to see that."[1]

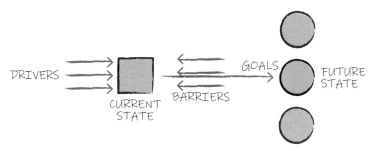

FIGURE 5-5

The current state, future state, drivers, and barriers—these represent the context that frames your strategy. Goals connect it all together.

A large retail chain wanted a customer portal for business customers. That's not a goal. That's a product: we will have a portal for business customers. The retail chain had two goals:

- Make it easier for customers to do business with them, and

- Provide more personalized marketing to customers.

Doing *this* and expecting *that* applies to specific activities. If we build a portal, customers will use it to self-serve. That's more of a tactical objective, something concrete to achieve. A goal is directional, not concrete. If we improve customer service (the goal), users will be more engaged (future state). The goal never says how to accomplish it (a customer portal). Instead, it states that in order to reach the future state, you are going to head in this direction.

A product or service answers the question: How? How will we improve customer service? We will build a portal with self-service features. To fulfill the goal and reach the future state, we will build a customer portal (Table 5-1).

---

1 Kalbach, Jim. "UX Strategy Blueprint." EXPERIENCING INFORMATION. Jim Kalbach, 12 Aug. 2014. Web. 03 July 2017. *https://experiencinginformation.com/2014/08/12/ux-strategy-blueprint/.*

TABLE 5-1. Example goals and their products

EXAMPLE GOAL	EXAMPLE PRODUCT
Make it easier to enjoy music	iPod
Make it easier to collaborate	SharePoint
Make it easier to market across channels	Sitecore

None of these goals prescribe how something will happen, only that you want it to happen. They're the direction you go in. Not what exists when you get there.

THREE TYPES OF GOALS

Often, talk about goals refers to user goals or someone's personal goals. While important, when you identify and define the organization's strategy, you focus on your organization's, department's, or project's goals. Eliciting goals can be as simple as asking. The problem? If you ask five people about their goals, not only do you get different goals, you get different types of goals. Three types of goals, actually.

Organizational goals

Organizational goals identify what the organization, as a whole, wants to accomplish. When you see people talk about big "S" strategy, they're talking about organizational goals. For example, an international coffee company's organizational goal might be to expand their customer base.

Department/business-line goals

Department or business-line goals describe what a specific department inside of an organization wants to accomplish. While an international coffee company has an organizational goal to expand the customer base, the department/business-line goals should support and enable the organizational goals. The ecommerce department might have a goal to improve the conversion rate for new visitors. By improving the conversion rate, the ecommerce department helps expand the customer base.

Project goals

Project goals detail what a specific project wants to accomplish. For example, the ecommerce department might kick off a project to improve personalization on the website. By improving personalization, they hope to improve conversions and expand the customer base.

In your organization and on your project, all three types of goals should line up and reinforce one another (Figure 5-6).

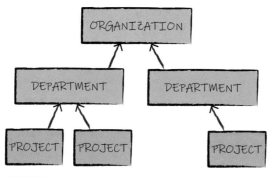

FIGURE 5-6

All of your organization's goals should align so that project goals help achieve departmental goals that help achieve organizational goals.

Using our example from above, the project's goal to improve personalization helps the department's goal to improve conversion, which helps the organization's goal to increase the customer base (Figure 5-7). When project and department goals support the organization's goals, we say they "ladder up."

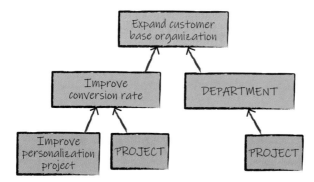

FIGURE 5-7

The goal to improve personalization helps the goal to improve conversion, which helps the goal to increase the customer base.

Even though strategy identifies this complex context surrounding a product or project and its goals, to begin to understand or devise strategy, you start with goals.

Innovating at the Right Altitude

Two consultants flew to Indiana to talk to a client about a customer portal. At a standard suburban intersection, the client's one-story, nondescript office-plex squatted behind a gas station and across from a strip center, the kind you see throughout American suburbs. A phalanx of line managers crowded one end of a conference room table. The two consultants probed the managers about their goals, their challenges, and their needs.

On hearing these, the first consultant asked the client how they envisioned customers would use the portal. The second consultant declared the portal would be built in IBM WebSphere. The first consultant had a problem to explore. The second had a solution to implement.

Projects exists in one of two contexts:

- Exploring possible solutions
- Pursuing a single solution

Although collaboration structure remains the same, projects in exploration require a slightly different approach than projects working on a specific solution.

PROJECTS IN EXPLORATION MODE

Projects in exploration mode have not decided on a solution. Not only is the solution not known, the problem may not be known.

For projects in exploration mode, you imagine ways to frame problems and different ways you can solve them. Rather than working toward a solution, you are working toward an understanding and what the solution could be.

If you haven't settled on a solution and you're trying to understand your options, then you're exploring. You're looking for new ways to innovate, new ways to solve a problem. In projects in exploration mode, you use collaboration to generate and explore multiple options.

PROJECTS IN SOLUTION MODE

You have seen projects in solution mode. In these projects, the problem is known and the solution is known. In solution mode you are building a customer portal in WebSphere. For projects in solution mode, you design ways to implement the solution, iterate on those ideas, and test them. In solution mode, you Think-Make-Check your approach to the solution. In solution mode, you use collaboration to iterate and refine how you will implement the chosen solution.

MOVING BETWEEN EXPLORATION AND SOLUTION

At different times, you focus on exploration or solution. However, it's common for collaboration to range. You'll find discussion shifts from one context to another.

When exploring possible solutions, you might dive into a specific solution to think about implementation. This helps you understand the different solutions you're exploring. When working through a specific solution, you might jump to exploring and wonder whether a different solution would make implementation easier.

These jumps are part of the Think-Make-Check process. You follow ideas to their logical conclusions to see if they go where you think they'll go. This also helps optimize your decisions. Given what you know now, maybe you should have done something differently.

Focus Teams on the Right Goals

Whether your project is in solution or exploration mode changes the kinds of conversations you have about goals, vision, and barriers. Most of the time you will work in solution mode where barriers, goals, and vision will focus very much on an individual project.

Making sure your goals ladder up from the project to the department and broader organization helps your team make product-level decisions, as well as communicate the product's value to the rest of the organization. Being able to distinguish between project, department, and organizational goals is critical to clearly communicating value.

In the next chapter, we'll look at ways to ensure you and your team have identified the right goals for a project and made sure the entire team is aligned to the same goals.

[6]

Identify Project Goals with Goal Mapping

SOMEONE SHARED A DASHBOARD they'd designed. I asked, "Why did you make this dashboard? How does this dashboard help the organization?" They didn't know. I asked, "How do you know what's good?"

It's tough to make good decisions if you don't know the project's goals. This leaves teams rudderless and adrift. They paddle the boat, and don't go anywhere specific. You can help your team navigate better when you identify the project's goals.

Any time someone asks why, your team should agree on the goals and on what goals are most important. In this chapter, we'll look at how a goal map can help you think about and align your team on one set of prioritized project goals.

I use a goal map as a part of formal discovery and kickoff workshops. I also use an abbreviated, conversational version when I join random meetings for unfamiliar projects. We'll look at the workshop version first and then talk about how to adjust the approach for more informal settings.

How Goal Mapping Works

Goal mapping uses a common approach to generate and prioritize a list of items (Figure 6-1):

1. Individually, everyone generates what they perceive as the project's goals and then shares their goals with the group.

2. Working together, everyone groups all goals by similarity. These are "themes."

3. Working together, everyone agrees on a name for each theme.

4. Working together, everyone prioritizes the themes from most important to least important.

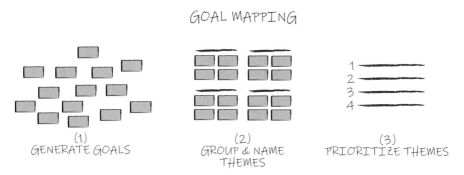

GOAL MAPPING

(1) GENERATE GOALS

(2) GROUP & NAME THEMES

(3) PRIORITIZE THEMES

FIGURE 6-1
Generate and group goals into themes—then, prioritize the list of themes.

At the end of the activity, the team will have produced three, concrete outcomes:

- Goals from everyone on the team

- Thematic trends for the team's goals

- A prioritized list of team goals

WHEN TO MAP PROJECT GOALS

Map and align on goals at the beginning of a new project to make sure the team stays aligned around what's most important.

Goal mapping also helps in the middle of projects when teams disagree about how to accomplish something. These disagreements signal deeper misalignment on project goals.

INPUTS AND QUICK STARTS

As a kickoff workshop exercise, goal mapping works great if you start with nothing, a big blank dry erase board or sheet of paper. If you'd rather seed the discussion, find a pre-existing list of goals for the project. If you can't find a pre-existing list of goals, ask each teammate to share a list of what they think the goals are. You will want three goals from each person.

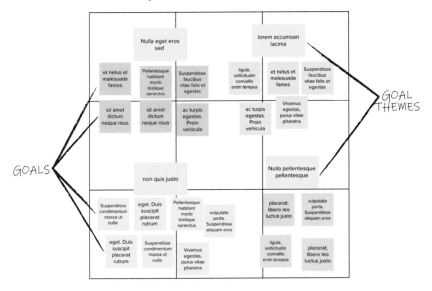

FIGURE 6-2
Goal maps have three parts: the goal map, movable items for goals, and movable items for themes

Goal map

Draw or project a goal map on a whiteboard or wall or draw the map on a piece of paper (Figure 6-2). Use a blank space, or use a 3×3 grid to help less experienced participants with grouping.

Individual goals

Once identified, goals may be moved. Capture each goal in a separate group next to the team member's name. Use movable sticky notes or pieces of paper, or make them easy to erase and rewrite.

Goal themes

While the team groups goals into themes, themes may also be moved. Capture each theme on the goal map.

Find templates, framing material, and remote resources on the website:

http://pxd.gd/strategy/goal-map

Activity 1: Generate and Share Everyone's Project Goals

Everyone has their own reason for participating in a project. Everyone has their own perception for why the project exists as well as their own agenda. To work together, it's important to recognize everyone's individual goals, so everyone feels included and valued as a member of the team. Likewise, it's important for everyone to agree on why the project is important, so you have a shared framework for making important decisions.

In this activity:

- Each team member will work individually to generate 3–5 goals they have for the project. These can be their personal goals or what they perceive to be the organization's goals.

- Each team member will share their goals with the broader group.

If your organization has already defined goals for the project, use the pre-defined goals to start the discussion, rather than skipping this activity. If you do skip goal generation, start with Activity 2, grouping, to ensure the team identifies 3–5 overarching goals (later in this chapter).

THE FRAME

WHAT WILL YOU DO?	List 3–5 project goals
WHAT'S THE OUTCOME?	A list of goals from each team member
WHY IS IT IMPORTANT?	Ensures the team accounts for and includes everyone's goals
HOW WILL YOU DO IT?	Working alone

To frame goal generation, say something like:

> "Everyone has a unique perspective about the goals for this project. Each of us will take a few minutes to list 3–5 goals we think are important, so we can understand what everyone wants to accomplish."

FACILITATE GOAL GENERATION IN PRIVATE OR AS A GROUP

Choose to generate goals individually, in private, or as part of a group discussion. Both techniques offer advantages and disadvantages.

Facilitate goal generation in a group discussion to align quickly

Generating goals as a group mixes group discussion with brainstorming. Open goals up to group discussion where all team members can volunteer their goals to everyone. Make sure everyone in the group offers at least one goal, and preferably at least three.

In group discussions, everything said will influence what the next person says. This helps groups align and reduces the breadth of goals. Generate goals as a group with small, aligned teams who know or have worked with each other.

In a group discussion, you ask one person to share their goals with the group. Generation and sharing happen at the same time. If you generate goals in private, add a second step where everyone takes a turn and shares their goals with the group.

Facilitate goal generation in private to expose more individual goals

To help team members feel more included and preserve variance in group members' goals, have the team capture 3–5 goals in private. Request they list their goals before the discussion or ask everyone to take three minutes to write down 3–5 goals.

Generating goals in private helps individuals on newer teams share what's important to them with the rest of their teammates. Generating goals in private is critical for remote teams where time, distance, and culture can hide nuance in team conversations.

Based on the team dynamic, make a judgment call on whether the team needs to be more inclusive (generate goals privately) or to be more aligned (generate goals as a group).

Encourage participants to trust their instincts

For some participants, someone else has the responsibility or authority to declare relevant goals. They may resist listing what they think the goals should be.

Reassure these participants two ways: first, the group needs to make sure its goals align with the department and organization. You will use the goals you identify in this activity to make sure the team is on track. Second, goals issued from the top do not always address important needs that only team members have seen. For example, team members might realize they should architect the project's code to support continuous integration.

SHARE GOALS WITH THE ENTIRE GROUP

Whether the team generates goals in private or as part of a group discussion, participants can share goals in different ways. As the group shares their goals, capture them on the goal map (Figure 6-3).

Share all goals in turn

Have everyone take a turn to share their 3–5 goals and place them on the board. Since everyone takes a turn, other team members may not speak up when they have a question, so look for opportunities to clarify and better understand goals.

Sharing in turn works whether you generated goals in private or as part of a group discussion. Sharing in turn works especially well for smaller groups in person or remote. Sharing in turn takes too long for groups larger than eight people.

Share unique goals in turn

In groups larger than seven people, have each person take a turn and share just one of their goals. Place the goal on the board and ask if anyone else has a similar goal. Place similar goals on the board near the first one.

Some participants will want to explain how their goal is similar, yet different. Use this opportunity to help the group discuss what is the same and different.

For larger groups, asking for similar goals as you go will reduce the total number of goals shared and help use less time to share all goals.

Share goals with introductions

Since goal generation often occurs during project kickoffs with new teams, combine goal generation and sharing with introductions. At the beginning of the kickoff meeting, ask everyone to take a turn, introduce themselves, and share their top three goals.

If the team captured goals on individual notes or cards, have them place their goals on the board. If they didn't capture goals individually, capture each goal as it's shared and place it on the board. Paraphrase to make the goal more concise or easier to understand, and make sure the author agrees with how you captured the goal.

Share goals without group discussion

Instead of discussing goals in a group or discussing in turns, have team members capture goals on sticky notes and place their goals on the board as soon as they are done.

Unlike sharing in turns, team members don't need to wait for everyone to finish before they can move to the next step. For large groups, either in-person or remote, placing their goals on the board lets faster participants finish instead of making everyone wait.

Because they don't share the goals out loud, plan additional time for discussion and clarification during the grouping activity.

Goal Map

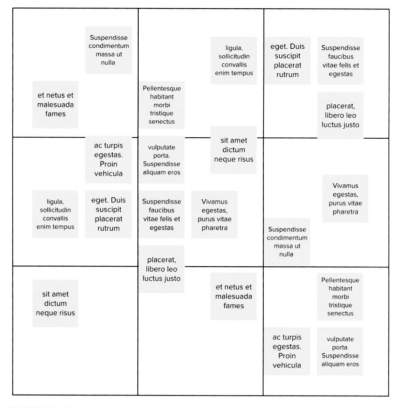

FIGURE 6-3

Capture goals on the board either altogether or grouped by author

PROBE RESPONSES TO GET TO PROJECT-SPECIFIC GOALS

When you ask someone about their goals, the range of answers will astound you. Even though they may not state a project goal, make no mistake, there's one hidden in their response. You just have to find it.

Analyze to get to project-specific goals

Instead of a goal for the project, they may share a departmental or organizational goal. While departmental and organizational goals are important, project goals best help guide the conversation:

- Project goals are concrete and align with the team's ongoing activities.

- Project goals match what the team has focused on for the current project.
- Project goals match the project's defined scope.
- Project goals offer a starting point from where you can expand into more abstract departmental and organizational goals.

As team members share their goals, clarify and discuss to make sure you have collected project goals. Ask yourself these questions to make sure you're looking at a project goal:

- Is the goal unique to the project?
- Is the goal unique to the department?
- Is the goal unique to the organization?

Based on how you answer those questions, probe to understand and uncover the project goal. Ask: How does this project help accomplish that goal (Table 6-1)?

TABLE 6-1. Probing to uncover project goals

QUESTION	IF YES	IF NO
Is the goal unique to the project?	Capture as-is	If the goal is not unique to the project, then it may be a departmental goal.
Is the goal unique to the department?	Ask how the project supports the departmental goal	If the goal is not unique to the department, then it may be an organizational goal.
Is the goal tied to the organization?	Ask how the project helps the department support the organizational goal	If it is not specific to the organization, it is too broad to be useful. Probe to ask how the organization can fulfill the goal.

An example: Understanding how the goal "make more money" applies to our sample project

Let's say we work for a global coffee company that roasts its own coffee to serve in its international chain of stores. And let's say we start a project to add ecommerce functionality to the website.

On our team, we have a developer, a product owner, and a designer. We kick off the project with a formal goals activity, and someone suggests our goal is to "make more money."

The goal to "make more money" is too broad to be useful. Most commercial organizations want to make more money. A global coffee company that wants to make more money is like every other coffee company, so the goal is too broad to be useful.

In response, ask what they mean by "make more money." Perhaps they respond with "increase share of the pocketbook." Improving how much money each customer gives you represents a specific way our coffee company wants to "make more money."

While you've converted a less useful, non-specific idea to a specific organizational goal, you still need to understand how that goal applies to the ecommerce project. How does the ecommerce project help our coffee company "increase the share of the customer's pocketbook"?

Our team asks themselves: how does ecommerce help us increase the amount of money customers spend with us each year? Ecommerce helps customers buy stuff anytime from anywhere. The developer also suggests, "ecommerce opens up new ways to sell things—like you could sell coffee subscriptions or coffee-of-the-month clubs that you can't really do in stores."

Now you've discovered two goals for the project:

- Allow customer to buy anytime from anywhere

- Allow new merchandising models

These project-specific goals reframe the goals, "to make more money" or "to increase share of the pocketbook," into a useful, shared understanding of where the team should be going. As the team makes technical, business, and design decisions, they understand they need to ensure those decisions support those two project goals.

Don't forget the non-project goals

When you elicit goals, you want to focus on project-related goals. This doesn't mean you should forget organizational and departmental goals. Make note of them. You will need them later to communicate project value with the rest of your organization. For now, though, you should have amassed a hefty stack of project goals.

Probe beyond features to find underlying goals

Often, when you ask someone about a goal, they respond with a feature: we want to build a shopping cart. When they articulate their goal as a feature, ask, "Why?" Why do they want to build a shopping cart? The answer to why they want to create a service or feature is usually the goal. If it's not, ask why again. And again until you find the goal behind the feature.

Don't worry about being right; goals evolve

You may worry about whether or not you will identify the right goals. This is fair. Over time, the team's understanding about the project and its goals will grow by leaps and bounds. The assumptions you have at the beginning of a project will change.

FINISH AND MOVE ON TO THEMES

After everyone shares their goals, and you've analyzed goals to get to the right project-specific level, verify everyone agrees with how the goals have been captured and no one has any other goals to add. Once the team has shared and captured all their goals, change activities to look for themes:

> "Now that we've captured everyone's goals, let's group them by similarity, so we can find themes common to everyone's goals."

Activity 2: Group Goals to Find Common Themes

Even with small teams, after goal generation you will have 15–25 goals, more different than similar. Teams can't keep track of 15–25 goals, much less achieve them, so you need to refine the total list of goals to the more manageable number of 3–5 goals.

To transform larger numbers of goals into a manageable set of 3–5, group goals by similarity to identify common themes.

In this activity:

- Working all together, the team organizes similar goals into groups.

- Working all together, the team names each group of goals to create a set of overarching themes.

THE FRAME

WHAT WILL YOU DO?	Group project goals by similarity
WHAT'S THE OUTCOME?	A list of overarching goals or themes
WHY IS IT IMPORTANT?	Reduces a large number of goals into a more manageable number you can achieve
HOW WILL YOU DO IT?	Working together, sort goals into groups and name them

To frame the goal grouping, say:

> "We can only really work toward 3–5 goals at one time, so let's group all the goals we have by similarity, so we can find themes and identify a smaller number of overarching goals we all agree on."

FACILITATE GROUPING GOALS BY SIMILARITY

Everyone contributed their perspective when they shared their goals. Now, you need everyone to come together under a shared perspective, so the team needs to work together. Physically move goals on the board to group them (Figure 6-4).

Goal Map

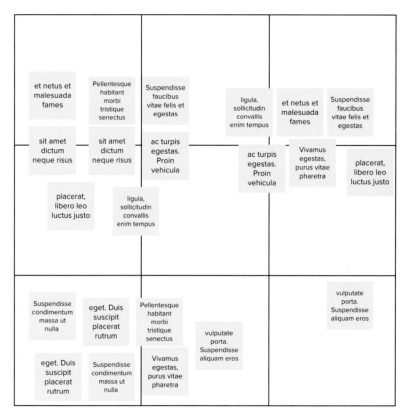

FIGURE 6-4
Sort goals by similarity

For teams new to working with each other or new to this process, you can lead the discussion. For teams where you want to force them to speak and work with one another, have them work together.

For inexperienced teams, lead the discussion to group goals
If this is one of the first times the team has collaborated, timid team members may hesitate before they join in. To overcome hesitation in new teams, lead the discussion to group goals.

As everyone shares their goals or places them on the board, common themes begin to emerge. Use these common themes to kickstart the discussion. Group goals by similarity and narrate what you do. Some goals clearly belong together. When you find a goal you're not sure about, ask the group for their input. When you come across a goal you don't understand, ask the author to clarify.

To force collaboration, have the team group goals

Sometimes you want to force the team to work together. With all goals collected on a wall or board, ask the team to work together to sort goals into thematic groups. This forces team members to talk to each other and negotiate how they group goals and can help new teams get to know one another. Work with the team but hang back and let them work together.

ANALYZE GROUPS TO COMBINE OR BREAK APART

Discuss groupings with the team. For any groups that seem similar, ask why the team separated them. If discussion suggests it, combine the groups together. Similarly, look for groups that collect goals that seem less related, and ask why the team grouped them together. If it appears goals are too different, break them into separate groups.

When complete, it's not uncommon to see one or two large groups, medium or small groups, or even goals that form their own, lonely little group. If you have more than about 10 groups of goals, look for more ways to combine the groups. In the next activity, the group should prioritize as few as 5 goals and no more than 7–10.

NAME EACH GROUP OF GOALS

Once the team has moved goals into groups, name each group. The name should be an overarching goal that describes and encompasses all of the goals in that group (Figure 6-5). For example, say you had a group of three goals:

1. Reduce time to choose and order.

2. Increase purchase options.

3. Reduce store order and wait time.

You could identify an overarching goal that describes all three: make it easier to order online.

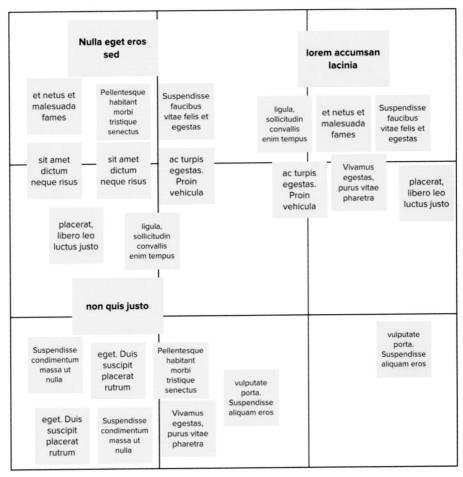

FIGURE 6-5
Describe each group as an overarching goal

FINISH AND MOVE TO PRIORITIZATION

From where you started, the team will have grouped goals into a more manageable number of overarching goals. Likely, you still have more than 3–5 goals. Prioritization will help the team focus on a specific, manageable number of goals:

> "Now that we've identified a more manageable number of goals, we will prioritize them from most to least important, so we all agree on what we're working toward."

Activity 3: Prioritize Project Goals

For any group of goals, teams must understand what goals are more or less important. Priorities support decisions when two goals conflict. At a basic level, goals determine whether a button appears at the top or bottom of the screen and whether or not you include a feature.

When teams prioritize goals together, everyone agrees to and understands why one goal is more important than another. This helps the team agree on product decisions.

In this activity, the team works all together to rank goals from most to least important.

If you started with 3–5 goals, then you may have jumped directly to the prioritization activity. If the team started by generating goals, then make sure you have grouped them down into overarching goals, so you have at least 5 and no more than about 10 goals to rank. If you have more than 10 goals, look for ways to group the goals by similarity (see Activity 2, page 78).

THE FRAME

WHAT WILL YOU DO?	Prioritize goals
WHAT'S THE OUTCOME?	A prioritized list of goals
WHY IS IT IMPORTANT?	Helps team understand what goals are most important, so they can resolve product decisions
HOW WILL YOU DO IT?	Working together, rank goals from most to least important

To frame goal prioritization, say:

> "We will prioritize the overarching goals from most to least important, so later on, we can use the goals to help us make decisions about the product."

FACILITATE GOAL PRIORITIZATION

Prioritization is as easy as asking everyone: "What goal is most important?" When someone suggests the most important goal, move it to the top of the board. Some groups may hesitate to suggest a most important goal, and you can help incite the discussion.

Prompt discussion with resource limits

When teams hesitate to suggest a primary goal, use resource constraints as a metaphor. Tell the participants: If they can only afford to achieve one goal, what one goal would they choose? The goal they would pay for above all others is the most important goal.

Seed discussion with an example goal

When teams hesitate, suggest a most important goal to seed the conversation. Choose a goal you think or believe would make a good primary goal and ask the team if they agree. Continue to choose and rank goals and ask the team to agree or disagree.

Spur discussion by being wrong

A colleague of mine begins with the goals already prioritized. About halfway down, he purposely places less important goals higher in the list to spark discussion. Sometimes when people don't feel comfortable offering an idea, they feel comfortable identifying a mistake.

Reassure team about more senior stakeholders or being wrong

Some teams hesitate before ranking goals. Setting goals isn't their job. More senior stakeholders set and prioritize goals. This may be true, and that doesn't change these activities.

Goal generation and prioritization isn't about the team setting and prioritizing goals. It's about the team clearly understanding what they *think* the goals and importance are. Once the team has aligned, they can share their goals to anyone else to evaluate how aligned they are with the rest of the organization.

The list of ranked goals works like a prototype the team can Check with different stakeholders across the organization. As you'll see in Chapter 8, the team will be able to evaluate these goals over and over, again and again, as you work on the project.

RANK GOALS FROM MOST TO LEAST IMPORTANT

Continue to rank goals from most to least important (Figure 6-6). When team members rank two goals as equal, ask what goal they'd pick if they only had resources for one. Continue ranking goals until you have identified the five most important goals.

Goal prioritization

FIGURE 6-6

Rank the overarching goals from most to least important

lorem accumsan lacinia

vulputate porta. Suspendisse aliquam eros

Nulla eget eros sed

non quis justo

Teams shouldn't focus on more than three goals and can never focus on more than five. I want to repeat that because it's important. In over 20 years of leading cross-functional teams, I have never seen a team able to focus on and achieve more than five goals. Anything more than five goals is extraneous noise. Anything more than three goals is a bonus.

Probe for opportunities to reorganize goals

In some cases, additional discussion reveals previously unclear similarities between goals. When you identify these opportunities, discuss whether the goals should be grouped differently. Sometimes, it makes sense to group goals with more important goals. This reduces your overall list of goals and helps avoid ties in the ranking.

Pyramid rank goals to allow for ties

Ideally, the team can rank goals in a single line from most to least important. If the team can't decide between two goals, you can keep these ranked as a tie. Ties should only appear at lower levels in the ranking. Do everything you can to ensure only one, most important goal.

If you would like to encourage ties, rank goals on a pyramid (Figure 6-7) with the most important goal at the top, two goals at the second level, and three goals at the next level. Still, do not rank more than five goals. (If you use three levels on the pyramid, you will finish with six goals.)

FIGURE 6-7
Use a pyramid to rank goals when you have ties

Probe for dissenting opinions

As priorities solidify, probe for dissenting opinions. Almost always, someone disagrees with how the team has prioritized some goals. Surface this disagreement now. If you don't, the disagreement will surface and slow decisions later in the project.

When you identify disagreements, probe to understand the team member's perspective. As a member of the team, their input should be valued and respected. Work with the team to address the issue and find a resolution. Sometimes the team differs less on the goal and more on its definition. Discussion allows the team to reach consensus.

When disagreement stems from something more intrinsic, goal ranking may need to change, or the dissenting team member will need to concede to the rest of the team. Forge a consensus where everyone can agree—or agree to not disagree.

FINISH AND HIGHLIGHT WHAT YOU ACCOMPLISHED

At the end of these activities, the team has a prioritized list of 3–5 goals that act as a north star as you make product decisions. Highlight this achievement:

> "We've created a prioritized list of goals for this project. We can refer back to these goals, and use them to help make decisions as we go forward."

Identify Goals in Casual Conversations

I use the structured process described in this chapter to kick off new projects and internal initiatives or as part of discovery workshops for clients. However, I don't always join a project at the beginning. Sometimes I'm asked to join a random meeting to provide some perspective or expertise.

In casual and ad hoc conversations, it's difficult to make decisions and offer advice if you don't know the goals. I joined a call about a new internal website where the organizer asked my feedback on wireframes. Before I answered, I asked why we wanted to build the website. What goal did we want to achieve?

We didn't do a formal goal generation, grouping, and prioritization exercise. Meeting attendees provided more than one goal, and I asked what goal was more important. Knowing the team's goals and the most important goal, I was able to provide useful feedback on the wireframes. Knowing the goals helps the Check.

Shared, Prioritized Goals Fuel Better Teams

When teams identify and rank their goals, they take their first step toward working together. You build the foundation for this collaboration when you have every team member offer their individual perspectives about the goals. Team members feel listened to and valued as their goals stay on the board, and they begin to see and understand each other as they discuss how goals should be grouped and ranked.

In larger experience machines, teams that feel listened to and valued become more engaged and take more ownership over the product experience. And when you align on goals at the beginning of a project, you bake the team alignment and the vision it supports into every future decision made by the experience machine.

With activities like these, teams learn to collaborate because they practice listening to and valuing each other's perspectives. They begin to speak their shared language. A prioritized list of goals can act as a constant point of reference for every team discussion after this.

Now that the team knows what it wants to accomplish, it needs to understand and agree on what it wants to do. What is the vision of what they want to build? How will the world be different when they're done? What does success look like?

[7]

Identify a Concrete Vision for Success

If the three little pigs all agreed on their goal to build a place to live that would shelter them from weather and keep them warm, why did each pig build a different house?

Even though goals point to what direction to go in, they don't tell you where to stop. Goals are a direction, not a destination. Everyone on the team might be building the house, but everyone's building a different house. You can help your team members all imagine the same house.

Just as everyone on the team should have the same answer when asked about the project goals, everyone needs to share the vision of how the end state will appear. In this chapter, we'll apply some principles from systems thinking that can help teams create and envision the future together.

I often pair this exercise with the goals activities from the previous chapter as part of kickoff and discovery workshops. It's also useful any time you want to think about where you are now and where you want to go. Just like with goals, we'll look at the more formal version first and then explore variations you can use in other circumstances.

How Future-State Envisioning Works

Future-state envisioning uses a brainstorming technique called framing to generate a concrete vision of what the ideal future could look like (Figure 7-1). It's based on a technique explored by Russel Ackoff[1] in his book and writing on *idealized design*.[2] It ends by mapping the future state to specific metrics the team can use to measure their progress:

1. Individually or as a group, everyone generates what they perceive as issues with the present, current state.

2. Individually or as a group, everyone generates what they perceive as successes that exist in the present, current state.

3. Working together, everyone generates concrete descriptions of what people do in the ideal future.

4. Individually or in groups, everyone identifies metrics that can be used to measure what happens in the future.

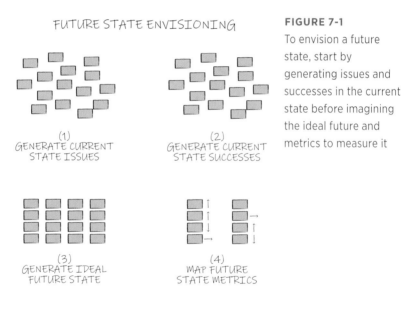

FUTURE STATE ENVISIONING

(1)
GENERATE CURRENT
STATE ISSUES

(2)
GENERATE CURRENT
STATE SUCCESSES

(3)
GENERATE IDEAL
FUTURE STATE

(4)
MAP FUTURE
STATE METRICS

FIGURE 7-1

To envision a future state, start by generating issues and successes in the current state before imagining the ideal future and metrics to measure it

---

1   Russel Ackoff was a prominent systems thinker and professor of management at the Wharton School.

2   Ackoff, Russell Lincoln, et al. *Idealized Design: Creating an Organization's Future.* Wharton School Pub., 2006.

At the end of this activity, the team will have analyzed the current state and populated the worksheet with four outputs:

- A list of current state issues
- A list of current state successes
- A concrete vision of the future
- A list of metrics to measure success in the future

WHEN TO ENVISION THE FUTURE STATE

Envision the future state at the beginning of a new project to make sure everyone on the team works toward the same, concrete vision. It works best after the team has identified and prioritized goals. The goals help frame how the team thinks about and discusses the future vision.

You can use this activity when redesigning sites, apps, systems, or even business processes, and it works the same way if you're starting something totally new.

Output three, the concrete vision of the future, also helps any time teams need to imagine the broader context, so they can answer specific implementation questions.

INPUTS AND QUICK STARTS

Current state analysis requires no specific inputs other than the team's tacit understanding of the project. For example, our gibbons want to add ecommerce to a coffee company's website, so they would approach this activity with that in mind.

Future-state envisioning works great when you start with a blank canvas. You can also gather information from objective research. It's all grist for the mill. These seeds kickstart discussion, help you explore more depth during the collaborative discussion, and reduce overall discussion time.

Seed discussion with pre-existing lists of features and issues

For redesigns and retooling, it's not uncommon for organizations to gather lists of known issues or features. Use existing lists to seed discussion or ask team members to brainstorm issues, successes, and future state ahead of time.

Seed discussion with user research

Leverage user research about pain points, current needs, and issues as well as how users speak about features. User research provides a treasure trove of information about current state issues and successes as well as desired future states.

MATERIALS YOU'LL USE

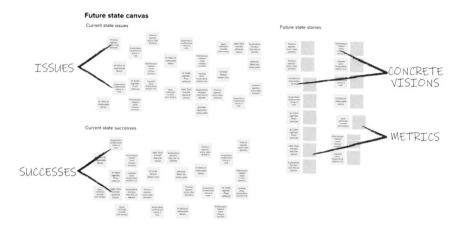

FIGURE 7-2

The future state canvas uses two areas to collect the outputs from the current state issues and successes and a third area to collect outputs of the concrete future vision

Future state canvas

Draw or project the worksheet on a whiteboard or wall or draw or print the worksheet on a piece of paper (Figure 7-2).

Issues, successes, and concrete visions

Once captured, these may be moved. Use movable sticky notes or pieces of paper, or make them easy to erase and rewrite.

Find templates, framing material, and remote resources on the website:

http://pxd.gd/strategy/future-vision

Activity 1: Generate Issues That Exist in the Current State

You wouldn't deliver your product if it didn't make things better. Intrinsic to making things better is changing the negative things about the current state. Before you start envisioning the ideal future, spend some time thinking about the issues that exist now that you might want to change.

In this activity team members work individually or all together to generate a list of issues that exist with the current state.

If your organization has collected a list of issues to address or you have relevant user research, use this information to seed the discussion and prompt team members to generate more issues.

THE FRAME

WHAT WILL YOU DO?	List issues that exist in the current state
WHAT'S THE OUTCOME?	A list of things to fix
WHY IS IT IMPORTANT?	Ensures the team accounts for as many issues as possible when they envision the future state
HOW WILL YOU DO IT?	Work all together to generate as many issues as possible

To frame the generation of current state issues, say:

> "While we work on the new [product/site/system/platform/etc.], we want to make sure we don't end up with the same problems we have today, so let's make a list of all the things we would like to change."

FACILITATE GENERATION OF CURRENT STATE ISSUES

Ask everyone:

"What is broken in the current system? What could be better? What's terrible?"

Generate and discuss issues as a group. Teammates and clients will have no problem rattling off things they don't like. Projects start because the organization wants something to change or improve. Direct questions to quiet team members to make sure everyone contributes. If you capture the issues for your team (instead of them writing them down on their own), paraphrase to make the issues more concise or easier to understand, and make sure the author agrees with how you captured the issue (Figure 7-3).

FIGURE 7-3

Capture current state issues on the board or worksheet

If you worry group discussion may prematurely limit the team's ideas, ask everyone to write down three issues in private. Then have everyone share and discuss their issues.

Capture each issue on an individual note or card and place issues on the board or worksheet. If you share issues in a group discussion, capture each issue and add it to the board as it's shared.

Probe for issues related to quality and efficiency

As the team shares and discusses current state issues, ask why something happens as well as why it's an issue. Understand who is affected and why it's important. Also look for opportunities to uncover issues related to quality and efficiency:

- In the current state, what is inefficient?
- What takes too long to do? What requires extra steps?
- What is too difficult to do? What should be easier?
- What is confusing? Frustrating?
- What barriers or obstacles make the current state difficult?
- What unintended consequences occur?

Probe for issues that inhibit change, evolution, or customization

Most products live in a context that's constantly evolving, so look for issues that inhibit change:

- What processes prevent the system from adjusting?
- What restricts change? Is it a process? People?

Probe for issues that affect specific groups

Issues may also describe suboptimal outcomes:

- What issues affect customers?
- What issues affect price or sales?
- What issues make maintenance difficult? Or inhibit marketing?
- What causes low performance for departments or employees?

Probe for issues connected to the project goals

Use your project goals as prompts to identify additional issues. Follow where the discussion leads and capture any issues whether they relate to the project, department, or organization. State each goal as a question in the negative.

TABLE 7-1. Use project goals to probe for current state issues

PROJECT GOAL	CURRENT STATE ISSUES
Improve functionality	What features don't exist?
Improve efficiency and quality	What features don't work?
Improve conversion and use	In what contexts does it not work? Why don't people sign up?
Maximize or find new customer value	What customer outcomes are not addressed?

Group issues to identify themes (optional)

In some cases, you have too many issues or want more clarity. Group issues by similarity and identify themes. Do this the same way you grouped project goals to identify themes (see page 78). Sometimes when you envision the ideal future, it's more useful to think about themes of issues rather than individual issues. Use your judgment. Are the issues your team captured too specific and detailed? Or do they give you a good sense of what the product can fix?

Limit time to keep discussion moving

Almost certainly, teams can spend hours to identify things to improve, optimize, and change. Even then, you won't have identified everything. That's OK. The goal is less about identifying issues. When you identify current state issues, you frame how the team thinks about the future vision. The goal isn't a comprehensive list of issues, but to ground the future vision in real problems that exist today.

Limit time for current state issues to 10–15 minutes. That provides enough time to identify common and pressing issues and primes the discussion for the future vision.

FINISH AND MOVE ON SUCCESSES

Once time has elapsed, verify that you captured all issues and everyone agrees with how you captured them. Move to discuss current state successes:

> "Now that we know what we want to fix, let's look at what we don't want to change."

Activity 2: Generate Successes That Exist in the Current State

Current state issues identified the dirty bathwater. Current state successes highlight the baby you don't want to throw out. Collect a list of features, processes, and outcomes the team doesn't want to affect.

THE FRAME

WHAT WILL YOU DO?	List successes that exist in the current state
WHAT'S THE OUTCOME?	A list of things to keep
WHY IS IT IMPORTANT?	Ensures the team protects and continues successes when they envision the future state
HOW WILL YOU DO IT?	Work together to generate as many successes as possible

To frame the generation of current state successes, say:

> "We want to make sure we don't lose anything that's good about the current state, so we'll identify things we would like to stay the same when we envision the future."

FACILITATE GENERATION OF CURRENT STATE SUCCESSES

Ask everyone what they like about the current state. What works? What shouldn't change?

As you identify successes, capture them on the worksheet. Paraphrase to make the successes more concise and easier to understand and make sure authors agree with how you phrased them (Figure 7-4).

Future state canvas

FIGURE 7-4

Capture current state successes on the board or worksheet

While teammates and clients have found it easy to list problems, they generate successes more slowly. Sometimes people don't notice something unless it gets in the way or annoys them. To reveal the good things the team may not notice, ask about what's normal:

- What tools or features help the user get their job done?

- What keeps everything on track and working well?

Probe for other people's successes

Issues and successes can be subjective, so it's easy to slip into your own perspective. To identify additional successes, ask the team what other people might like:

- What do executives like about the current state?

- What helps your boss get their job done?

- What do customers like?

Probe for successes related to project goals

Just like you can use project goals to probe for issues, they can help you probe for successes. Phrase the project goal as a positive question to probe for current state successes related to that goal.

TABLE 7-2. Use project goals to probe for current state successes

PROJECT GOAL	CURRENT STATE SUCCESSES
Improve functionality	What features do exist?
Improve efficiency and quality	What features do work?
Improve conversion and use	In what contexts does it work?
Maximize or find new customer value	What customer outcomes are addressed?

FINISH AND MOVE ON TO THE FUTURE VISION

Once success generation slows, the team has a decent sense of what works in the current state and what you don't want to change. In rare cases, the current state is so broken, the team won't identify any successes. Do one last pass to ensure you've identified key successes. Once everyone agrees, move to describe the future state vision.

Activity 3: Generate Concrete Visions of What People Do in the Ideal Future

Everyone in the room already knows what success looks like. However, your team envisions that success in different ways. Like the three little pigs, some see success as a straw house while others see success in sticks.

In this activity:

- Team members will imagine an ideal, successful future and describe what people do.

To build a successful product, you need a concrete vision of what success will look like. In the future, when this project is a success, what will specific people do? Describing a vision of success in terms of specific people and behaviors reveals a concrete set of behaviors and outcomes the team can build for.

If your organization has documented features they want to see in the new product, use those to seed the discussion and ask participants to reframe them in terms of what people will do.

THE FRAME

WHAT WILL YOU DO?	Describe what people do if the product is successful
WHAT'S THE OUTCOME?	A list of people, tasks, and behaviors
WHY IS IT IMPORTANT?	Provides concrete outcomes the team can design for
HOW WILL YOU DO IT?	Working all together

To frame the generation of a concrete future vision, say:

> "Our goals tell us what direction we should go in, but we need to define what success looks like. After the project has launched, how do we know we built the right thing? Let's describe what a successful future looks like."

CONSTRAIN THE VISION TO WHAT'S POSSIBLE

Because you want a concrete vision of what a successful future will look like, two rules ensure the vision is possible:

- It must be feasible with today's technology

- It must be legal

Technological feasibility ensures your team can build the vision it imagines. While magical thinking and science fiction provide interesting ideas, if you can't build the vision, then you can't ship the product, and it can't be a success.

Likewise, you shouldn't pursue a vision that violates ethics, laws, or regulations. Unless you aspire to villainy.

PUSH THE VISION BEYOND WHAT'S PREFERRED

Feasible and legal are the only two constraints. It doesn't need to be viable because you can't know that yet. It doesn't need to be popular, and it doesn't need to avoid the CEO's pet peeves or use the CTO's favorite new technology. None of that matters.

Sometimes, it's useful to encourage groups to imagine the craziest, most far-fetched ideas. This kind of activity expands the team's creativity. If you feel the team needs to broaden their thinking, creative exercises can help. However, when you generate a concrete future vision, you want to focus on not only what is possible, but what possibility we should choose to represent success. What can you build and then say you succeeded?

FACILITATE THE GENERATION OF CONCRETE VISIONS OF SUCCESS

Ask everyone:

> "Imagine the product launches and it's a wild success and everyone gets a raise. Two years after launch, what do people do?"

The people can be users, customers, support staff, the CEO, the maintenance team, frontline managers, the customer's friends and family, or anyone else. Two years from now the world has changed for the better. Anyone in the world could be affected.

The concrete vision follows a specific format:

[User] will [task]

You can expand the format toward a user story:

[User] will [task], so they can [goal]

If you've worked through goals, current state issues, or current sate successes, kickstart the discussion with specific behaviors the team has already mentioned. For example, during the goals discussion, someone may have mentioned customers will compare products. Capture that as a vision statement. Or expand it into more of a user story: "Customers will compare products, so they can find the one that works best for them."

As the group describes future behaviors, capture them on the worksheet. Make sure each vision follows the format: [User] will [task] (Figure 7-5).

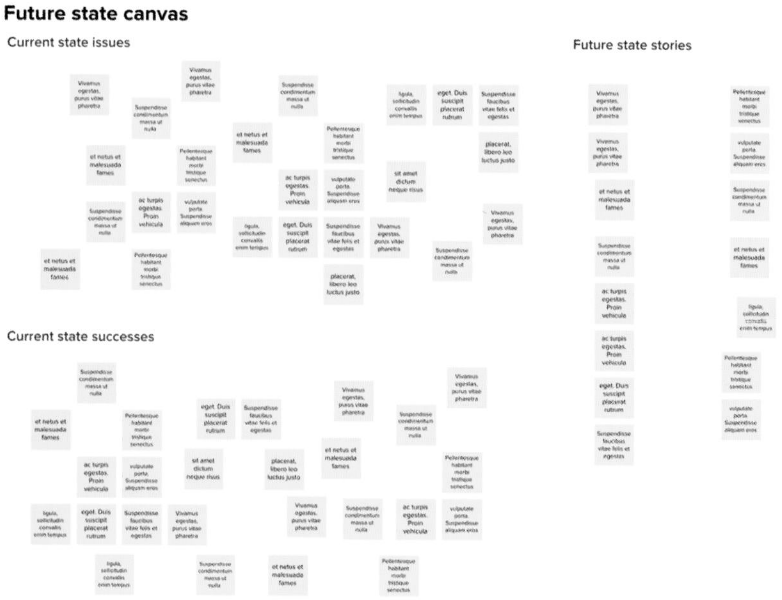

Future state canvas

FIGURE 7-5

Capture vision statements on the board or worksheet. Leave space next to each one, so you can add metrics during the next activity.

Probe for behaviors at all levels

One or more users or stakeholders occupy more of the team's headspace, but many different people have a stake in the project's success. Probe the team to envision what other stakeholders will do in a successful future:

- What will executives and managers do?

- What will other departments and business lines do? What will support staff do?

The same applies to end users, both customers and employees:

- What will coworkers do?
- What will the customer's friends and family do?

Probe for behaviors that address current state issues

In the excitement of envisioning a utopian future, don't forget current state issues the team wants to improve or fix. For any current state issues not addressed by a vision statement, ask how the future vision addresses the issue.

In some cases, a current state issue ceases to be a problem because of how the future is envisioned. For example, if a current state issue is you can never find creamer, the future state may envision rich, creamy coffee that never needs cream.

Use current state successes as constraints

As the group identifies concrete visions, watch for places where the future vision conflicts with a current state success. Usually, these conflicting future visions address an issue the team didn't articulate. Ask the author to describe their vision in more detail. Why does it represent a successful future? Can this vision of a successful future occur and the current state success both exist in the future? Or must the team choose one?

Probe for ideal visions of the future

The group's background as well as framing around current state issues and successes ensures concrete visions extend practices and processes that exist in the current system. The future vision continues present thinking. This framing limits the reach and imagination of future innovations. These visions are easier to sell and implement, but they may not be enough.

It may be useful to push the team to imagine an ideal future that has no ties back to the current system. Ask everyone:

> "Imagine that last night, a fire destroyed everything. All data was lost, every building burned, all the files are gone, and you have to create a new product from scratch. If you could build anything you wanted, what would it look like? What would people do when it was a success?"

Many teams restrict what is possible in the current system. Often, more ideal products aren't feasible because that's just not how things are done. However, when you remove restrictions present in the current system, the ideal becomes much more feasible.

Remember, the question isn't what can the organization do, it's what can the team do that's technologically feasible and legal?

Reassure the team about scope

When you frame the question with phrases like "if you could build anything you wanted" and words like "ideal," project and product managers fear scope increases and unfulfilled project goals. Reassure the team this exercise identifies what people will do when the project is a success and does not affect scope, deadlines, or budget. Knowing what success looks like makes no promises or commitments about how it's built or when.

FINISH AND MOVE ON TO MEASURING SUCCESS

Once you have collected concrete visions of success on the worksheet, you've generated very valuable information about your product. Instead of a list of features, you have specific descriptions about what people will do. Instead of requirements, your team has described outcomes.

You could stop there. A concrete vision described as a list of specific behavioral outcomes is a pretty great vision. The last step is to identify how you will measure success. Tell everyone:

> "Now that we know what people are doing in a successful future, let's identify metrics we can use to measure that behavior and track our success."

Activity 4: Map Metrics to Future Behaviors

When you envision the future in terms of what people do, you not only describe an outcome you can build toward, you also describe something that can be measured, tracked, and evaluated.

In this activity the team will identify metrics that measure each vision statement.

Specific metrics measure and validate success. Ending with metrics prepares the team to base design decisions on specific, measurable hunches and hypotheses they can test and validate.

THE FRAME

WHAT WILL YOU DO?	Identify a metric for each vision statement
WHAT'S THE OUTCOME?	A list of metrics that measure future behaviors
WHY IS IT IMPORTANT?	Identifies metrics the team can use to test and validate product decisions
HOW WILL YOU DO IT?	Working together or in groups

To frame the identification of metrics, say:

> "Each of the concrete visions describes a specific user behavior, and because it's a specific behavior, we can measure it. For each of the concrete visions, we want to identify a metric we can use to track it. We can use these metrics to measure our success and test and validate product ideas."

FACILITATE THE IDENTIFICATION OF METRICS

Review each vision statement and work with the team to identify a metric or metrics that measure the behavior. When you define vision as a person that does a thing, you can track and measure that behavior.

For example, if the vision is, "a customer will compare types of coffee to find the right one for them," you can define several metrics:

- Percent of shoppers who compare coffee
- Percent of shoppers who compare coffee and complete a purchase

The trick of these metrics is they sound like quantitative numbers you can get out of your analytics system. Don't think about how the behavior would be measured, only that you could measure it. With product comparison, for example, you can track comparisons on the website if the user clicks on something to make a comparison. What if the design helps the user compare just by looking at a list of products instead of clicking a button? Your analytics system can't measure that. But your research team could measure that interaction with user testing or interviews.

Capture metrics to the right of each concrete vision (Figure 7-6). Future behaviors can have one or more relevant metrics. Capture all that seem relevant.

Future state canvas

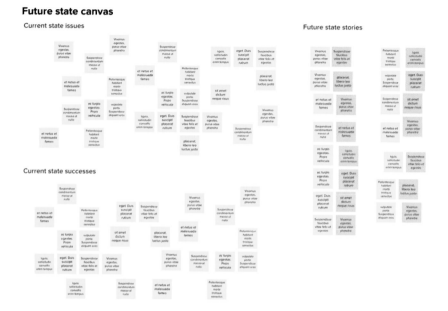

FIGURE 7-6
Capture metrics next to each concrete vision

Identify baselines for metrics

For many metrics, the team can gather data about current behaviors to use as a baseline. Sometimes the data is right on point. Sometimes it's inferred. Let's use personalization as an example.

Let's say the team believes personalized content on the homepage will be more attractive to customers. Since the current site does not personalize, you can't compare it to future personalization. However, if personalized content is more enticing to customers, you may predict that bounce rates will go down because customers like what they see. Or maybe time spent on the homepage will go down because customers click personalized content more quickly than non-personalized content. Or maybe a smaller percentage of customers use search or navigation because they click through the personalized content instead.

Of course, it's probably better to measure how likely it is that customers who view personalized content buy coffee compared to customers who don't see personalized content. But the point stands. Some metrics won't have explicit baselines, so you may need to infer a baseline from a related behavior.

Help the team identify direct and inferred baselines. This frames product development as a measurable, scientific activity, so you can reduce the impact of opinions.

Specify direction the metric should move

Nothing communicates a project's value at the start or success at the end than comparing it to a pre-existing baseline. Organizations improve good things and reduce bad things. Before a project launches, communicate project value in terms of whether it will improve, reduce, or maintain a current metric. A focus on metrics helps stakeholders understand the impact the project will have on the organization in the same language managers and executives use to evaluate success and failure.

After a project launches, measure metrics before and after launch to communicate actual value. The metrics should move in the predicted direction. Regardless of direction, the team has clear metrics they can use to learn and evaluate product decisions.

Don't worry about too many metrics

At this point, the team isn't selecting key performance indicators. Identify a breadth of metrics and baselines the team can use as inputs for future project work. It's better to identify a bunch of potential metrics and not use them than to rely on common metrics that don't measure what you have identified as the concrete vision.

You can't start tracking behaviors if you don't identify that you want them tracked. You're about to build the ideal product. You need to know what metrics to track, so the team can engineer the right tracking in the right places.

FINISH METRICS AND WRAP UP

With metrics captured, identify next steps to make sure the outputs remain actionable. First, identify who will track down applicable baseline metrics. Second, decide how the future vision will be documented, stored, and shared.

Identify who needs to reference and use the outputs. Both current state issues and successes as well as concrete future visions translate into business, functional, and technical requirements. Future vision statements transform into user stories for agile teams and test cases for the test lead. Identify specific team members to feed the outputs from this activity into the rest of the team's work.

Vision Focuses the Team on Success, not Features

In four easy steps, you helped the team envision concrete user behaviors it can build for as well as specific metrics it can use to test and validate product ideas. Before this activity, the team was building a product. Now, instead of a collection of features, the team envisions the product in terms of how it enables specific user behaviors. More important, when the team chose a metric, baseline, and direction for change, they turned each behavior into a testable hypothesis.

When all is said and done, the real output isn't the list of current state issues, successes, or future visions. This activity changes how the team thinks about the product and success. This powerful change isn't like a light switch that just gets flipped on. It's more like a fire you have to feed over time.

In the next chapter, we'll look at ways to keep the project goals and the future state vision at the front of everyone's attention throughout your product's lifetime.

[8]

Document and Share
Project Goals and Vision

IT FEELS NICE WHEN the team works together and aligns on strategic ideas like project goals and the concrete vision. However, if you forget the goals and vision in two weeks, then you wasted your time. You can help your team keep the project goals and vision top of mind. Your team will make product decisions using the goals and stay on track toward the future vision.

In this chapter, we'll look at ways to document and share the project goals and vision, so they help your team stay aligned. We'll also look at how to share the goals and vision with other people in your company, so reviews and check-ins with managers and executives run smoother.

Document Goals to Provide Important Context

After you identify and prioritize project goals, you have a nice list of goals. Now it's time to clean them up, so you can keep them in front of the team as well as share them with everyone else in your organization.

When you share the project goals, you provide important context that explains decisions to others who aren't familiar with the myriad nuances surrounding the project. Good goals make sense to both the team as well as additional stakeholders across the organization.

An important part of this context, the project goals focus on outcomes that anyone can understand. While the CEO may not understand why you placed a specific button at the top of the screen, they understand your goal to reduce tech support calls. Rather than argue about where the button goes, talk to the CEO about the best way to reduce support calls.

DOCUMENT PROJECT GOALS AS A PRIORITIZED LIST

Share project goals as prioritized lists. Goals keep the team aligned and communicate rationale to external stakeholders. Prioritized goals support decisions when two goals conflict with each other (Figure 8-1).

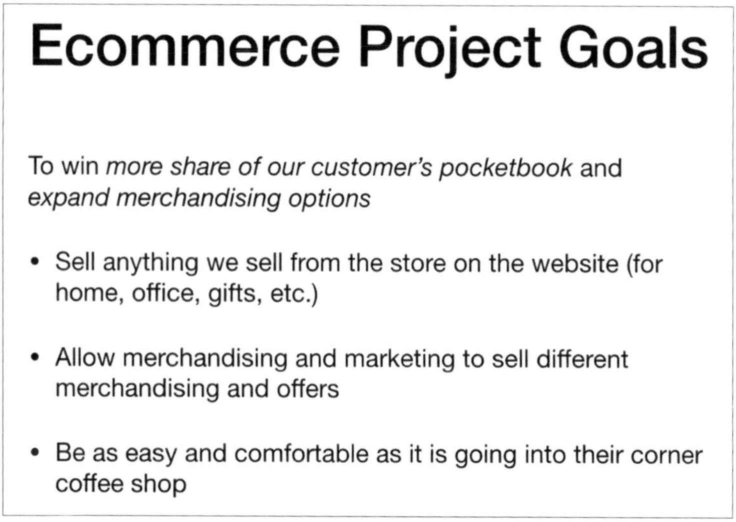

Ecommerce Project Goals

To win *more share of our customer's pocketbook* and *expand merchandising options*

- Sell anything we sell from the store on the website (for home, office, gifts, etc.)

- Allow merchandising and marketing to sell different merchandising and offers

- Be as easy and comfortable as it is going into their corner coffee shop

FIGURE 8-1
Document goals in prioritized lists to support team decisions

The project goals activity creates an output that's already in the format of a prioritized list, so it's easy to clean up and share as quickly as possible. If you prioritized goals on the pyramid, document goals in a hierarchy (Figure 8-2).

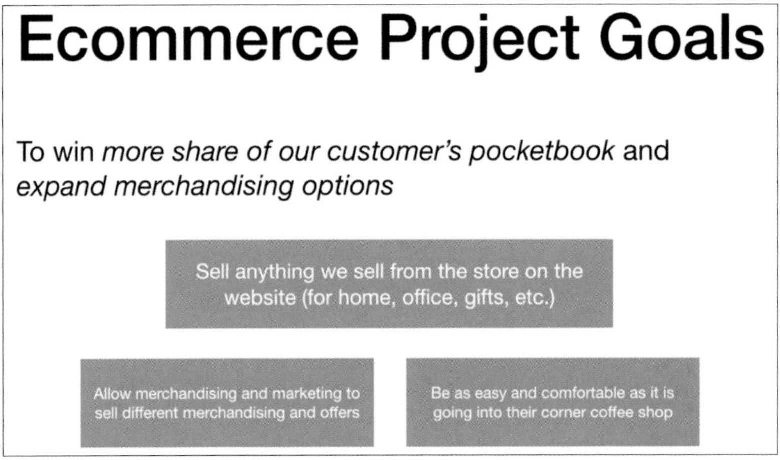

Ecommerce Project Goals

To win *more share of our customer's pocketbook* and *expand merchandising options*

Sell anything we sell from the store on the website (for home, office, gifts, etc.)

Allow merchandising and marketing to sell different merchandising and offers

Be as easy and comfortable as it is going into their corner coffee shop

FIGURE 8-2
Document project goals in hierarchies

Document Vision to Show the Big Picture

While goals provide context about where you're going, the vision paints a picture of what the future will look like, so people want to go there. Unfortunately, where goals come out as a list that's easy to document and share, it takes more work to convert your concrete vision stories into an easy-to-share vision.

A good vision tells a brief story.

Stories package ideas into human-friendly narratives that explain where you will start, the problem you will overcome, and what the successful future looks like. Good vision statements tell the story of the project's success.

This story should act like an elevator pitch, short enough to share in chance hallway encounters or as a brief introduction when speaking about a project.

Identify the most important and interesting vision stories

Your team identified quite a few future state behaviors, so you can't include all of them into a brief story. Select the future state behaviors that seem most important or most interesting. When possible, select future states that echo popular ideas in your company to take advantage of existing mindshare.

String the stories together into a couple of paragraphs that describe what success looks like in the future. Finish the vision with a description of the human impact. For example, if you allow customers to subscribe to their coffee and order smaller batches, note how that means their coffee will be fresher (Figure 8-3).

Ecommerce project vision

In the future after ecommerce has been added to the website:

- Customers will order their favorite coffee, ground to their specifications to be delivered to their homes or offices. Educational content helps them choose coffees they will like best and what grind to use. They'll subscribe to their coffee and receive smaller batches more frequently, so their coffee is always fresher.

- Marketing and merchandising will tailor products and offers to match individual customer buying habits. Customers buy more and are more satisfied with their purchases.

FIGURE 8-3
Use important and interesting future scenarios to document vision as a brief story

Check the Goals and Vision with the Team

Even though you created the project goals and vision all together, make sure to check the documented version with the team. Check the final wording and format and revisit the project goals and vision at the beginning of every discussion.

REVIEW FINAL WORDING AND FORMAT WITH TEAM

You and a subset of the team may work apart after collaboration to document the goals and vision. Wordsmith phrasing to make goals clear and concise and describe the future vision in clear, concrete terms.

Share these final versions with the rest of the team. Listen to and address any feedback to ensure everyone on the team agrees with how you have described the goals and vision. If the entire team aligns around and shares the goals and vision, you've laid the foundation for everyone to trust everyone else's decisions.

REFERENCE THE PROJECT GOALS AND VISION AT THE BEGINNING OF EVERY DISCUSSION AND REVIEW

North stars aid navigation only when referenced. When the team comes together to share learnings and work, display the goals and vision at the beginning of the discussion. When evaluating options, reference goals to support decisions.

Although goals and vision should not change during the course of the project, they are difficult to articulate. As the team works on specific parts of the project, you may discover the initial goals and vision were incorrect. Every time you use goals and vision to rationalize a decision, you provide the opportunity to review and adjust the goals and vision and to improve them and make them more accurate.

START WITH GOALS AND VISION WHEN SPEAKING WITH STAKEHOLDERS

When you review material with others outside of the project, start with the goals and vision. When you begin with the project goals and vision, you give managers and executives the opportunity to review your north star and make sure you're still on track. If the team is off, the stakeholder will tell you.

When you share the vision, it creates a context for any project-related discussion, so stakeholders understand what you are trying to do. Prioritized project goals describe your decision framework, so stakeholders know how to evaluate and respond to everything you share.

Teams Need to Constantly Reference Goals and Vision

Teams find goals and vision useful to document and communicate. Goals and vision support decisions to resource projects as well as onboard new team members. However, as north stars, teams must reference goals and vision on a continual basis to take advantage of the alignment they provide. Revisit and reference goals and vision at every opportunity, especially to evaluate options and rationalize project decisions.

The project goals align with what your organization wants to do. The vision represents how the future will change for your users. In the next part, we'll look at how you can help your team understand users, so they can build the future that's in store for them.

 Find templates, framing material, and remote resources on the website:

http://pxd.gd/strategy/

[*III*]

Users

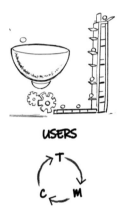

BEYOND JUST THE PRODUCT, the user lives at the center of every deci-sion the entire experience machine makes about anything it does. As a shared vision, the user keeps teams aligned and building the same product for the same people. The activities in this section help teams collaboratively understand and analyze their users as well as how to share and communicate that vision to the broader organization.

Your team can work better together, and you're going to help them do it. In this part we examine the basic elements of users. Because we always talk about research whenever we talk about users, we will also look at ways to rightsize user research to match the information you need for the product you're building.

To support the team's ongoing analysis of and learnings about their users, we'll look at the attribute grid as a living document and how to convert the wall of sticky notes and user data into easy-to-read and scan stories about who the user is.

[9]

Users and User Research

EVERY DESIGN PROJECT STARTS with personas. The user hides in the folds of our gray matter. For every product, service, or interface you design, you imagine the user who will use it, and everyone on the team imagines a different user.

Just like with project goals and vision, when everyone on the team imagines the same thing, you collaborate more easily and effectively. Documenting the user makes the user real and lets everyone on the team imagine and design for the same person.

That being said, have you ever noticed personas often look different and capture different information? We're going to talk about how to model users, so you and your team can collaborate on better designs, and the experience machine will crank out better products and services. In this chapter, we'll examine the different attributes you can use to document a user model. We'll also spend some time on how to determine the type of research you need, if any.

The attributes we discuss in this chapter form the foundation for the following collaborative activities on prioritizing users, understanding user needs, and documenting your user models as personas.

Personas vs. Profiles vs. Roles vs. Archetypes

Some people take exception if you suggest you don't need user research to make a persona. Some teams sieve oceans of quantitative data to craft personas, while others quilt personas together from patches of qualitative research. Though some argue for one approach over the other, both are valid.

A persona is a *model* of a user. How you create that model depends on what you need to do. User insights are like fuel for an engine. Not everyone needs high-octane, quantitative insights. Some people get by fine with regular fuel.

Some people refer to these user models as personas. It doesn't matter if you call them personas or profiles, actors, roles, archetypes, or whatever. Whatever you call it, it's a *model* of your user.

These models help your team design better products because they document and communicate the most important information about users that your team needs. We break these user attributes into three types: tasks, contexts, and influencers.

Tasks, Contexts, and Influencers

When you think of a user, you might imagine what they're doing, where, and maybe even why. When we talk about how we understand the user, we refer to:

- Tasks, what the user does
- Contexts, where and when the user does it
- Influencers, why the user does it

When you describe or identify insights about users, group them into one of these three areas (Figure 9-1).

FIGURE 9-1
Define users by what they do (task), where and when they do it (context), and why they do it (influencers)

TASKS: WHAT USERS DO

Tasks describe what your user does. The user's tasks tell us what functionality we need to build. Teams find it easy to talk about tasks. Interfaces help users accomplish one or more tasks.

Tasks can be broad or narrow. Something like buying coffee beans online can have numerous steps, including searching for coffee, evaluating whether you like the coffee, deciding to buy, adding to cart, and checking out. All of these steps help the user complete the broader task of buying coffee online.

You can break this down even further. For example, the "Add to cart" step can be broken down into more minute steps:

1. Scan screen for "Add to cart" button

2. Find "Add to cart" button

3. Move mouse to "Add to cart" button

4. Press mouse down to initiate button selection

5. Release mouse to complete button selection

6. Notice confirmation message

7. Read confirmation message

8. Understand coffee was added to cart

As a general rule, when you think about tasks, work with enough detail to help you make decisions about what you're designing. The way you describe the task should be actionable.[1] It should help you make decisions. Think of this as the task's *fidelity*. How much detail do you need about a task to design for it?

Use building a house as an analogy. If you're planning a house, you need the blueprint. If you're building a house, you need to know how many doors you need. If you're helping people move through doors, you need to know what the doorknob looks like. Although you may draft a blueprint, build a house, and help people move from one room

---

1 Mulder, Steve, and Ziv Yaar. *The User Is Always Right: A Practical Guide to Creating and Using Personas for the Web.* Berkeley, CA: New Riders, 2007.

to another, you won't do all three at the same time. Choose the correct task fidelity to have the information you need without spending time on information you don't.

CONTEXTS: WHERE, WHEN, HOW, AND WITH WHOM

Context describes where, when, and how users complete a task. Knowing the user's context helps make the product easier to use.

Often, context describes the user's device, like a laptop or phone, as well as the channel, like email or the web. Context can also describe if the user completes the task at home or in an office, during the day or at night, once a day or once a year, with family and friends or alone.

INFLUENCERS: WHY THEY DO IT

Influencers describe why the user does something. Tasks tell us *what* to build, and context tells us *how* to design it. Influencers help us design the *right* thing.

Pains and gains

An influencer can be positive or negative. You can climb the apple tree to pick an apple or to escape a pack of wolves. In either case, you climb the tree. Being eaten by wolves is a *pain* you want to avoid. Getting closer to apples is a *gain*. Users move away from pains and move toward gains.

Intended and unintended

Pains and gains can be intended or unintended. The user may unintentionally move closer to apples while they intend to get away from wolves. The user may encounter unintended pains and gains. Tasks often have multiple unintended consequences. For example, climbing the tree may result in splinters, an unintended pain. Similarly, the user may see a beautiful view of the horizon, an unintended gain, when they climb the tree.

Tasks, context, and influencers help teams think about how users climb trees. But if we zoom out one level, we might wonder why the user is running around a forest filled with wolves and apple trees in the first place.

Motivations, Goals, and Jobs-to-Be-Done

Influencers provide insight into why a user does what they do, but they don't explain what the user wants to get done. If the user's task is to buy coffee, why do they want to buy coffee? Do they want to take a break? Do they want to wake up? Be nourished? The answer to *why* the user wants to buy coffee represents the user's goal or "job-to-be-done" (JTBD).

As a concept, jobs-to-be-done appear in innovation and lean startup communities. Product innovation consultant Anthony Ulwick defines jobs-to-be-done: "The core functional job is defined in a single statement, such as 'cut a piece of wood in a straight line,' 'pass on life lessons to children,' or 'monitor a patient's vital signs.'"[2]

In *About Face 3*, interaction designer Alan Cooper refers to a similar concept as a goal, the answer to the question: "*Why* is a user performing an activity, task, action, or operation in the first place?"[3]

Whether you call it a goal or job-to-be-done, you want to describe the user's primary motivation, the fundamental need the user wants to fulfill.

When you understand the user's fundamental need, "you understand the meaning of activities to your users, and thus create more appropriate and satisfactory designs."[4] For the experience machine, "A deep understanding of the core functional job enables a company to create product or service offerings that get the job done significantly better than competing solutions."[5] When your team understands the user's fundamental need, their base goals, the core job the user wants to get done, your organization can create more innovative and more successful experiences.

Motivations, tasks, contexts, and influencers—that's a lot of information to keep track of for each of your users. Fortunately, you can focus on only the user attributes you need for the product you're building.

---

2   Ulwick, Anthony W., and Alexander Osterwalder. *Jobs to Be Done: Theory to Practice.* Houston, TX: Idea Bite, 2016.

3   Cooper, Alan, Robert Reimann, and Dave Cronin. *About Face 3: The Essentials of Interaction Design*. Indianapolis, IN: Wiley Pub., 2007.

4   Cooper, Reimann, and Cronin, 2007.

5   Ulwick and Osterwalder, 2016.

THE MILLER, HIS SON, AND THEIR DONKEY

As a child, I loved the Random House Pictureback *Tales from Aesop*[6] and the story about the miller, his son, and their donkey.

A miller and his son walk along the road to sell their donkey in town. A passing traveler criticizes the miller for making his son walk when he could ride. So, the miller places his son on the donkey, and they continue on their way.

A little while later, a traveler criticizes the son: "How ungrateful you are to ride while your father walks." Hearing this, the son dismounts to let his father ride.

Further along, another traveler comments, "It seems so foolish that either of you would walk when you could both ride." At this, both the miller and his son climb atop the donkey and continue to town.

Seeing the miller and his son atop the poor beast, another says, "How cruelly you force your donkey to bear both your burdens!" Taking the traveler's words to heart, the miller and his son lash the animal's feet to a pole and carry him on their shoulders the rest of the way to town.

---

6 Aesop, and J. P. Miller. *Tales from Aesop*. New York: Random House, 1976.

As the miller and his son cross a bridge into town, a crowd gathers to laugh at the foolish pair carrying a donkey on their shoulders. The crowd's loud jeers scare the poor beast. The donkey struggles, the ropes loosen, and the donkey falls over the bridge to his death in the river below.

The miller and his son, with no donkey to sell, return home empty-handed.

Every passerby recommended better ways for the miller and his son to travel to town. No one helped them sell their donkey.

NO ONE TALKS ABOUT USER GOALS/JTBD

Although the miller and his son want to sell their donkey, everyone helps them get to town. You'll see this same problem over and over again. User goals and jobs-to-be-done are invisible. Just like you talk about the visible parts of an interface and overlook the invisible parts, people don't talk about jobs or goals. If no one talks about goals/JTBD, how do they talk about what users need or want?

Marketing teams talk about marketing personas

Historically, marketers succeeded when they focused on demographic segments. Clayton Christensen shares examples like feminine hygiene and baby care products where demographic segments closely align to the job. If you understand the demographics, you understand the job.[7]

Marketing teams also use psychographics like values, opinions, attitudes, interests, and lifestyles to create marketing personas that model different types of customers. Marketing personas based on demographics and psychographics can communicate and advertise to customers, but they don't help you improve or innovate the user's experience.

Any time someone defines users based on demographics (married women, 35–45) or psychographics (prefers low cost over quality, values time with friends), you know you're not talking about user goals/JTBD.

Technical teams talk about features and technology

Just like marketing teams focus on what they know (marketing segments), technical teams focus on what they know (features and technology). Throughout their careers, technical teams achieved success when they focused on features and implementation.

Any time someone mentions features or technology, you're not talking about user goals/JTBD.

Organizations talk about products and services

Innovation consultants Anthony Ulwick and Lance Bettencourt[8] note that many companies focus on the products and services, or on products and services from the competition. This focus on products and services aligns with the marketing and technical teams. Marketing teams think of how they'll market products and services. Technical teams think of how they'll build the products and services.

Any time someone speaks in terms of products and services, help them dig to get to the user goals/JTBD.

---

7 Christensen, Clayton, Scott Cook, and Taddy Hall. "Marketing Malpractice: The Cause and the Cure." *Harvard Business Review*, Dec. 2005.

8 Bettencourt, Lance and Anthony W. Ulwick, "The Customer-Centered Innovation Map." *Harvard Business Review*, May 2008.

Users talk about solutions and specifications

Even users won't talk about their goals. Ulwick describes how users often talk about solutions, specifications, needs, or benefits. Ulwick uses customer comments about a razor as an example. When asked about razors, customers might mention they want a specific solution like a lubrication strip or describe specifications like lighter weight or a sleeker look. Users may also describe needs and say they want the razor to be reliable or dependable. Lastly, users may mention the benefits they'd like to see in the razor, like "a better shave" or "an easy clean-up."[9] Solutions and specifications are concrete and easier to describe than more abstract goals.

When people talk about solutions or specifications, you know you need to probe a little to identify their underlying goal.

The miller and his son knew they wanted to sell their donkey. Marketing teams, technical teams, organizations, and users prefer to focus on how the miller and his son get to town.

---

9 Ulwick, Anthony W. *What Customers Want: Using Outcome-Driven Innovation to Create Breakthrough Products and Services.* New York: McGraw-Hill, 2009.

Project Goals Reveal the Attributes Your User Model Needs

Your user model needs a certain amount of fidelity. The more attributes you include, the more fidelity your model has (Table 9-1).

TABLE 9-1. Different types of user models include more attributes and have more fidelity

		TYPE OF USER MODEL		
		"User"	Role "Sales manager"	Persona "Sammy, sales manager"
TYPE OF ATTRIBUTE	**Tasks** What will the user do?	X	X	X
	Context When, where, how, and with whom do they do it?		X	X
	Influencers What pains and gains affect what they do?			X

Based on the project's type of goal, the user model needs different types of user attributes. Use your project's goals to determine the attributes to include in your user model (Table 9-2).

Once you identify the user attributes you need, identify the information you need to fill in those attributes. You've now identified the user research you need.

TABLE 9-2. User model attributes based on type of project goal

TYPE OF PROJECT GOAL	USER ATTRIBUTES TO INCLUDE IN THE MODEL
• Add content and functionality	**Tasks** What do users do?
• Improve efficiency • Reduce errors • Improve output quality	**Contexts** When, where, how, and with whom do they do it?
• Improve conversion • Improve adoption • Improve retention • Increase engagement • Increase social activity	**Influencers** What pains and gains affect interaction?
• Maximize customer value • Defend existing markets from disruption • Innovate new markets • Disrupt existing markets	**Goals and jobs-to-be-done** What fundamental needs drive the user?

Four Types of User Research

The vast world of available user research methods breaks down into two sources:

- Direct observation
- Indirect observation

Direct observation refers to research you collect yourself. You directly observe the users. To directly research what users do in the real world, you watch them. To directly see what users do in the digital world, you watch their behavioral analytics, what people click on and see, when, and how often.

Indirect observation refers to research provided by someone else. To learn what users do through indirect observation, ask people who interact with your users. With indirect observation, interview other people to learn what your users do. This can be people in sales, customer support, and other users. This is also other user researchers. What is direct observation to you is indirect observation to the person you tell it to.

Whether direct or indirect, research provides insights in two flavors:

- Behaviors
- Attitudes

Behavioral research documents what users do. Design ethnography, analytics, and stakeholder interviews provide information about what users do, how they behave.

Attitudinal research documents what users say they want or say they do. User interviews allow you to directly observe what users say. Search analytics, customer support logs, customer feedback, user surveys, and diary studies let you indirectly observe what users say.

What people say they do and what they actually do are two different things. Behavioral research is more accurate than attitudinal research.

RESEARCH METHODS PROVIDE DIRECT OR INDIRECT, BEHAVIORAL OR ATTITUDINAL RESEARCH

User research methods map onto a grid that compares direct and indirect observation to behavioral and attitudinal research (Table 9-3).

TABLE 9-3. Direct or indirect observation and behavioral or attitudinal research maps to specific research methods

<table>
<tr><td colspan="2"></td><td colspan="2">TYPE OF RESEARCH INSIGHT</td></tr>
<tr><td colspan="2"></td><td>Attitudinal
What users say they want or do</td><td>Behavioral
What users actually do</td></tr>
<tr><td rowspan="4">TYPE OF RESEARCH</td><td>Direct observation
Where you observe the user</td><td>• User interviews</td><td>• Analytics observation

• Ethnographic observation</td></tr>
<tr><td>Indirect observation
Where other people observe the user</td><td>• Search analytics
• Customer support logs
• Surveys
• Diary studies</td><td>• Stakeholder interviews</td></tr>
</table>

Select Research Methods Based on User Attributes and Project Goals

Some say behavioral research like analytics and observation are the only way to understand users. In fairness, watching users does generate the most accurate information. Unfortunately, direct, behavioral research requires more time and resources.

Direct behavioral observation isn't the only way to research users. To choose a research method, focus on the attributes you need to create the user model. Just like attributes align to project goals, so do research methods (Table 9-4).

The user attributes you need will identify your research objectives. For example, if you have a goal to improve conversions, then user interviews should include questions about tasks, contexts, and influencers. In contrast, if you have a goal to reduce errors, then the user interviews only need to include questions about tasks and context.

MODIFY RESEARCH METHODS BASED ON TIME, COST, AND DIFFICULTY

You have several options to collect research. Direct observation almost always provides more accurate information than indirect observation and almost always requires more time, money, and skill.

Direct, behavioral research isn't the only way to understand your users. Many teams use profiles based on indirect observation or what the team believes they already know about the users. Sometimes called proto-personas,[10] ad hoc personas,[11] or assumptive personas,[12] these types of user models use less accurate research to focus teams around user-centered thinking and test-driven design.

---

10 Gothelf, Jeff. "Using Proto-Personas for Executive Alignment." UX Mag. N.p., 1 May 2012. Web. 12 June 2017. *https://uxmag.com/articles/using-proto-personas-for-executive-alignment.*

11 Norman, Donald A. "Ad-Hoc Personas & Empathetic Focus." Don Norman's Jnd.org. N.p., 16 Nov. 04. Web. 12 June 2017. *https://jnd.org/ad-hoc_personas_empathetic_focus.*

12 Browne, Jonathan. Assumption Personas Help Overcome Hurdles to Using Research-Based Design Personas. Publication. N.p.: Forrester Research, 2009.

TABLE 9-4. Research methods based on project goals and user attributes needed

PROJECT GOAL	TYPE OF USER ATTRIBUTE	DIRECT OBSERVATION	INDIRECT OBSERVATION
• Add content and functionality	**Tasks** What do users do?	• User interviews • Analytics	• Stakeholder interviews • Competitive analysis
• Improve efficiency • Reduce errors • Improve output quality	**Contexts** When, where, how, and with whom do they do it?	• User interviews • Analytics observation • Ethnographic observation	• Stakeholder interviews • Competitive analysis
• Improve conversion • Improve adoption • Improve retention • Increase engagement • Increase social activity	**Influencers** What pains and gains affect interaction?	• User interviews • Ethnographic observation	• Stakeholder interviews
• Maximize customer value • Defend existing markets from disruption • Innovate new markets • Disrupt existing markets	**Goals and jobs-to-be-done** What fundamental needs drive the user?	• User interviews	• Stakeholder interviews • Surveys • Customer feedback • Diary studies

Distinguish your collaboration goals from research goals. One should not hinder your efforts toward the other. Regardless of what research you start with, you have many ways to collaborate with your team and to create user profiles.

Good User Models Evolve With the Product

Personas help the experience machine think more clearly about its end users. The user profile creates a model your team can design for, return to, and refine over time. Better models are better, but they shouldn't be static. If you start with less accurate models, work to improve them over time as the team learns more about their users.

It's tricky to figure out what information the team needs to build the best product. Use project goals to identify the most relevant user attributes and let project goals and attributes guide any research you need. But don't let missing research stop you from moving forward. Research provides better understanding, and user models allow better collaboration.

This all assumes you know what users are important. The next activity helps teams identify what users need to be on their radar.

Identify Users with the Bull's-Eye Canvas

The miller took his donkey to market to sell. People made fun of the miller. The donkey fell in a river and drowned. You don't want that to happen again, so who do you design for? The miller who owns the donkey? The people who made fun of him? Or the donkey that drowned?

It's difficult to make the right product decisions if you're not sure who they're for. Teams risk building the right features for the wrong users. Help your team identify the right users, so they build the right product for the right people.

Everyone on the team should understand who you're building for and why. This chapter uses a bull's-eye canvas to identify a product's users and agree on who's important. We'll look at a formal version of this activity you can use as part of project kickoff or discovery workshops, but the approach works just as well in ad hoc conversations where you want to verify the user before providing feedback.

How User Identification Works

User mapping uses a bull's-eye canvas to generate users and map them based on how they interact with or are affected by the product (Figure 10-1). The bull's-eye uses four, concentric circles to organize users by how the product affects them. The center circle represents the product. Users who interact directly with the product go in the second circle. The third circle contains anyone they communicate or collaborate with, and the fourth circle is for anyone else affected by the product. To complete the canvas, the team works through three activities:

- Working together, the team generates a list of direct users (people who will use the product).

- Working together, the team identifies indirect users (people who communicate or collaborate with direct users).

- Working together, the team identifies extended users (people who are affected by the product).

When done, the team will have produced three lists of users:

- A list of direct users to design for

- A list of users affected by the design to keep in consideration

- A list of users to deprioritize

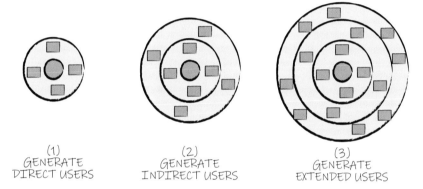

(1)
GENERATE
DIRECT USERS

(2)
GENERATE
INDIRECT USERS

(3)
GENERATE
EXTENDED USERS

FIGURE 10-1

Use the bull's-eye canvas to generate and map users who interact with or are affected by the product

WHEN TO IDENTIFY USERS

Use the bull's-eye canvas at the start of a project to align the team around the same list of users. The bull's-eye canvas also works to identify users for journey mapping and flows (Part IV) or interface ideation (Part V).

The bull's-eye canvas helps teams understand how a product affects users. Usually, team members have an idea of who will use a design. However, like with the team's other assumptions, there's a lot of misalignment. Getting everyone on the same page helps the team share the same vision.

INPUTS AND QUICK STARTS

Because teams often already have some assumption about who the users will be, the bull's-eye canvas works well if you start with no inputs. You may also request a list of users or existing personas. Even if the team does not have a documented set of users, you can poll teammates and collect a list of users before you start the activity.

If you've previously worked through project goals and future vision, then the team has already mentioned lots of users, especially in the future scenarios that each start with a specific type of user. Use the users from future scenarios to seed discussion.

MATERIALS YOU'LL USE

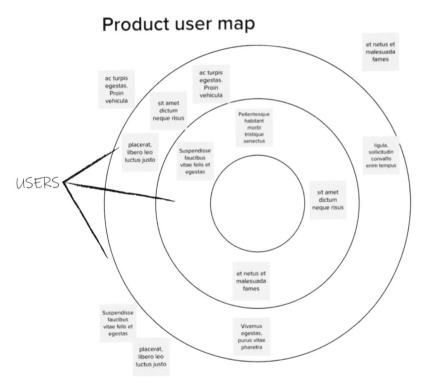

FIGURE 10-2

Product user maps have four parts: the bull's-eye canvas and three different groups of users

Bull's-eye canvas

Draw or project the bull's-eye canvas on a whiteboard or wall or draw the canvas on a piece of paper. Use three or four concentric circles (Figure 10-2).

Users

Users may move around the canvas during discussion. Sticky notes make it easy to add, move, and remove users. However, if using a dry erase board, you can easily write and erase users.

 Find templates, framing material, and remote resources on the website:

http://pxd.gd/users/user-target

Activity 1: Generate Direct Users

Usually, the people who interact directly with the product are the most important users. In this activity the team will work together to generate a list of people who will use the product.

Often, the team knows who will use the product, and will easily generate a list. If you gathered a list of users as an input, place users on the canvas to kickstart discussion.

THE FRAME

WHAT WILL YOU DO?	List people who use the product
WHAT'S THE OUTCOME?	A list of users who interact directly with the product
WHY IS IT IMPORTANT?	Helps team understand who they should build the product for
HOW WILL YOU DO IT?	Working all together

To frame generation of direct users, say:

> "Let's identify the system's users, so we can optimize the experience for the right people. We want to list people who will directly interact with the system and its interfaces."

FACILITATE GENERATION OF DIRECT USERS

Ask everyone:

> "Who will interact with and use the product?"

The center circle represents the product. As the team lists direct users, capture them in the second circle of the bull's-eye canvas (Figure 10-3).

If you collected a list of users as inputs to this activity, think aloud while you place them on the canvas and ask the team if they agree with your placements.

Probe for the user's proper relationship to the product

If participants identify people you believe are not direct users, probe to understand what the users do with the product. Ask what part of the product the user interacts with. Team members may identify unexpected ways users interact with the product. If the user will interact directly with the product, add them to the second circle of the canvas.

It's also common to identify users affected by the product, either indirectly or in more extended ways. As you discuss and understand how the product affects the user, place the user in the appropriate circle on the canvas.

Product user map

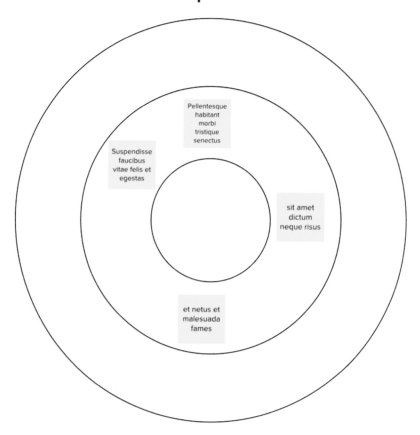

FIGURE 10-3
Capture direct users in the second circle of the bull's-eye

Probe for other users

Teams wear blinders about the product's users. They focus on one user and ignore others. It's not that they don't know about other users. Rather, they've prioritized one set of users over others, and it's not uncommon to focus on the wrong users.

Ask who else will use the product to probe for other users and remove your team's blinders.

A technical services organization wanted to redesign their website to help procurement managers order more services. Very quickly, they discovered engineers and technicians drove most orders and most traffic to the site. Although procurement managers wrote the checks, the organization wanted to build the site for the wrong users.

Look for any other users, no matter how insignificant they seem. The goal is to generate a wide and comprehensive list of potential users.

When the team doesn't know the system's users

For new products or teams, it's possible you don't know who the user is. You really can't go much further. Pivot to create a concrete future vision (see Chapter 7). That alignment will help identify potential product users.

FINISH AND MOVE TO INDIRECT USERS

When discussion around direct users slows, tell the team you're ready to focus on indirect users, people who communicate or collaborate with direct users without using the product themselves:

> "Let's move on to the next circle of the canvas and talk about users who talk to or work with the direct users."

Activity 2: Generate Indirect Users

Teams usually focus on people who interact directly with the product. However, users often communicate and collaborate with other people while they use our products. These indirect users affect the needs of the direct users. So, who do your users talk to and work with?

In this activity, the team works together to generate a list of users who the direct users must talk to or work with.

THE FRAME

WHAT WILL YOU DO?	List indirect users
WHAT'S THE OUTCOME?	A list of users who direct users need to communicate and collaborate with
WHY IS IT IMPORTANT?	Helps the team understand how to optimize the product to support how direct users will use it
HOW WILL YOU DO IT?	Working all together

To frame discussion around indirect users, say:

> "Now that we know who will use the product, let's look at who they collaborate with, so we can make it easy for our users to get their jobs done. We want to list anyone our users talk to or work with."

FACILITATE GENERATION OF INDIRECT USERS

Ask everyone:

> "Who will our users talk to or work with while they use our product?"

As the team lists indirect users, capture them in the third circle of the bull's-eye (Figure 10-4).

Probe for connected users

Trigger questions can identify additional indirect users:

- Who do users talk to while using the product?
- Do users share information with anyone?
- Does someone else review or approve what users do or choose?
- Who do your users work with?
- Who do they complain to?
- Who watches them while they use the product?
- Who do they report to?
- Who provides information users need while using the product?

Product user map

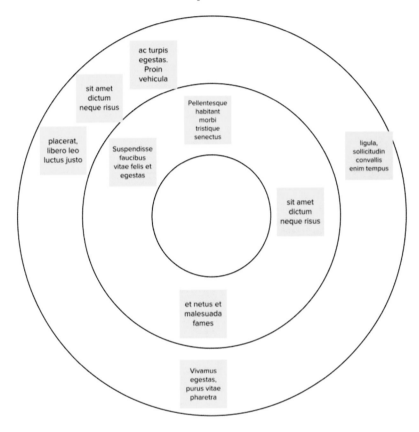

FIGURE 10-4
Write the indirect users in the third circle of the bull's-eye canvas

Probe for anti-users

In some cases, users may avoid contact with some people while using the product. You can understand these relationships to optimize the product to either support or prevent this behavior. Ask the team if there is anyone users avoid or hide from while using the product.

Capture anti-users in the third circle of the canvas. Differentiate them from other indirect users with an X next to their name.

After the team has identified indirect users, it's time to talk about more extended users:

> "Let's move on to the next circle of the canvas and talk about anyone who might be affected by what direct users do with the product."

Activity 3: Generate Extended Users

In the fairy tale "Rapunzel," a witch catches a husband stealing lettuce for his wife. To avoid the witch's punishment, the husband agrees to give the witch his first child.

In this story, the witch and the husband represent direct users. Each directly participates in agreeing to the bargain. The wife is an indirect user. She doesn't interact with the agreement, although she interacts with her husband.

Many months later, the wife gives birth to a daughter who the witch collects as payment for stolen lettuce. Rapunzel is the extended user. Although she never stole lettuce, risked a curse, or entered into a witch's bargain, she spends her youth in a tower letting a witch climb up and down her hair.

Extended users represent people who neither use the product, nor interact with those who do, the direct and indirect users. Despite their distance from the product, they feel its effects. While every design produces unintended consequences, a little foresight reduces unintended, negative consequences.

In this activity, the team works together to generate a list of extended users, people affected by the product.

THE FRAME

Direct and indirect users provide a solid foundation for your team to think about who else may be affected. Frame discussion to focus on anyone who could be affected by the product or by the direct and indirect users.

WHAT WILL YOU DO?	List extended users
WHAT'S THE OUTCOME?	A list of users who may be affected by the product or its direct or indirect users
WHY IS IT IMPORTANT?	Helps teams avoid unintended consequences that may run counter to the project's goals
HOW WILL YOU DO IT?	Working all together

To frame discussion around extended users, say:

> "We have a good idea about who will use the product, as well as who they talk to and work with. Now let's look for anyone else who may be affected."

FACILITATE EXTENDED USER GENERATION

Ask everyone:

> "Who will our indirect users interact with?"

Capture extended users around the edges of the bull's-eye (Figure 10-5).

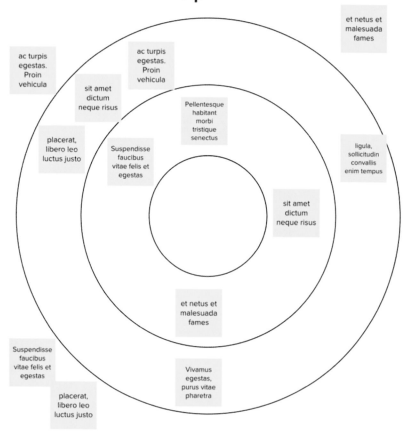

Product user map

FIGURE 10-5
Write extended users around the edges of the bull's-eye

Probe for policies or processes used by indirect users

Many unintended consequences extend not from the product, but from policies, processes, or outcomes triggered by indirect users. Look for prominent indirect users whose day-to-day actions affect large numbers of people. For example, stealing lettuce doesn't affect Rapunzel. It's the witch's policy of requesting first-born children and the father's policy of agreeing.

Build the Right Product for the Right User

After you identify extended users, the team will have identified an ecosystem of people who will use and be affected by the product. This shared vision of who has a stake in the system will guide and influence ongoing discussions about the product. The bull's-eye canvas helps teams reflect and consider who is affected by their product decisions.

Once the team has created a shared vision of the user landscape, it's time to reexamine the team's initial assumptions about who they will build for. The team will have populated the bull's-eye canvas with many different user groups.

In the next chapter, we'll learn how the user profile canvas helps teams understand a user's tasks, context, influencers, and motivations.

[11]

Explore User Attributes with the Profile Canvas

SOMEONE SHARED A REPORT interface they were building. "Looks nice," I said. "What's the user trying to do here? Why do they look at this report?" They didn't know. How can I provide feedback if I don't know what the user's trying to do?

Once you start designing and building, your users and their needs should drive most decisions. Teams have the same two problems with users that they have with other aspects of the project. Either they haven't all agreed on who their users are, or they haven't learned the right information about their users. You can help your team come to a shared understanding about the user that includes the exact information they need, and nothing more.

In this chapter, we'll look at how teams can gather around the user profile canvas and discuss, explore, and agree on who their users are, their tasks, contexts, influencers, and even goals and jobs-to-be-done.

Even though I typically create user profile canvases to kick off project discovery, you can create them any time and are encouraged to revisit them constantly.

How the User Profile Canvas Works

The user profile canvas creates a visual checklist that helps teams think about a user's tasks, contexts, and influencers. The user profile canvas creates a single space where the team can collect a user's attributes. Information collected can derive from research insights or the team's tacit knowledge about the user (Figure 11-1). In a short span of time, a team can synthesize a great deal of information about a user:

1. Working together, the team generates a list of tasks and contexts.

2. The team works together to identify the user's goal or job-to-be-done.

3. The team generates a list of the user's pains.

4. The team generates a list of the user's gains.

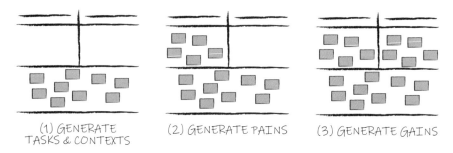

(1) GENERATE TASKS & CONTEXTS   (2) GENERATE PAINS   (3) GENERATE GAINS

FIGURE 11-1

Generate the user's tasks and contexts before focusing on influencers like pains and gains

The team starts with tasks and then moves to the user's goal because it is easier for people to list tasks. The tasks also give us a hint about what the underlying goal really is.

Create a user profile canvas for each target user. At the end of the activity, the team will have gathered a trove of good information about a user's tasks, contexts, and influencers.

WHEN TO EXPLORE USER ATTRIBUTES

Explore user attributes at the beginning of projects when the team starts to align on their shared vision of the product. You can also use this method at any point in a project when you don't have good alignment or clear documentation about the user's tasks, contexts, or influencers.

INPUTS AND QUICK STARTS

The user profile canvas assumes you have one or more users to profile. If you don't have a list, help the team identify a list of users to profile (Chapter 10). If you have more than 3–5 users to profile, help the team rank users, so you can focus on the most important ones.

To start, write the user's name at the top of the canvas. If you know the goal or JTBD, write that as well. (If not, the team can identify the goal or job-to-be-done in activity 3.)

MATERIALS YOU'LL USE

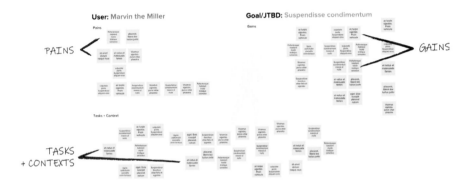

FIGURE 11-2
The user profile canvas helps teams collect a user's tasks, contexts, pains, and gains

User profile canvas

Draw or project the canvas on a whiteboard or wall or draw the canvas on a piece of paper (Figure 11-2). You don't need the walking stick figure, but I like how it points the user toward gains and away from pains.

Individual pains and gains

Once captured, pains and gains may move as the team discusses the user's attributes.

Tasks and contexts

Once captured, these may move as well. It's common for teams to group tasks by topic (coffee) or type (education) or channel (mobile).

Find templates, framing material, and remote resources on the website:

http://pxd.gd/users/profile-canvas

Activity 1: Generate Tasks and Contexts

Teams find it easy to talk about user tasks, so we start there. However, there's a catch. Every time the user does something, they might do it with someone, and they definitely do it somewhere, at some time, at some frequency. To capture tasks, the team also needs to capture that task's context.

In this activity team members will work together to generate a list of the user's tasks and their context.

THE FRAME

WHAT WILL YOU DO?	List the user's tasks
WHAT'S THE OUTCOME?	A list of user stories/scenarios
WHY IS IT IMPORTANT?	Helps team understand and optimize functionality for the contexts where the user performs the tasks
HOW WILL YOU DO IT?	Working all together

To frame discussion around user tasks and contexts, say:

> "Let's list each of the user's tasks and its context, so we can understand what the user is trying to accomplish."

FACILITATE TASK AND CONTEXT GENERATION

Ask everyone what the user does. As the team identifies tasks, capture each one at the bottom of the canvas. If you've drawn the canvas on a whiteboard, write the tasks on the board or on sticky notes (Figure 11-3).

Each task should follow a specific format: [task] + [context]. For example, if Regular Joe's task is to order coffee for the office, you would capture it in this way:

> Order coffee for office + at work on desktop during day once every 2 weeks with coworker

This captures the task as well as context that includes where, when, what device, how often, and with whom. Not all tasks will have or need this much context. Use your best judgment to determine what's enough. Some tasks have more, and some have less, and you'll go back and edit others to add more context as discussion progresses.

Mix discussion and brainstorming to generate tasks and context all together as a group. Encourage people to mention a task and context and then capture it themselves on the board. If you have more than 5 people, split into groups with 3–5 people each, and give each group a separate user to explore.

To draw out quiet participants and gather a broader set of perspectives, request that team members generate lists of tasks + contexts in private before coming together to share and place on the canvas.

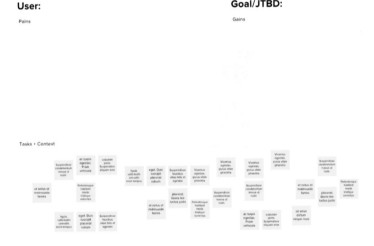

FIGURE 11-3
Capture user tasks at the bottom of the canvas

Probe for additional tasks

Make sure to probe for additional tasks with questions or statements. Sometimes a gentle push kicks participants into an avalanche of ideas. As the team thinks of additional tasks, capture them on the canvas:

- Are there other tasks the user might do?

- Users may also...

Probe for related tasks

Each task can have related tasks. Ask about additional tasks that happen before and after:[1]

- Does the user do anything to prepare for the task?
- Does the user need any information or material before they complete these tasks?
- How does the user know when to do the task?
- If the task is ongoing, how does the user stay on track?
- How do they know to adjust or change what they're doing?
- Do they do anything once the task is done?

Capture pains, gains, and goals as they come up

Good discussions about tasks reveal user pains, gains, and goals. As the team identifies these, capture them in the appropriate sections of the canvas to ensure you remember them and reinforce everyone's input is valid and listened to. If the team becomes sidetracked, remind them you will work on pains, gains, and goals soon, and refocus the team on tasks + contexts.

GROUP TASKS BY SIMILARITY

Sometimes it's useful to sort tasks into logical groups. Ask the team to group the tasks, and groups will emerge organically. Two common ways to organize tasks may help the team later when they map journeys or touchpoints (Part IV):

- Group by similarity: these tasks relate to riding donkeys, those tasks relate to other travelers, and so on.
- Group by time: these tasks happen first, these tasks happen last

FINISH AND MOVE TO GENERATE PAINS

Once the team has identified and grouped the tasks, you're ready to analyze them and understand their core goals:

> "Let's talk about the user's core goal."

---

1 Bettencourt and Ulwick, 2008.

Activity 2: Analyze Tasks to Identify the User's Goal

Use the generated tasks to understand the user's core goal to drive a really great product experience.

Quite possibly, someone has already blurted out the user's goal. Quite possibly, they haven't. Goals are fuzzy. The fuzziness around finding the user's goal has to do with getting to the right altitude. In *The User Is Always Right*, Steve Mulder shows how you can discuss the user's goals at different levels (Figure 11-4).

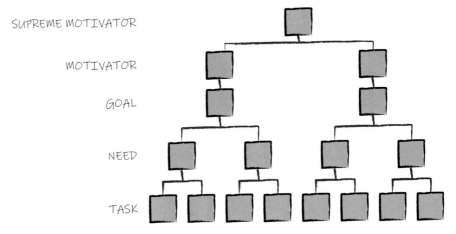

FIGURE 11-4
Steve Mulder illustrates how a user's goal varies based on its level

At lower levels, you clearly talk about tasks, discrete, time-specific actions taken by the user. In the fable about the miller and his son, one task is to ride the donkey. Another is to listen to fellow travelers belittle you. All tasks assume a certain kind of interface. Riding assumes a donkey. Being belittled assumes language.

In contrast, a goal is timeless. Being timeless, it can't rely on any specific technology or interface.

Users complete tasks to accomplish goals, so you can imagine tasks like rungs on a ladder that leads up to the goal. An easy way to identify a user's goal is to take a task like "ride the donkey" and ask: "Why is the user riding the donkey?"

The miller answers, "to go to town." Go to town could be the goal, but you can also ask why the miller wants to go to town: "to sell my donkey."

Going to town is a fine goal and lives lower on the hierarchy than the miller's higher goal to sell the donkey. What goal should you design for? That depends. Do you design for lower goals where you have more control? Or do you focus on higher goals that offer more potential value?

That depends on your project. For every project, you'll move up to a level that feels "right."

THE FRAME

WHAT WILL YOU DO?	Identify the user's goal
WHAT'S THE OUTCOME?	A single goal or goals
WHY IS IT IMPORTANT?	Goals help the team design for pains and gains that determine the quality of the experience
HOW WILL YOU DO IT?	Ask why a user does a task until you arrive at the underlying goal

To frame the analysis around the user's goal, say:

> "Let's figure out why the user does these tasks. What is the user really trying to accomplish? What is their goal?"

PROBE FOR GOALS WITH THE 5 WHY'S

Asking "why" is the easiest way to take a task and understand the underlying goal. You may have heard to ask why five times.

Practitioners use this technique, often called the 5 Why's,[2] to take a problem and learn the root cause. When you see a problem, ask yourself why it's happening. When you get that answer, ask why again. And again and again until you arrive at the problem's root cause. In the world of lean thinking, this type of analysis roots out problems in a system, so they can be fixed. As any toddler knows, 5 Why's can reveal the root issue behind anything. And it works that way with tasks.

To uncover goals, choose a task or group of tasks from the user profile canvas and ask, "why does the user do this?"

---

2 Discussed in *The Toyota Way.*

You might ask:

- "Why does the miller walk on the road?" To get to town.

- "Why does he want to go to town?" To sell his donkey.

- "Why does he want to sell his donkey?" To make money.

- "Why does he want to make money?" To pay his cell phone bill.

- "Why does he want to pay his cell phone bill? It's the only way he can order coffee with the app.

While every passerby offered advice for how to get to town, no one offered advice for how to buy coffee with the mobile app. Or how to make money. Or how to sell his donkey. We can map the farmer's answers on Mulder's hierarchy (Figure 11-5), and you can see how root cause analysis also reveals problems at different altitudes that you can choose to solve.

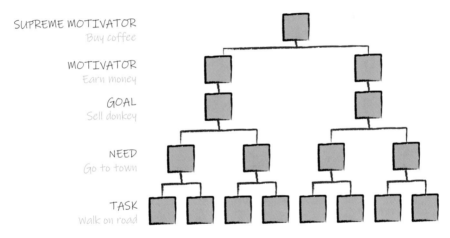

SUPREME MOTIVATOR
Buy coffee

MOTIVATOR
Earn money

GOAL
Sell donkey

NEED
Go to town

TASK
Walk on road

FIGURE 11-5
5 Why's reveals problems to solve at different levels

The power of user goals comes in how you answer those why's. What if the miller gave you different answers (Figure 11-6)?

- "Why does he want to sell his donkey?" Because he has too many donkeys.

- "Why does he have too many donkeys?" Because his farm only has so much room.

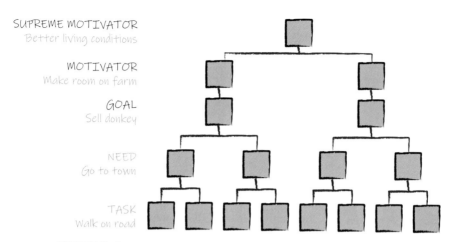

SUPREME MOTIVATOR
Better living conditions

MOTIVATOR
Make room on farm

GOAL
Sell donkey

NEED
Go to town

TASK
Walk on road

FIGURE 11-6

Different 5 Why's answers reveal different problems to solve

In both cases, better donkey-to-town transportation helps the miller sell his donkey. Real innovation emerges when you help the miller achieve his core goal. Is his core goal to buy coffee or manage donkey population?

STACK GOALS INTO A LADDER

Each time you ask "why," move up the ladder of user needs. Use the profile canvas to record the answers (Figure 11-7).

FIGURE 11-7

As you ask why and move up the goals ladder, capture the why's on the profile canvas

Once you feel like you've arrived at the right user goal, discuss with the team to come to a consensus. Often you discover the right altitude because you go one or two steps too high. Importantly, the team decides to focus on one or more goals. That doesn't mean there aren't other goals that could be targeted. The team makes the decision that they will focus on *this* goal.

FINISH AND MOVE TO USER PAINS

With the user's goal identified, the team now has a clear way to evaluate user pains and gains. Pains are always easier to generate, so start there:

> "Now that we've identified the user goal we think is most important, let's look at the pain points and issues that hamper the user as they move toward their goal."

Activity 3: Generate User Pain Points

The only thing easier to imagine than user tasks are their pain points. Now that you understand the user's tasks and goals, capture the annoyances, barriers, and negative outcomes the user tries to avoid.

Users must overcome annoyances and barriers with every task, and people love to talk about negative side effects. Knowing these annoyances and side effects will help the team better understand the core goal and job-to-be-done, as well as identify problems the product can help users overcome.

THE FRAME

WHAT WILL YOU DO?	Generate the user's pain points, barriers, and risks
WHAT'S THE OUTCOME?	A list of user pains
WHY IS IT IMPORTANT?	Reveals constraints that influence the user's behavior and decisions
HOW WILL YOU DO IT?	Work as a group to brainstorm a list of user pains

To frame discussion around user pains, say:

> "Let's talk about user pain points and barriers, so we can look for ways to improve the user's experience."

GENERATE PAINS

Ask everyone:

> "What do users hate about doing these tasks? What do they find most annoying?"

As the team generates pains, capture them on the left side of the user profile canvas (Figure 11-8).

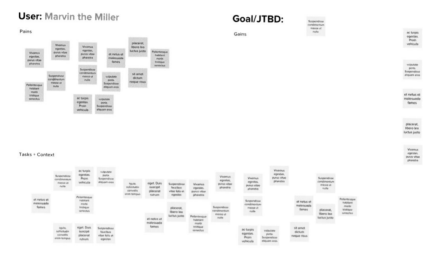

FIGURE 11-8

Capture user pains on the left of the user profile canvas

The team will generate three types of user pains:

- Barriers that make completing the task more difficult

- Annoyances that make tasks frustrating

- Negative side effects users try to avoid while completing a task

Probe for each type of user pain.[3]

---

3 See also Ulwick, Anthony W., and Lance A. Bettencourt. "Giving Customers a Fair Hearing." *MIT Sloan Management Review*, April 1, 2008; Bettencourt, Lance and Anthony W. Ulwick, "The Customer-Centered Innovation Map." *Harvard Business Review*, May 2008; and Osterwalder, Alexander, et al. *Value Proposition Design: How to Create Products and Services Customers Want*. Wiley, 2014.

Probe for barriers

Barriers describe anything that prevents users from completing tasks or achieving their goals. Barriers also describe anything that makes the user's job more difficult.

Probe the team about any barriers. Ask if there are any barriers that prevent the user from achieving their goal. Probe for barriers with specific questions:

- Is it too expensive?
- Do they not understand what they need to do?
- Do they not have enough time?
- Do they lack necessary training?
- Do they not have access to information or tools they need?

Probe for annoyances

Annoyances describe anything that frustrates the user. Ask:

> "What do users find annoying or frustrating? What would they change to make things easier?"

Use specific questions to probe for annoyances:

- Are there any missing features?
- Are there any common malfunctions?
- Is performance a problem?
- What common mistakes do your customers make?
- Does anything take too much time?
- Does anything cost too much money?
- Does anything require too much effort?
- What makes the job challenging?
- What could be more efficient?
- What requires troubleshooting?
- What workarounds do they use?

Probe for negative side effects

Negative side effects describe undesirable outcomes that happen when they complete the task. Ask:

> "Even if the user succeeds, are there any side effects they dislike?"

Probe with specific questions:

- Are users concerned with how they will be perceived?
- Do they feel guilty? Scared? Embarrassed?
- What do users worry will go wrong?
- Do users worry about extra fees or costs?

RANK PAINS BY SEVERITY

After the team identifies pains, understand what pain points cause the most trouble. Rank each pain in order of severity from most severe to least severe (Figure 11-9).

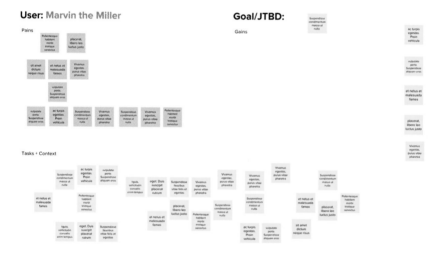

FIGURE 11-9

Rank pains in order of severity, from most severe to least severe

THE FINISH

With a list of pain points, prioritized in order of severity, it's time to shift the discussion to user gains:

> "Now that we understand the user's pains, let's talk about what users like."

Activity 4: Generate User Gains

Pain points and barriers loom large in our minds. Helping users avoid pain points and overcome barriers makes their lives suck less, but it doesn't make the world better. User gains like expected outcomes and unexpected moments of delight provide a clear roadmap of highlights your product can aim for.

At the most basic level, users have specific expectations about any interaction. Understand these expectations to ensure your team creates the right experience.

THE FRAME

WHAT WILL YOU DO?	List user's expected and unexpected gains
WHAT'S THE OUTCOME?	A list of user gains
WHY IS IT IMPORTANT?	Reveals constraints that influence the user's behavior and decisions
HOW WILL YOU DO IT?	Work as a group to brainstorm a list of user gains

To frame discussion around user gains, say:

> "Let's talk about what the user gains, so we can make sure the experience meets their expectations."

GENERATE GAINS

Ask everyone:

> "What will users gain when achieving this goal? What do they expect to achieve?"

As the team generates gains, capture them on the right side of the user profile canvas (Figure 11-10).

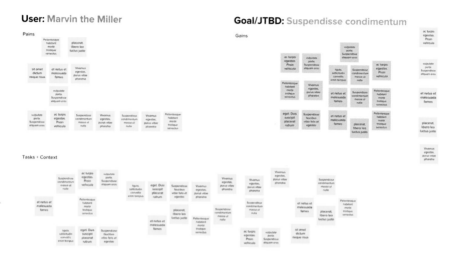

User: Marvin the Miller

Goal/JTBD: Suspendisse condimentum

FIGURE 11-10

Capture user gains on the right of the user profile canvas

The team will generate three types of user gains:[4]

- Required and expected gains the user must achieve to consider themselves successful

- Desired gains that make the experience better

- Unexpected gains that delight the user

Probe for each type of user gain[5] and create a complete picture of what will make the product better for your users.

Probe for required and expected gains

For some experiences, the user requires and expects certain outcomes. For example, if you eat at a coffee shop, you expect to sit, and you require the food to be edible and tasty.

---

4 These four types of user gains echo the five types of customer preferences explored with Kano analysis. For another way to explore user gains, check out "Kano Model." Wikipedia. Wikimedia Foundation, June 7, 2017. Web. June 28, 2017. *https://en.wikipedia.org/wiki/Kano_model*.

5 See also Ulwick and Bettencourt, 2008; Bettencourt and Ulwick, 2008; and Osterwalder, Pigneur, Bernarda, and Smith, 2014.

In Kano analysis, required and expected gains are called "must-be's," as in they must be present in the experience. When you design an experience, if it doesn't fulfill the user's required and expected gains, it's immediately a failure, so the team needs to identify those expectations and requirements.

Ask:

> "What expectations do users have when completing these tasks? What gains are required for them to be successful?"

Probe for gains with specific questions:

- What specific features are required?
- What outcomes does the user expect?
- What outcomes or features has the user experienced in the past?
- What outcomes or features do competitors provide?
- How does the user know they were successful?
- How does the user measure performance or quality?
- How does the user determine value or cost?

Probe for desired gains

Unlike required and expected gains that "must be" part of the experience, desired gains represent outcomes that make the experience better. Desired gains are like icing on the cake. The cake can be fantastic without the icing. Icing makes it better.

The Kano model refers to desired gains as "attractors." When users compare two otherwise identical experiences, the experience that provides more desired gains will be more attractive to your users.

Ask what outcomes will make the experience better for users. Probe with specific questions:

- What kinds of savings would make customers happy? Time? Money? Effort?
- What quality would customers wish for more of?
- What outcomes make users feel better?
- How can you reduce the user's risk?

Probe for unexpected gains

Unexpected gains represent those moments of unexpected delight users never expected or knew to expect. There's no hard-and-fast way to identify unexpected gains because they're unexpected. I'll share a personal example.

One day I open the Maps app on my MacBook to find a restaurant. Later that day, on the way to the restaurant, I open the Maps app on my iPhone to get directions to the restaurant. Rather than needing to search for the restaurant on my phone, the restaurant was already listed as the first option. Not expecting this, I was delighted.

Since delights represent the unexpected, they are harder to come up with. Ask:

"How might we make the experience even better?"

Additional probing questions:

- What do customers dream about?

- What time, cost, or effort savings would make them happy?

- What would be a big relief to customers?

RANK GAINS BY VALUE TO THE USER

Just like with user pains, it can be useful to rank gains from most to least desirable (Figure 11-11).

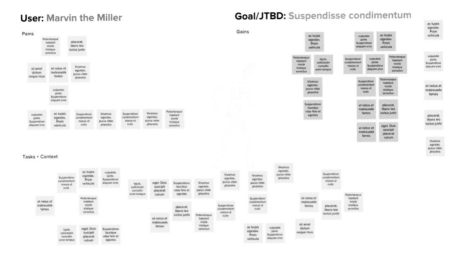

User: Marvin the Miller

Goal/JTBD: Suspendisse condimentum

FIGURE 11-11

Rank gains in order of preference, from most desirable to least desirable

Explore User Attributes to Build Better Products

Working through four topics, you've completed the user profile canvas. Not only do you have a list of user tasks, pains, and gains, you also have a set of user goals to guide the overall experience. You use each of these inputs to create user models.

For new projects, working through a profile canvas for each key user helps teams crystallize the tasks they can design for as well as understand the pains and gains that really affect the user's behavior.

You can also break these activities apart and use them separately. You can start with any task to discuss and identify a user goal. "Why" is a magical question. Similarly, from any task, you can probe for the pains or gains involved to help design a better product.

If you have multiple users, the team will have generated quite a wealth of information. You may have also noticed similar tasks, contexts, pains, and gains across the different users. You need a way to analyze and compare user attributes across all of your users. In the next chapter, we'll look at an attribute grid that lets you do just that.

User Needs and Preferences with the Attribute Grid

AS A ROAD BUILDER, how do you know when to optimize for the miller and his son, their donkey, or belittling passersby? Teams learn and assume so much information about their users, it's difficult to understand what information is important and use that information to make decisions. The attribute grid helps teams analyze user insights and understand what matters most. Your team will focus on the contexts and preferences that matter, and you're going to help them do it.

In this chapter, we'll learn how an attribute grid lets you corral and understand everything teams know about a set of users, so you can make better product decisions. When teams analyze user contexts and preferences with an attribute grid, they can improve usability and efficiency and reduce errors, and products that cater to user preferences have better conversions and higher engagement. To achieve these gains, you don't need to know everything about your users, just what matters.

Most important, unlike the traditional persona, an attribute grid can grow and evolve as the team learns more about their users over time.

How the Attribute Grid Works

Turning a stack of user research into one-page personas looks like magic. It's actually a straightforward, step-by-step process:

1. Capture insights and observations

2. Group, analyze, and refine the data

3. Identify primary and secondary users

The attribute grid helps teams capture and update research over time and makes it easy to edit, organize, and filter information. The grid uses contrast and color, so teams see similarities, differences, and patterns at a glance (Figure 12-1). Visualization makes analysis easier and more accessible to everyone on the team.

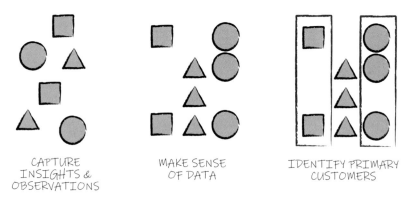

CAPTURE
INSIGHTS &
OBSERVATIONS

MAKE SENSE
OF DATA

IDENTIFY PRIMARY
CUSTOMERS

FIGURE 12-1

Use the attribute grid to understand user contexts and preferences and identify primary design personas.

With the attribute grid, the team documents user contexts, behaviors, and preferences that help the team build more usable products and more engaging experiences. The attribute grid helps teams capture insights and observations, make sense of the data, and identify primary and secondary user groups the product can support.

Once you've completed the analysis, you have three important product tools:

- A list of primary users

- A list of important attributes that guide product decisions

- The attribute grid, as an evergreen tool you can build on

FOUR-STEP PROCESS

Use a repeatable four-step process to analyze research with the attribute grid (Table 12-1):

1. Generate insights and observations to create the landscape.

2. Refine information for clarity to remove noise.

3. Interpret and analyze to reveal patterns.

4. Document to review and share to prioritize what's important.

TABLE 12-2. Attribute grid's four-step process

1. GENERATE TO REVEAL LANDSCAPE	2. REFINE TO REMOVE "NOISE"	3. INTERPRET TO UNDERSTAND	4. DOCUMENT TO SHARE
3–5 people	3–5 people	1–2 people	3–5 people
Fragment what you know Chunk into groups Assign values	Probe for better data Fragment and fuse to refine attributes Cut extraneous attributes	Rearrange columns and rows Filter to focus on items of a type (chunk) or quality (value)	Prioritize what's important Prioritize what challenges assumptions Stuff you thought was important Stuff revealed as important Review and collaborate

WHEN TO USE AN ATTRIBUTE GRID

The more you understand your users, the better the product, so use the attribute grid at any time during a project. And keep in mind that the grid is a living document; update it every time you learn more about your users. Use the grid in conjunction with user prioritization (Chapter 11), or work through the grid before you create user models like profiles and personas (Chapter 14).

INPUTS AND QUICK STARTS

The attribute grid can collect qualitative or quantitative insights from user research like observations, interviews, and surveys. Does better research provide better insights? Absolutely. However, when you don't (yet) have research, the attribute grid helps teams begin with what they already know or think they know about users.

Because the grid captures analysis in a structured format, start with any quantity or quality of information, and revisit over time to include better, more complete information. The grid grows as the team's knowledge grows.

In addition to tacit team knowledge and user research, use market and trend research to provide more information about user behaviors and preferences.

MATERIALS YOU'LL USE

The grid uses one column for each user group and collects analysis about each context and preference in a different row (Figure 12-2). That way, the team can see how all user groups compare across all attributes.

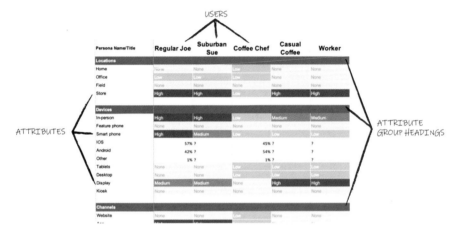

FIGURE 12-2

The attribute grid compares user groups (in columns) against context and preference attributes captured in rows.

Attribute grid

Draw or project the grid on a whiteboard or wall or draw or print the grid on a piece of paper. I recommend a spreadsheet program like Excel or Numbers.

Users and attributes

Collect analysis for users in columns and attributes in individual rows. When you interpret and analyze results, you will move rows and columns to reveal patterns. A spreadsheet makes it easy to move large numbers of rows and columns.

Include all users identified, or start with the most important users.

Attribute groups

After you have identified attributes, you will group them by similarity. Though attributes will move, the name of the attribute group won't move very often.

 Find templates, framing material, and remote resources on the website:

http://pxd.gd/users/attribute-grid

User Insights Captured in the Attribute Grid

Contexts: when, where, and how users engage

- Physical context: Where, when, and how do users engage?

- Information-seeking behaviors: How do users find information?

- Communication behaviors: How do users prefer to communicate?

- Collaboration and social behaviors: How do they interact with others?

- Preferences: what users prefer to engage with

- Content formats and preferences: What types of content do they use and prefer?

Specific content and functionality preferences: What content and functionality specific to this project are users interested in?

Activity 1: Generate Attributes to Reveal the Landscape

You know, or think you know, a lot about your users, and it's way more than you can keep in your head. To get it all down in one place where you can see it, collect insights from user research or tacit knowledge and include each insight as a separate attribute in the attribute grid. When you capture each insight as an individual, modular unit, the team can understand how much it applies to all users or even just some users.

THE FRAME

WHAT WILL YOU DO?	Collect attributes related to contexts and preferences
WHAT'S THE OUTCOME?	A list of attributes grouped by similarity
WHY IS IT IMPORTANT?	Identifies constraints, needs, and preferences that affect product usability and engagement
HOW WILL YOU DO IT?	Working in small groups on one attribute at a time

To frame attribute generation, say:

> "When, where, and how users engage has a huge effect on how they use the product. Let's analyze common contexts and user preferences, so we can make the product as good as possible."

COLLECT PHYSICAL LOCATION AND DEVICES

Physical contexts like device, channel, and frequency highlight constraints that affect a product's usability. Where and how the user interacts with a product provides key constraints around a user's product use.

- Where will users use the product? At home? The office? Front-line positions? In the field?

- What devices will users use to interact with the product? Laptops or desktops? Tablets? Smartphones? Feature phones? Kiosks? Display screens? Phones? Paper forms? Smart devices?

- What channels will users use? The web? An app? Chat? Voice? Email? SMS or text?

- How do users want to send or receive communications around the product?

As the team identifies locations, devices, and channels, capture each as a new row in the attribute grid.

SCORE EACH ATTRIBUTE

Use T-shirt sizes—small, medium, and large—to capture the answer for each attribute in a separate row in the grid for each user group (Figure 12-3). Small, medium, and large allow groups to generalize, rather than require specific research to score each attribute. T-shirt sizes also force teams to compare each user. Small, medium, and large is the same as asking: does this attribute apply to this user the same as, more than, or less than other users? Since you score each user relative to the others, score all users against an attribute before moving on to another attribute. Use the attribute grid to fill out an attribute's entire row before moving on to the next attribute.

Persona Name/Title	Regular Joe	Suburban Sue	Coffee Chef	Casual Coffee
Locations				
Home	None	None	Low	None
Office	Low	Low	Low	None
Field	None	None	None	None
Store	High	High	Low	High
Devices				
In-person	High	High	Low	Medium
Feature phone	None	None	None	None
Smart phone	High	Low	Low	Low
Tablets	None	None	Low	Low
Desktop	None	None	Low	Low
Display	Medium	Medium	None	High
Kiosk	None	None	None	None
Channels				
Website	None	None	Low	None
App	High	High	Low	None
In-store	High	Low	Low	High
Drive through	Low	High	None	None
Chat	None	None	Low	None
SMS	None	None	None	None
Email	None	None	Low	None

FIGURE 12-3

Capture analysis for each context for each user group.

Choose the right T-shirt sizes for each attribute

Use T-shirt sizes for everything, but they may mean something different for different attributes. Look at population and frequency as examples.

For *population*, small, medium, and large can describe how many people belong to a user group. Small, medium, and large relate to the group's population relative to the other groups.

For *frequency*, small, medium, and large mean something like low, medium, and high. Even then, provide some definition for each score. Low, medium, high can translate to daily, weekly, monthly; or weekly, monthly, yearly; or something else.

With value-related attributes like the importance of quality, low, medium, and high might mean not important, important, or very important. In addition, how the team defines T-shirt sizes may change during the discussion. You see this most often with frequency where the team's sense of frequency changes as they evaluate additional users or attributes. This change highlights a natural part of the discussion when the team expands their understanding of the customer groups.

If using a spreadsheet, add a note to the attribute that describes what small, medium, and large mean. Especially for attributes that measure a frequency, make sure to give each T-shirt size a specific value. Does small equate to several times a day, daily, weekly, monthly, or yearly? And what do medium and large mean?

Probe to adjust scores

As discussion flows, you may identify opportunities to update a previous score. Probe the team to understand if they agree.

Once you have filled out the entire grid, probe the team again to verify that everyone agrees. Probe for any disagreements: "Before we move on, does anyone disagree with any of the scores we captured?"

Assure naysayers it's their right to disagree: "Everyone gets a veto. Is there anything here you think the group got wrong? Reassure their inner voices: "Is there anything where that little voice at the back of your head is just screaming, 'this is all wrong'?"

COLLECT TIME, FREQUENCY, AND DURATION

Frequency and duration reveal key information about how to make your product usable:

- What time of day will users interact with the product? Morning? Afternoon? Evening? Late at night?
- How frequently will people use the product? Several times a day? Once a day? Once a week? Once a month? Once a year? Just once?
- When they interact, will users use the product for an instant? A short period of time? A longer period of time?
- When they interact will users focus fully on the experience? Will they multi-task? Not pay attention at all?

ANALYZE INFORMATION-SEEKING BEHAVIORS

How people use the product can be just as important. With some products, users access information. Probe for the user's information-seeking behaviors:[1]

- Will users know what they're looking for? Do they know what words to search or browse for? Do they have a good understanding of where to start?
- Will users have some idea of what they need, but not know the right words to use? Will they not know where to start?
- Will users know what they need to know? Do they think they need one thing, but really need another?
- Will users need to find things they've already seen?

ANALYZE WORK GROUP BEHAVIORS

For products designed for employees like intranet, workflow, and collaboration, analyze how employees work and collaborate:

- Do employees spend more time as individual contributors or as team contributors?
- Are employees given more or less autonomy?

---

1   Spencer, Donna. "Four Modes of Seeking Information and How to Design for Them." Boxesandarrows.com, Boxes and Arrows, 14 Mar. 2006, *boxesandarrows.com/four-modes-of-seeking-information-and-how-to-design-for-them/*.

- Do employs work with or without interruption?

- Do employees work directly with external or internal users?

- Do they manage other employees? Small teams? Large teams?

ANALYZE SOCIAL AND COLLABORATIVE BEHAVIOR

Whether or not products offer social and collaboration features as part of the product's feature set, users may participate in social media or collaborate using other products. Understanding the user's social behavior reveals opportunities to improve engagement and retention.

How do users engage with communities and groups?

- Do users join communities or groups?

- Do users manage communities or groups?

- Do users start new communities or groups?

How do users engage with community content?

- Do users read posted content and messages?

- Do users rate or review content (e.g., likes, thumbs-up)?

- Do users reply or comment on content?

- Do users share or recommend content?

How do users contribute content?

- Do users post articles or blogs (like Medium)?

- Do users post micro-blogs and status messages (like Twitter or Facebook)?

- Do users contribute resources (like tools, templates, worksheets)?

PROBE FOR FORMAT PREFERENCES

An unsuccessful product communicates all in video when users prefer text. Make sure you communicate the way users prefer:

- Do users prefer short text? Long text?

- Do users prefer only a few images or lots of images?

• Do users prefer photos and illustrations or diagrams and infographics?

• Do users prefer video? Audio?

ANALYZE CONTENT AND FUNCTIONALITY PREFERENCES

Users also have preferences related to the product's content and functionality. List the content and functionality planned for the product as rows in the attribute grid. For each type of content and piece of functionality, use T-shirt sizes to indicate each user's level of interest or need (Figure 12-4).

Persona Name/Title	Regular Joe	Suburban Sue	Coffee Chef	Casual Coffee
Content and funtionality				
Coffee descriptions	Low	Low	Medium	None
Drink descriptions	Medium	Medium	None	High
Order ahead	High	Low	None	None
Menu	Low	Low	None	High
Mugs	None	None	None	None
Travel mugs	Low	None	None	None
Snacks	Low	Low	None	Medium
Breakfast	Medium	Medium	None	None
Lunch	Low	Low	None	Low
Regular order	High	High	Medium	None
Previous order	High	High	Low	None
Ratings	None	None	Medium	None
Reviews	None	None	High	None
Coffee production stories	None	None	High	None
Coffee origin stories	Low	None	Medium	Low
Coffee trivia	Low	None	None	Low
Company trivia	Low	None	None	Low
Brewing tips	None	None	Low	None
Taste chooser	Medium	Low	None	None
Storage tips	None	None	Medium	None
Coffee date conversation tips	None	None	None	None

FIGURE 12-4
Assess each user's interest in product-specific content and functionality.

For example, you might list specialty drinks, help content, ratings, reviews, and share content. Identify the users that most want or need those features.

Remember to make a note on the cell to explain whether the T-shirt size reflects the user's interest, need, or frequency of use. For example, if you have an attribute around ordering ahead of time, does small, medium, and large indicate users are very interested in the idea, that they really need the idea, or that they use or would use that functionality all the time?

CAPTURE ANY ATTRIBUTES FROM USER, MARKET, OR TREND RESEARCH

Comb through available research to identify any possible context, behavior, or preference. Capture these insights. Even if an insight relates to only one group of users, evaluate all users against the attribute.

Include any and every possible attribute

You don't know what you don't know, and you don't know what's important. As you discuss contexts and preferences with the team, include anything and everything that comes up. Someone may suggest something you feel isn't important. Maybe you're right, but you won't know until you've completed the full analysis, so include everything.

FINISH GENERATION, THEN REFINE TO REMOVE NOISE

Once the team has generated and collected a comprehensive set of attributes, the team should have filled the grid with attributes. Less complex products should have at least 50 attributes. Complex products will quickly exceed that number.

Wrap up generation and move to review and refine the existing attributes.

Activity 2: Refine Attributes to Remove Noise

After collecting and scoring as many attributes as possible, the team faces a huge wall of noise, and buried somewhere in the noise, the team will find key insights that drive product success.

In this activity, the team will work together to verify values, improve the data, and remove extraneous attributes to improve the quality of the attributes in the grid.

THE FRAME

WHAT WILL YOU DO?	Review attributes to improve quality and remove what's unnecessary
WHAT'S THE OUTCOME?	A refined list of attributes grouped by similarity
WHY IS IT IMPORTANT?	Reduces list of all possible data to a list of more relevant attributes
HOW WILL YOU DO IT?	Work together to review all attributes

To frame attribute refinement, say:

> "We've collected a ton of information about our users. Let's review the attributes, remove unnecessary ones, and look for places where we can replace the T-shirt sizes with real data, so we make sure we have as accurate a picture of our users as possible."

GROUP ATTRIBUTES BY TYPE

It's common for teams to identify over 100 attributes for even small products. Grouping by similarity makes these long lists of attributes easier to manage. Review and group similar attributes with each other (Figure 12-5). And, as you identify new insights, modify groupings to best reflect all of the attributes.

Channels				
Website	None	None	Low	None
App	High	High	Low	None
In-store	High	Low	Low	High
Drive through	Low	High	None	None
Chat	None	None	Low	None
SMS	None	None	None	None
Email	None	None	Low	None

Goals				
Completing ritual	High	High	High	None
Boosting alertness	High	High	None	None
Sipping socially	Low	Low	None	High
Appreciating flavor	Low	Low	High	Low

Tasks/Jobs				
Research coffee	None	None	High	None
Buy coffee	Low	Low	Medium	None
Find a store	Medium	Medium	None	Medium
Try coffee	None	None	Low	None
Work	Low	None	None	Low
Use wifi	Low	None	None	Low
Meet friends	None	None	None	Medium
Take break	Low	None	None	Low

Content and funtionality				
Coffee descriptions	Low	Low	Medium	None
Drink descriptions	Medium	Medium	None	High
Order ahead	High	Low	None	None
Menu	Low	Low	None	High

FIGURE 12-5

Group and label attributes by similarity to make long attribute lists easier to process.

Remove irrelevant attributes

The trigger questions in Activity 1 include items relevant to specific types of products and experiences. Remove any attribute that adds little or no value to the team's understanding of the user. Look for attributes with no value (Figure 12-6). For example, if your product won't appear on display screens or kiosks, ignore those items.

Locations				
Home	None	None	Low	None
Office	Low	Low	Low	None
Field	None	None	None	None
Store	High	High	Low	High
Devices				
In-person	High	High	Low	Medium
Feature phone	None	None	None	None
Smart phone	High	Low	Low	Low
Tablets	None	None	Low	Low
Desktop	None	None	Low	Low
Display	Medium	Medium	None	High
Kiosk	None	None	None	None
Channels				
Website	None	None	Low	None
App	High	High	Low	None
In-store	High	Low	Low	High
Drive through	Low	High	None	None
Chat	None	None	Low	None
SMS	None	None	None	None
Email	None	None	Low	None

FIGURE 12-6

Items with no value often signal irrelevant attributes. "Field" might be relevant when we're designing an application for traveling technicians, but not for our coffee company. They can also reveal potential opportunities. What if stores did add kiosks? What if you could order ahead via SMS?

Similarly, attributes where all users have the same value may offer little value. For example, if you're building a mobile application, all users will rate mobile device use "high." Tracking mobile use adds no useful information.

Revisit and revise attribute values

Attribute values are never final. They represent the team's most recent perception of user contexts and preferences. User understanding moves through an iterative process. As you review and discuss attributes, your understanding changes. Encourage the team to revisit and change values to reflect their evolving, shared vision of the user.

WATCH FOR CONFLICTS THAT SIGNAL A NEW USER

As team members review values for a user group, listen for discussions where some members of a user group have one value while others have another value. For example, you may start with a single technical persona. During discussion, the team disagrees on whether they work at desktops or tablets and you discover some technical users work at desktops in an office while others squint at tablets in the field.

These conflicting values reveal an opportunity to split the single technical user into two separate users, field workers and office workers (Figure 12-7). Add a column for the new user, and copy the original user's column and paste into the new column. With two different columns, you can capture the conflicting values for each type of user.

Split or combine user groups to reveal useful requirements or constraints. Any user model compresses some real people into a single archetype. All of those people are similar. They're also different. You can split any user model into smaller and smaller groups until you're back down to one for every person.

Segment users to support better product design. Don't split user groups unless new groups reveal useful requirements or constraints. As with anything, do it when it makes sense.

Persona Name/Title	Regular Joe	Suburban Sue	
Devices			
In-person	High	High	
Feature phone	None	None	
Smart phone	High	Medium	
Tablets	None	None	
Desktop	None	None	
Display	Medium	Medium	
Kiosk	None	None	
Channels			
Website	None	None	
App	High	High	
In-store	High	Low	
Drive through	Low	High	
Chat	None	None	
SMS	None	None	
Email	None	None	
Goals			
Completing ritual	High	High	
Boosting alertness	High	High	
Sipping socially	Low	Low	
Appreciating flavor	Low	Low	
Tasks/Jobs			
Research coffee	None	None	
Buy coffee	Low	Low	
Buy drink	High	High	
Find a store	Medium	Medium	
Try coffee	None	None	
Work	Low	None	
Use wifi	Low	None	
Meet friends	None	None	
Take break	Low	None	
Content and funtionality			
Coffee descriptions	Low	Low	
Drink descriptions	Medium	Medium	
Order ahead	High	Low	
Menu	Low	Low	
Mugs	None	None	
Travel mugs	Low	None	
Snacks	Low	Low	
Breakfast	Medium	Medium	
Lunch	Low	Low	
Regular order	High	High	
Previous order	High	High	

FIGURE 12-7

Conflicting attribute values can mean you should split a single user into two or more user groups. When we realized Regular Joe's attributes were very different for order ahead and drive through users, we split him to add Suburban Sue.

FRAGMENT AND FUSE ATTRIBUTES TO IMPROVE THE USER MODELS

As you review and refine attributes, look for opportunities to split existing items into multiple attributes, so you can track more detailed user information. Likewise, look for places where it makes sense to combine several separate attributes into a single item. For example, if you have an attribute for "buy drink," you may want to split that into two separate contexts, one for "buy coffee" and another for "buy drink" (Figure 12-8). Add the new attribute as a new row and score each user. Add, remove, combine, and split items to match your product's unique users.

Research coffee	None	None	High	None
Buy coffee	Low	Low	Medium	None
Buy drink	High	High	Low	High
Find a store	Medium	Medium	None	Medium
Try coffee	None	None	Low	None
Work	Low	None	None	Low
Use wifi	Low	None	None	Low
Meet friends	None	None	None	Medium
Take break	Low	None	None	Low

FIGURE 12-8

Continue to split and combine attributes to create the best overall picture of your users. Here we split "Buy Coffee" to add "Buy Drink" because packaged coffee and made drinks are different. We split "Hang Out In Store" into four separate reasons for why users would hang out in a store.

IMPROVE FIDELITY OF DATA AND ATTRIBUTE VALUES

T-shirt sizes like low, medium, and high let teams quickly analyze contexts and preferences. However, T-shirt sizes are like sketching a screen. They offer a general idea about what's important, but they won't provide the full picture.

Identify items that need better data

As the team analyzes, identify more important items and look for ways to improve the fidelity of the data. For example, if you have T-shirt sizes for mobile operating systems like iOS, Android, and Windows, you may want more specific numbers before you commit to building a native app for a specific platform.

Identify available data

For items that need better data, identify how to include any existing data you already have (Figure 12-9). In some cases, pull data from analytics. For example, you might pull specific data on mobile phone operating systems from your current analytics platform like Google Analytics or Adobe's Marketing Cloud.

Identify both the data sources and who your team can contact to get access to the data.

Devices					
In-person	High	High	Low	Medium	Medium
Feature phone	None	None	None	None	None
Smart phone	High	Medium	Low	Low	Low
IOS	57% ?			45% ?	?
Android	42% ?			54% ?	?
Other	1% ?			1% ?	?
Tablets	None	None	Low	Low	Low
Desktop	None	None	Low	Low	Low
Display	Medium	Medium	None	High	High
Kiosk	None	None	None	None	None

FIGURE 12-9

When possible, replace T-shirt sizes with better data.

Plan to acquire missing data

Any data you need and can't get represents something that needs research. Match research methods to project goals as well as time, cost, and difficulty. (See "User research for creating user model" in Chapter 9.) Identify who will conduct the research and when. This single paragraph is super important. If you do not continually identify research needs and push for more research, everything the experience machine creates will come up short.

ADD ADDITIONAL USER INFORMATION

Your team knows a lot about its users, and you can collect any and all of that information in the attribute grid. This can include tasks, goals, and even relationships to other users.

Add tasks and goals

Add user tasks or goals to the grid and show how important they are to each user group (Figure 12-10). Multiple user groups will share tasks and goals. Pull tasks and goals from the user profile canvas (see Chapter 11). When teams see how users share tasks and goals, they can better prioritize what to build.

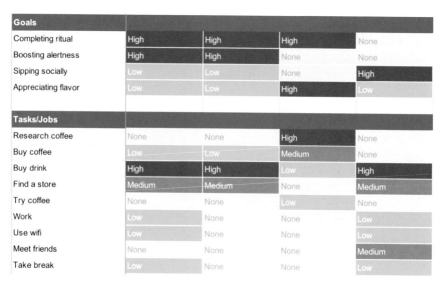

Goals				
Completing ritual	High	High	High	None
Boosting alertness	High	High	None	None
Sipping socially	Low	Low	None	High
Appreciating flavor	Low	Low	High	Low
Tasks/Jobs				
Research coffee	None	None	High	None
Buy coffee	Low	Low	Medium	None
Buy drink	High	High	Low	High
Find a store	Medium	Medium	None	Medium
Try coffee	None	None	Low	None
Work	Low	None	None	Low
Use wifi	Low	None	None	Low
Meet friends	None	None	None	Medium
Take break	Low	None	None	Low

FIGURE 12-10

Include tasks, goals, jobs, and engagement value to improve the team's understanding of the user.

Add relationships to other users

Add rows for other users to show how often each user interacts with the others or how much influence they have over each other (Figure 12-11). Reference users the team identified with the bull's-eye canvas (Chapter 10). When you analyze frequency of contact or amount of influence, you reveal insights about who users communicate and collaborate with.

Influence				
Regular Joe	Medium	Medium	Low	Low
Suburban Sue	Medium	Medium	Low	Low
Coffee Chef	None	None	High	None
Casual Coffee	Medium	Medium	None	High
Other store visitors	Medium	Medium	Low	None
Airport travellers	None	None	None	Low

FIGURE 12-11

Include other users as rows to understand how users interact with and influence each other.

FINISH REFINEMENT AND MOVE TO UNDERSTAND AND FIND PATTERNS

As the team refines, capture any new attributes that appear. When refinement begins to slow, shift the team's focus to interpret and understand attributes and find patterns:

> "It looks like we have a solid understanding of our users and their needs and preferences. Let's step back and look for patterns we can use to make our product better."

Activity 3: Understand Patterns and Outliers in User Behaviors

Even though the team knows a lot about a lot of users, you don't want to design everything for everyone. Good product teams identify a subset of all users they can design for to achieve the most value. This doesn't always mean ignoring some users at the expense of others. Sometimes several groups of users exhibit similar behaviors, contexts, and preferences. When you build for one of these users, the product supports similar users. You get more bang for your build.

With a good selection of refined attributes, the team examines how user groups compare to each other. To do this, the team looks for areas where users share attributes as well as areas where groups have opposite values.

THE FRAME

WHAT WILL YOU DO?	Reveal patterns in user behaviors and preferences
WHAT'S THE OUTCOME?	An understanding of how users are similar and different
WHY IS IT IMPORTANT?	Reveals key constraints and needs
HOW WILL YOU DO IT?	Working in a small group, rearrange and filter attributes

To frame attribute analysis, say:

> "With our refined set of user attributes, we will start to review and filter the attributes to find patterns. Let's start by looking for places where users are similar."

ZOOM IN AND OUT

To discover patterns, zoom out to the 50,000-foot view to see macro trends. And zoom in to find patterns at the 50-foot level.

You will change your perspective's altitude from close to far and back again as you work with the data. Shift your focus from users and columns to look at attributes in rows. Even though user models live in two-dimensional space, users live rich, multi-faceted lives. Use the grid like scaffolding to climb around and view users from different perspectives and develop richer understanding of what they need.

LOOK FOR MACRO PATTERNS THAT IDENTIFY SIMILAR USER GROUPS

Zoom out to view the entire user grid. Look at users as single columns. What users look similar? Look for patterns in dark and light to identify similar users. Move similar users adjacent to each other, so similar users get grouped together in the grid (Figure 12-12). Similar columns reveal opportunities where designing for one type of user allows you to meet the needs of several users.

REGULAR JOE AND
SUBURBAN SUE
LOOK SIMILAR

CASUAL COFFEE AND
WORKER
LOOK IDENTICAL

FIGURE 12-12
Zoom out to see similar user columns in the entire grid and move similar user columns adjacent to one another.

MOVE ROWS TO MAGNIFY SIMILARITIES AND DIFFERENCES

As you review attribute groups, notice where attribute values alternate lights and darks. Alternating colors make it difficult to see patterns. Move dark rows adjacent to other dark rows to make the patterns easier to see.

Often moving rows makes patterns easier to see for some users and harder to see for others. What makes the most sense? What reveals the best patterns? Move the attribute rows around to magnify the patterns you feel are more important.

IDENTIFY THE MOST IMPORTANT CONTEXTS, NEEDS, AND PREFERENCES

These patterns reveal requirements and constraints that define a successful product. To identify the most important attributes, look for attributes that affect every user as well as outliers. Look for the positive. What should the project do? Also identify things not to do, negative requirements. The team can revisit and remember these attributes later when they make product design decisions.

Identify important content

Some contexts suggest requirements for the entire system. For example, all users may use smartphones. Look for attributes that suggest content needs. If users want to know the product's weight before buying, you need to provide dimensions. Look for attributes that describe how you should create content. Users with no familiarity need more information. Knowledgeable users may need more specialized content.

As the group identifies important attributes, place an "X" in the "key" column to note them in the grid (Figure 12-13).

Persona Name/Title	Key	Regular Joe	Suburban Sue	Coffee Chef	Casual Coffee	Worker
Devices						
In-person	x	High	High	Low	Medium	Medium
Feature phone		None	None	None	None	None
Smart phone	x	High	Medium	Low	Low	Low
iOS		57% ?		45% ?	?	?
Android		42% ?		54% ?	?	?
Other		1% ?		1% ?	?	?
Tablets		None	None	Low	Low	Low
Desktop		None	None	Low	Low	Low
Display	x	Medium	Medium	None	High	High
Kiosk	x	None	None	None	None	None
Channels						
Website	x	None	None	Low	None	None
App	x	High	High	Low	None	None
In-store	x	High	Low	Low	High	High
Drive through	x	Low	High	None	None	None
Chat		None	None	Low	None	None
SMS		None	None	None	None	None
Email		None	None	Low	None	None
Goals						
Completing ritual	x	High	High	High	None	None
Boosting alertness	x	High	High	None	None	None
Sipping socially		Low	Low	None	High	High
Appreciating flavor	x	Low	Low	High	Low	Low

FIGURE 12-13

Mark important attributes in the grid, so you remember them later.

Identify important functionality

Like with content, the grid reveals requirements and constraints for functionality. Look for functionality relevant to the majority of users and for distinctions between desired capabilities and how users want to use that functionality. If users want to share information, do they want to email, print, tweet it? Do they want to share a link, images, descriptions, what?

Identify what's important to your organization

Finally, what attributes does your organization focus on? What attributes does the CEO think are important? Whether or not those attributes really are important, you need to address them because they're prominent in everyone's mind. You might believe they're not important, but the rest of the team does, so note them with the key column. As with everything, it's important to trust team members and what they think is important.

IDENTIFY THE MOST IMPORTANT USER GROUPS

With important attributes marked in the grid, zoom out to see your users as a whole, and think about what users are most important. When teams know their most important user, they focus on building products their users want.

The most important user differs based on the product. Sometimes the most important user is the group that represents the largest number of users. Sometimes it's the group that spends the most money. Other times it's the group that uses it most frequently or that does the most important thing. Sometimes the most important user groups are the ones that are both large and most frequent.

Note primary users in the grid (Figure 12-14). I use "primary" to describe the users the team should build for, and "secondary" for other users. Any users the team should specifically ignore should be labeled "negative," and users that are similar enough to another user can be marked "combined" to indicate they've been grouped with another user.

Photo						
Persona Name/Title	Key	**Regular Joe**	**Suburban Sue**	**Coffee Chef**	**Casual Coffee**	**Worker**
Description						
Persona type		Primary	Primary	Negative	Secondary	Combined

General						
Population	x	High	High	Low	Low	Low
Frequency	x	Daily (High)	Daily (High)	Weekly (Medium)	Monthly (Low)	Monthly (Low)
Criticality		High	High	Low	Medium	Medium
Influence		Medium	Medium	Medium	High	High
Engagement value		54	54	4	6	6

FIGURE 12-14

Note primary, secondary, combined, and negative users in the grid.

Identify primary design targets

What user groups have similar attributes? You can see these in the grid because they have similar patterns of light and dark. Should you combine similar users? If not, what user can you design for whose needs support the needs of similar users? The user you can target and who also supports other user types is another primary design target. The similar users are secondary design targets. Note this in the grid.

For our global coffee company, we chose Regular Joe and Suburban Sue for primary users because they both represent large portions of the customer base ("Population" is "high" for both), and they both visit stores more frequently than other groups ("Frequency" is "Daily/high" for both). In our example, even if you don't specifically think about the attribute values, you can lean back and see that both Regular Joe and Suburban Sue are darker than the columns for the other users.

After you identify the users that the attribute grid says are more important, identify any users the team or organization thinks are important. You may believe these early assumptions are no longer true, but the rest of the team will need to understand why the data suggests the team should build for different users. If there's a drift, you'll need to explain why when you share the user models with the broader team and organization.

Identify unique design targets

Look for users with different needs. Do these users represent unique requirements? Or should you ignore them? If they're users to ignore, note them as negative design targets. If they're not to be ignored, are they primary or secondary design targets? Does their uniqueness indicate the team should make special arrangements for them? Should you address them in a later project?

Design targets identify the most valuable users the experience machine should focus on. On a long enough timeline, all users are precious, and all products are used by everyone in delightful ways. In my experience, no project timeline is ever long enough, so who can your experience machine help now?

FINISH, CAPTURE MOST IMPORTANT USERS, ATTRIBUTES, AND ATTRIBUTE GROUPS

Ultimately, you check your analysis with the broader team and organization. You can't share everything, so focus on the most important users and attributes.

Make sure you've identified primary and secondary design targets and marked key attributes and attribute groups in the grid. Once you've completed analysis and captured the most important users and attributes, you have what you need to return to the larger team to check the nascent user models.

Identify user attribute groups to share and review

By design, the user profile grid stores every possible attribute, extending to hundreds of attributes for even simple products and experiences. The smaller group analyzes all attributes, so the larger team doesn't need to. With the larger group, identify three types of attributes to review:

- Those that challenge key assumptions—What's different than what we thought?

- Those that reveal unknown needs—What did you learn?

- Attributes important to the team—What are you still tracking?

Attributes that challenge key assumptions or reveal unknown needs surface critical information teams need to improve the product. Also identify attribute groups important to the team. Even if analysis reveals nothing new, reviewing these attributes helps verify the analysis is still correct and demonstrates you listened and understood what the team considered important.

Activity 4: Review to Build Shared Vision with Broader Team and Stakeholders

Shared vision isn't just about goals and interfaces. Shared understanding of your users helps the team and the rest of the organization make better product decisions and deliver better experiences.

Unfortunately, user analysis works best in smaller groups, so schedule time to share the analysis with the broader team and any necessary or influential external stakeholders.

THE FRAME

WHAT WILL YOU DO?	Check analysis of specific attribute groups
WHAT'S THE OUTCOME?	A shared understanding of your users
WHY IS IT IMPORTANT?	To ensure analysis of the user is correct
HOW WILL YOU DO IT?	Reviewing key attributes together as a group

To frame the review, say:

> "In a smaller group, we analyzed key user attributes to better understand requirements and needs. We want to review these attributes with the rest of the team to make sure our analysis is right and identify any inaccuracies. We'll look at user attributes in groups."

FACILITATE ATTRIBUTE REVIEW

To review attributes, review the entire attribute group, not just a single attribute. For example, if the team assumed users would use smartphones, and the analysis challenges that assumption, review the entire attribute group associated with devices (Figure 12-15). To better review and discuss laptops instead of phones, the team needs to see how users interact with all devices. Likewise, for attributes that reveal unknown needs, review the entire, relevant attribute group to share more context with the team, so they can understand and evaluate your analysis.

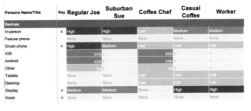

User devices

This attribute group lists possible devices a customer may use to interact with inside one of our coffee shops.

- In-person, smart phone, and menu displays are the most common ways customers will interact with us in the store.

- We assume feature phone users will order in-person.

- Why do we not have interactive kiosks?

Persona Name/Title	Key	Regular Joe	Suburban Sue	Coffee Chef	Casual Coffee	Worker
Devices						
In-person	x	High	High	Low	Medium	Medium
Feature phone		None	None	None	None	None
Smart phone	x	High	Medium	Low	Low	Low
IOS		57%			45%	
Android		42%			54%	
Other		1%			1%	
Tablets		None	None	Low	Low	Low
Desktop		None	None	Low	Low	Low
Display	x	Medium	Medium	None	High	High
Kiosk	x	None	None	None	None	None

FIGURE 12-15

If analysis challenges the team's assumptions about a specific attribute, it's useful to review the entire attribute group.

Frame the review with a description of the attribute group

For each attribute group, begin the review with a description of the group and the attributes it includes. Though groups may seem obvious to the smaller group that conducted the analysis, the larger group will need a description, so they know what they're looking at.

Report top-line conclusions for each attribute group

For each attribute group, describe why the team should care. Does the analysis challenge existing assumptions? Reveal unknown needs? Does analysis confirm earlier assumptions? Explain what you want the larger group to evaluate.

Check each attribute value in each group

Once the team understands how you grouped the attributes and what to evaluate, discuss values for each attribute and each user. You analyzed each attribute and user with the smaller group. Analyze important attributes and users a second time with the entire team to invite additional perspectives and improve the user models.

Discuss and capture changes to attribute values

As the team discusses attributes and identifies changes, update the grid directly or make a note and update the grid after the review. Updating the grid in real time is better, so everyone can see you listened to and applied the changes.

After the team reviews and updates important attribute values, update
the grid and zoom out to reassess user groups with three questions:

- Are similar user groups still similar?

- Do updated attribute values create new patterns?

- Do updated attribute values change the primary and secondary
  design targets?

In most cases, user groups and design targets won't change. However,
focus on how they should change. Making no change is the easy way
out. It's what usually happens, so make sure you take the easy way out
because it's right, not easy.

The updated attribute grid will document and illustrate a comprehensive, visual model of the product's users. Over time, as the team
updates the grid with new and refined data, review those three questions to reassess the user models. The attribute grid enables the continuous delivery of user understanding as the team's knowledge improves
over time.

Although the grid's visual lights and darks capture a comprehensive
view of each user, the grid only suggests user requirements. The grid
tracks *why* you should design the product a certain way, but it does not
tell you *how*. To capture and share design guidelines and requirements,
make user models to share with team members and the organization.

The Attribute Grid Lays the
Foundation for Personas

The attribute grid represents everything the team knows about its
users, both what's important as well as what isn't. This wealth of information provides fertile ground to imagine new products and features
that will help users. However, it's difficult to understand users at a
glance. This is why we often create personas that provide an overview.

An overview of user needs, pains, and gains helps us imagine new
products that fill those needs. However, once you start to build these
features, you no longer need to know the user's needs. Now you need
to know how to build for that user. In those cases, personas should

no longer display user needs but instead should display guidelines for building for them. In the next chapter, we'll look at the best ways to communicate user attributes for both circumstances.

[13]

Document and Share User Models

A team shared a persona with a client. After listening to the presentation, the client asks, "Why do we need this? What does this do for us?" The persona, though informative, failed to share anything useful.

User models are the TL;DR of user research. Also called personas, profiles, or archetypes, user models transform a wall of sticky notes or endless attribute grid into a simple format that team members understand, so they can build products that users need and love.

Most user models document information like pain points, needs, and goals (Figure 13-1). Once documented, what do you do with that information? Well, that depends on where you are in the process. Put another way, what the team needs to do changes how you should document your user model.

Regular Joe

Morning coffee is how I start my day

Channels

Mobile app

In-store

User goals

- Be comfortable at work because I am there so much
- Kickstart my brain to prepare for the morning grind

Pain points

- Long lines in morning
- Jostling crowds risk spilling my drink
- Dripping latté foam on my work shirt

Monthly coffee buy

FIGURE 13-1

User models document user information like pain points, needs, and goals (gibbon photo by Eric Kilby, *www.flickr.com/photos/ekilby/4877055767*).

User models condense a broad variety of information about a user into something your team can understand at a glance. The best user models communicate the point in less space—like a brief or infographic. Unfortunately, most teams don't include people who can write briefs and design infographics. To make good user models, you have to learn how to write briefs and create infographics.

You won't learn how to write briefs or create infographics here. However, you will learn enough to put together the right user information in the right format. Your team will create more user-centered products, and your user models will help them do it.

To do this, we'll look at the ingredients that go into a user model, the different ways your teams may use them, and the different ways you can communicate various types of information.

User Models Answer Four Different Questions

Different initiatives and projects ask different questions about their users (Figure 13-2). Broadly, think about projects as innovation or implementation.

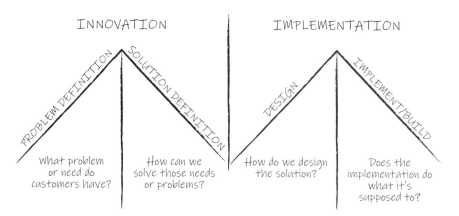

FIGURE 13-2

At different stages, teams ask different questions about their users

QUESTIONS FOR INNOVATION PROJECTS

Innovation project teams don't know what the solution should be, yet. So they can't answer implementation questions. In fact, innovation projects may not even know what problem they want to solve. Innovation teams have two big questions:

- What problem or needs do users have? What can we make better for users?
- What ways can we solve those problems? What solutions can we pursue for our users?

Projects focused on innovation typically shift into implementation as they identify solutions to implement.

QUESTIONS FOR IMPLEMENTATION PROJECTS

During implementation, teams take a solution from idea to product with two different questions:

- How should we build the solution? What design will help our users?
- Did we build it right? Does the solution do what we thought it would for our users?

With user models, tailor the information you include to match the questions your team needs to answer.

Two Types of User Models: Rationales and Guidelines

If you think about projects as implementation or innovation, you can create two kinds of user models:

- User models that reveal how you should *innovate*
- User models that tell you how you should *implement*

MODELS THAT REVEAL RATIONALES FOR INNOVATION

During innovation phases, teams need help to understand what problems users have and a way to generate possible solutions. Innovation teams need models that communicate user needs, pain points, goals, contexts, and influencers.

During innovation phases, teams need models that provide the *rationale* for what to build. If a user model shows users need to understand where a coffee shop is located, that need gives the team a reason to solve that problem.

MODELS THAT PROVIDE GUIDELINES FOR IMPLEMENTATION

In implementation, instead of rationale, teams need guidelines for how to build the solution. Instead of needs, pain points, and goals, teams need guidelines for how to design the interface and communicate messages. Rationale tells the team that users need a way to locate stores. Guidelines tell the team to make store locators mobile-friendly because users view them on their phone.

COMPARING RATIONALE AND GUIDELINES

So far, we've split user attributes into tasks, contexts, influencers, and goals. Those four types of user attributes look different when you show rationales or guidelines (Table 13-1).

TABLE 13-1. Differences in how rationale and guidelines communicate user attributes

	RATIONALE **What to build?**	GUIDELINES **How to build?**
GOALS	Why is the user trying to do this?	
TASKS	What capabilities do users need?	What content and functionality should we build?
CONTEXT	When and where do users need to engage?	How do we build content and functionality to make it usable in the appropriate contexts?
INFLUENCERS	What outcomes and preferences influence user behavior?	How do we build to increase adoption and engagement?

User models that provide *rationale* help teams understand user research and user needs, so they identify worthwhile problems and worthwhile ideas for how to solve those problems. User models that offer *guidelines* help teams decide what content and functionality to build, determine how to make it usable, and improve adoption and engagement.

The different types of information your team needs when they're in innovation or implementation will change the type of user model you create.

User Models Come in Three Formats

Along with the type of information the model should include, the format will change based on how the team uses the model. User models appear in three common formats:

- *References* remind people about a user
- *One-sheets* document a single user
- *Side-by-sides* compare and contrast multiple users

REFERENCES

The design process references users in many places. When you show a wireframe and mention that you designed the screen for a specific user, you're making a reference. You note the user when you illustrate touchpoints, and you identify the target user when you design an interface (Figure 13-3). In both cases, you don't include a complete user model. Instead, you remind the audience about the user.

User

Regular Joe
Morning coffee is how I start my day

Scenario

As **Regular Joe** exits train, he places mobile order for coffee, picks it up, and continues to work.

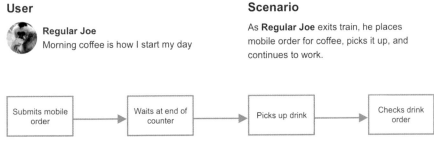

FIGURE 13-3
We use references to remind teams how to check something we've made (gibbon photo by Eric Kilby, on Flickr).

Though a user reference seems insignificant, references provide critical information the team needs to check whatever we've made. User references must provide enough information for the team to recall the user and relevant attributes. In the Think-Make-Check process, user references provide the critical information teams need to check.

ONE-SHEETS

When you think of a persona, you probably think of a one-sheet. One-sheets document one specific user with an in-depth, detailed view of all relevant attributes (Figure 13-4). During thinking and making, one-sheets give team members rationale or guidelines, so they can answer their innovation or implementation questions.

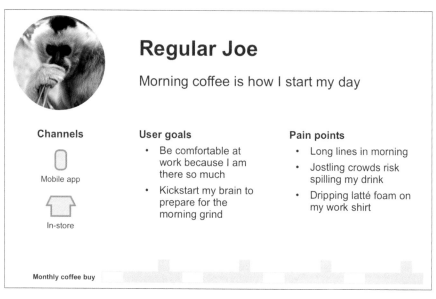

Regular Joe

Morning coffee is how I start my day

Channels

Mobile app

In-store

User goals

- Be comfortable at work because I am there so much
- Kickstart my brain to prepare for the morning grind

Pain points

- Long lines in morning
- Jostling crowds risk spilling my drink
- Dripping latté foam on my work shirt

Monthly coffee buy

FIGURE 13-4

One-sheets document a single user to help team members during thinking and making (gibbon photo by Eric Kilby, on Flickr).

One-sheets carry a dual responsibility. They tell viewers what's important as well as provide further detail when viewers need to dive in.

SIDE-BY-SIDES

To understand how different user models compare to one another, display them side-by-side (Figure 13-5). Side-by-sides communicate more information than a reference and less information than a one-sheet and explain how users are similar or different.

Teams use side-by-sides to help choose what user to think about. Side-by-sides can also identify each user's unique guidelines, so teams can evaluate their work.

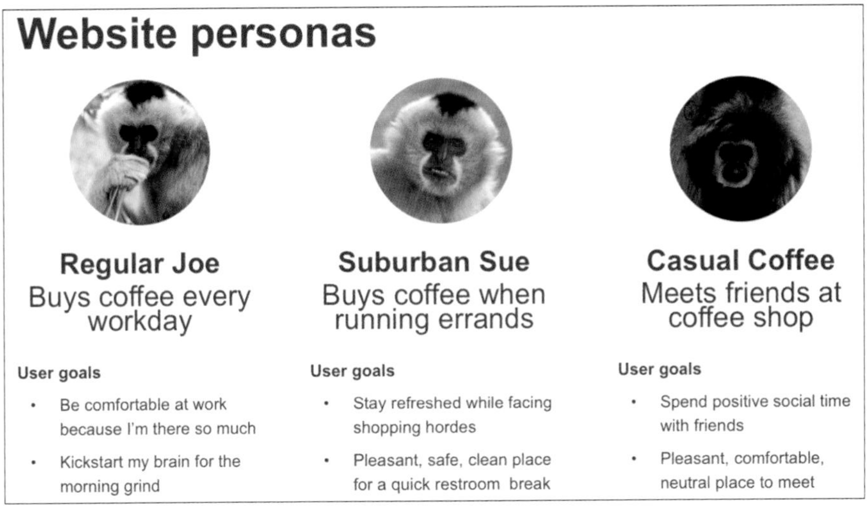

Website personas

| **Regular Joe** | **Suburban Sue** | **Casual Coffee** |
| Buys coffee every workday | Buys coffee when running errands | Meets friends at coffee shop |

User goals

- Be comfortable at work because I'm there so much
- Kickstart my brain for the morning grind

User goals

- Stay refreshed while facing shopping hordes
- Pleasant, safe, clean place for a quick restroom break

User goals

- Spend positive social time with friends
- Pleasant, comfortable, neutral place to meet

FIGURE 13-5

Display user models side-by-side to illustrate how users compare to one another (photos by Eric Kilby [*www.flickr.com/photos/ekilby/4877055767* and *www.flickr.com/photos/ekilby/4144806327*] and Jeremy Couture [*www.flickr.com/photos/jeremy-couture/5661976950*]).

Three Ways to Communicate User Attributes

Whether you make one-sheets, side-by-sides, or references, user models communicate user attributes. You communicate user attributes three ways:

- Lists
- Binary values
- Individual values

USE LISTS WHEN YOU DON'T NEED OR KNOW VALUES

Sometimes, you don't need to communicate how much of something. If you only need to communicate that something exists, use a list (Figure 13-6).

Coffee shop activities

- Buy morning coffee

- Buy breakfast

- Buy afternoon coffee

- Buy snack

- Use wifi for work

- Use wifi for personal use

- Social meet with friends

For example, you might want to tell team members what devices users have: a Galaxy S8, X-Box, iPad, BluRay player, and so on. You don't need to explain how much Xbox, just that the user has one. You also use lists when you don't know how much of something.

Positive lists

A list of user devices demonstrates a positive list. It lists things that exist or things to do or things to consider. Positive lists handle the majority of what you need a list to do.

Negative lists

We almost always imagine lists as positive, a list of things that exist or things to do or things to consider. You can also create lists of things that don't exist or things to avoid. For example, you might list devices users don't have: an Apple Watch, Google Home, and an Apple TV. Sometimes it's more helpful to think about what doesn't exist or things to avoid.

USE BINARIES TO CONTRAST TWO ATTRIBUTES

Binaries display two attributes at opposite ends of a single continuum (Figure 13-7). Like lists, binaries show an attribute exists. Unlike lists, binaries display a value for each attribute.

Coffee shop activities

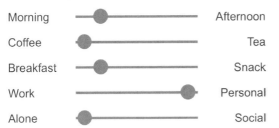

Morning — Afternoon

Coffee — Tea

Breakfast — Snack

Work — Personal

Alone — Social

FIGURE 13-7

Binaries display two attributes as opposite ends of a single continuum

Because binaries show two attributes on one continuum, they require less space than other ways to communicate attributes. If you use the right attributes, binaries can be easier to understand. For example, you might communicate items used at the dinner table and place forks and spoons at opposite ends of a continuum. It makes sense that if you use forks more, you use spoons less, and vice versa.

Binaries are easy to understand when they compare attributes that make sense as opposites. This opposition, whether implied or actual, illustrates a clear distinction between two attributes. Use binaries when you want to suggest a user is more one attribute than another.

Binaries work best when attributes make sense as opposites. What if instead of forks and spoons, you created a binary with forks and plates? Even if research suggested it was true—if you use your fork more, you use your plate less—it doesn't make sense on a continuum. Since user models should clearly communicate when team members and stakeholders look at them, create binaries with attributes that make sense as opposites.

Binaries can hide the values behind user attributes. Let's say you show temperature with warm at one end of the continuum and cool on the other. Because warm and cool really do represent opposite values, you haven't hidden any information. What if you created a continuum with warm at one end and comfortable at the other (Figure 13-8)? Is it true that as I get warmer, I become less comfortable? Sometimes. How you measure warm is different from how you measure comfort, so placing them on a single continuum distorts and hides the values behind each. Sometimes this is OK. Sometimes it's not.

Warm ——————⬤——————— Comfy

FIGURE 13-8
Binaries can hide individual attribute values

USE INDIVIDUAL VALUES TO COMPARE AND CONTRAST MORE USER DATA IN LESS SPACE

Values display information about a single attribute (Figure 13-9).

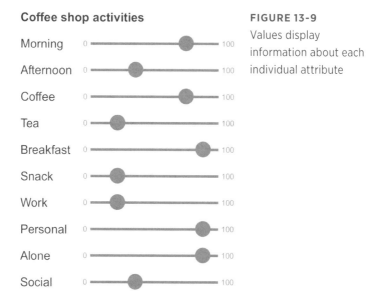

Coffee shop activities

Morning, Afternoon, Coffee, Tea, Breakfast, Snack, Work, Personal, Alone, Social (0–100 sliders)

FIGURE 13-9
Values display information about each individual attribute

When you display values for individual attributes, it's like you take a binary, break it in half, and display both attributes, each with its own value. Because you display each attribute with its own value, this approach requires more space than either lists or binaries.

Similarly, when you show values for every attribute, you show more information, so it's harder to understand at a glance. However, because you show values for every attribute, the individual values communicate user data and assumptions in the most accurate way. Where binaries contrast two attributes against each other, individual values show several attributes side-by-side for easy comparison and contrast.

The attribute grid in Chapter 12 shows a value for every attribute for every user. The attribute grid allows teams to visually compare and contrast attributes using color to visualize values as a DNA strip. You can also show value using numbers, length, or size (Figure 13-10).

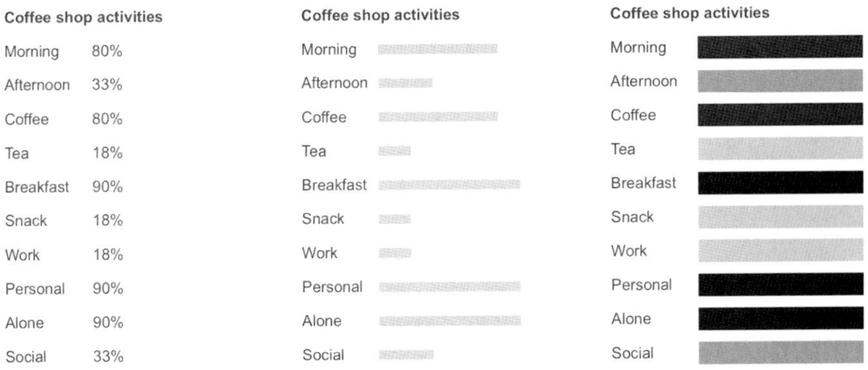

Coffee shop activities		Coffee shop activities		Coffee shop activities	
Morning	80%	Morning	▬▬▬▬▬	Morning	████████
Afternoon	33%	Afternoon	▬▬	Afternoon	████████
Coffee	80%	Coffee	▬▬▬▬▬	Coffee	████████
Tea	18%	Tea	▬	Tea	████████
Breakfast	90%	Breakfast	▬▬▬▬▬▬	Breakfast	████████
Snack	18%	Snack	▬	Snack	████████
Work	18%	Work	▬	Work	████████
Personal	90%	Personal	▬▬▬▬▬▬	Personal	████████
Alone	90%	Alone	▬▬▬▬▬▬	Alone	████████
Social	33%	Social	▬▬	Social	████████

FIGURE 13-10
You can communicate attribute values using color, numbers, length, or size

CHOOSE THE BEST WAY TO COMMUNICATE ATTRIBUTES

Choosing what attributes to communicate is pretty easy. Figuring the best way to communicate them is harder. Whether you choose a list, binaries, or individual values, each method has advantages and disadvantages (Table 13-2). The best way to display user attributes is the one that helps you communicate what you need with the least amount of effort.

TABLE 13-2. Advantages and disadvantages to different methods to communicate user attributes

	LIST	BINARY VALUES	INDIVIDUAL VALUES
EASY TO UNDERSTAND	High	Medium	Low
SPACE REQUIRED	Low	Medium	High
CONTRAST ATTRIBUTES	None	Medium	High
COMPARE ATTRIBUTES	None	Low	High
ATTRIBUTE VALUES	None	Low	High

Communicate User Identity with Names and Images

The user's identity is the most important part of the user model. You'd think attributes are more important, but without the ability to refer to a user, the team has no way to reference their attributes.

Identity performs two jobs. First, it identifies each user and makes them memorable. Second, memorable identities help teams better remember users and help user models spread throughout the broader organization.

Communicate user identity with names, visuals, or both.

IDENTIFY USER MODELS WITH GOOD NAMES

When teams hear the user's name, they should remember the user's tasks, contexts, influencers, and goals.

For a long time, user models had real names like John Smith or Zhang Wei. Designers believed personas with real names helped developers imagine the persona as a real person and build products that better met their needs. Unfortunately, it's hard to get to know a piece of paper, and a name like Zhang Wei or John Smith doesn't communicate user needs very well.

An actual name can communicate user needs if you add a title like "Zhang Wei, HR Manager" or "John Smith, Subscriber." Sometimes a title or role helps teams recall the user's needs.

I've seen user models given alliterative names to make them more memorable like "Sam, the subscriber" or even "Sam Subscriber." The name helps the model sound more real, so the team will empathize with and talk about what Sam needs and wants.

Although real names humanize user models, real names also attach human histories and biases. Who's more likely to watch professional sports? Sam Subscriber or Samantha Subscriber? Who's more likely to quit their job to raise the kids?

All names invoke stereotypes and biases. Sometimes you want team members to remember a user is male or from Asia. In contrast, if stereotypes about Asian men cause the team to make bad, less optimal decisions, then ditch the real name and use a title. Instead of "Sam Subscriber," name the user model "Subscriber."

When you choose how to name the user model, determine what the team needs more or less of (Table 13-3). Does the team need more empathy for users? Do stereotypes improve or hamper how well they understand user attributes?

TABLE 13-3. Advantages and disadvantages to different ways of naming user models

	EMPATHY GENERATED	ATTRIBUTES COMMUNICATED	STEREOTYPES TRIGGERED
NAME Sam Jones	High	Low	High
NAME + DESCRIPTOR Sam Subscriber	Medium	High	Medium
DESCRIPTOR Subscriber	Low	High	Low

IDENTIFY USER MODELS WITH GOOD VISUALS

User models often include a photograph of a person to make the model seem more real. Like with names, actual photographs evoke stereotypes.

To counter negative effects of user photographs, use illustrations that remove the bias. The right illustration can hide age, gender, and ethnicity to control what stereotypes the model will trigger.

Stereotypical images aren't necessarily bad. On one project, one segment of users lived and worked in China, where their behavior differed widely from US users. The team frequently based decisions on assumptions about US behavior. To counter this, we gave the Chinese user model a photographic headshot. Seeing a different ethnicity reminded the team to stop and think about how behavior in China and the United States was similar and different.

Of course, neither headshots nor illustrations communicate much about user attributes. To improve the amount of information the visual communicates, use icons that hint at roles and behaviors.

Visuals can also communicate user context. Instead of a headshot, use a photo of a representative user in the physical location. For example, instead of a photo portrait, show a photo of a barista behind an espresso machine. Like icons, broader images hint at what the user does and where, while also giving the user model a more relatable visual.

Like with names, choose the image for your user model that best supports the team's needs (Table 13-4).

TABLE 13-4. Advantages and disadvantages to different ways of visualizing user models

	EMPATHY GENERATED	ATTRIBUTES COMMUNICATED	STEREOTYPES TRIGGERED
Headshot photo[1]	Medium	Low	High
Headshot illustration	Low	Medium	Medium
Icon	Low	Medium	Low

---

1 Gibbon photo by Eric Kilby, *www.flickr.com/photos/ekilby/4877055767.*

	EMPATHY GENERATED	ATTRIBUTES COMMUNICATED	STEREOTYPES TRIGGERED
Context photo[2] 	High	High	High
Context illustration 	Medium	High	Medium

Change Names and Visuals Based on the Audience

There's no rule that you have to communicate user models the same way to everyone. Change how you refer to users based on your audience (Figure 13-11). For example, for executive presentations, you might use photos with context to provide more information. And for your team, you might use an icon because they've internalized more of the information. Every time you refer to a user, communication with your audience is more important than consistency.

Regular Joe
Morning coffee is how I start my day

Regular Joe
Buys coffee everyday

FIGURE 13-11
Change how you reference the user model based on what the audience needs to understand (gibbon photo by Eric Kilby, on Flickr).

---

2 Gibbon photo by Cazz, *www.flickr.com/photos/cazzjj/15716471788*.

Five Other Things to Include in User Models

Don't limit user models to lists of attributes. Include any additional details that provide the team with information they can use to make product decisions.

ILLUSTRATE USER RELATIONSHIPS

In some cases, product success depends less on individual users and more on groups. In many business contexts, one person chooses the product, another approves the choice, and someone else writes the check. Families can follow similar patterns for expensive home goods like cars, furniture, or appliances. One adult recommends options while another vetoes or approves.

Illustrate relationships as attributes or diagram the user's network to make relationships clear (Figure 13-12). Is it enough to know who the user talks to or works with? Or does the team need to see how the various users are connected?

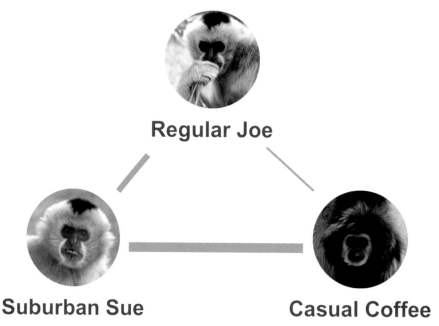

FIGURE 13-12

For products where relationships impact the experience, illustrate user relationships as part of the user model (photos by Eric Kilby and Jeremy Couture, on Flickr).

SHOW USER'S PLACE IN THE USER LIFECYCLE

If you segment users by where they exist on the user lifecycle, it can be useful to illustrate how a user model relates to other users (Figure 13-13). You might have models for potential users, new users, established users, and lapsed users.

User lifecycle

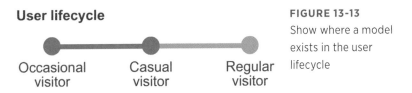

Occasional visitor   Casual visitor   Regular visitor

FIGURE 13-13

Show where a model exists in the user lifecycle

SHOW USER'S LOCATION IN THE PRODUCT LIFECYCLE

Some products move through a lifecycle that touches multiple users, so you can map when and where the user interacts with the product or process. For example, you could reveal when different users interact with a bag of coffee. Service blueprints show how several employees interact with a service and its user (Figure 13-14).

User's place in the coffee lifecycle

Cofee roasted   Coffee distributed   Coffee purchased   Coffee ground   Coffee ground   Coffee shared

FIGURE 13-14

With some products, reveal when and where the user interacts with the product

ADD METRICS TO USER MODELS

Add existing metrics to user models to help the team better understand each user. For example, if you segmented users by prospective users, recent users, and returning users, you probably have analytics for each group. You might know the percentage of total visitors in a user group, average screens per visit, or average cart size. Add metrics to tie the user model to real data.

Show Multiple Users Side-by-Side

When we think of personas and user models, we imagine a single page with a headshot, snappy quote, and abstract charts that tell us about a single user. The one-sheet—because it condenses a single persona to "one sheet" of paper—is the most used and least useful format to document and share user models. If the product has more than one type of user, the one-sheet isn't as useful as a side-by-side.

For projects with more than one user model, teams need to understand how those users compare to each other. When you document several user models side-by-side, your team sees how product decisions help or hinder different users. Your team can see the impact of its product decisions.

Show user models side-by-side in two ways:

- Columns communicate less information, good for guidelines or research overviews
- Grids communicate more information, good for research details

Choose the best format to leverage the advantages you need for your team. Side-by-sides should be easy to scan, so team members quickly understand the information presented and find the information they need. Clearly mark each user's identity and break columns and rows into discrete chunks of information.

USE COLUMNS TO SHARE DESIGN GUIDELINES
AND RESEARCH OVERVIEWS

Place multiple models next to each other in columns or rows to provide teams with an overview of important users (Figure 13-15). List important design targets or highlight users you will *not* design for.

When I review user models with stakeholders, I often show a list of users we will design for and a separate list of other users we identify as non-targets. Knowing who you're not designing for is just as useful as knowing who you will design for.

Website personas

Regular Joe	**Suburban Sue**	**Casual Coffee**
Buys coffee every workday	Buys coffee when running errands	Meets friends at coffee shop

User goals	User goals	User goals
• Be comfortable at work because I'm there so much	• Stay refreshed while facing shopping hordes	• Spend positive social time with friends
• Kickstart my brain for the morning grind	• Pleasant, safe, clean place for a quick restroom break	• Pleasant, comfortable, neutral place to meet

FIGURE 13-15

Use columns to list users and provide an overview of who they are (photos by Eric Kilby and Jeremy Couture, on Flickr).

The column format can communicate guidelines on *how* to build (Figure 13-16). For each user, provide brief goals, content, and interaction tips. You might note a user always uses their mobile, whereas small children constantly interrupt another user. Choose small details that provide outsized information to help the team build more useful products.

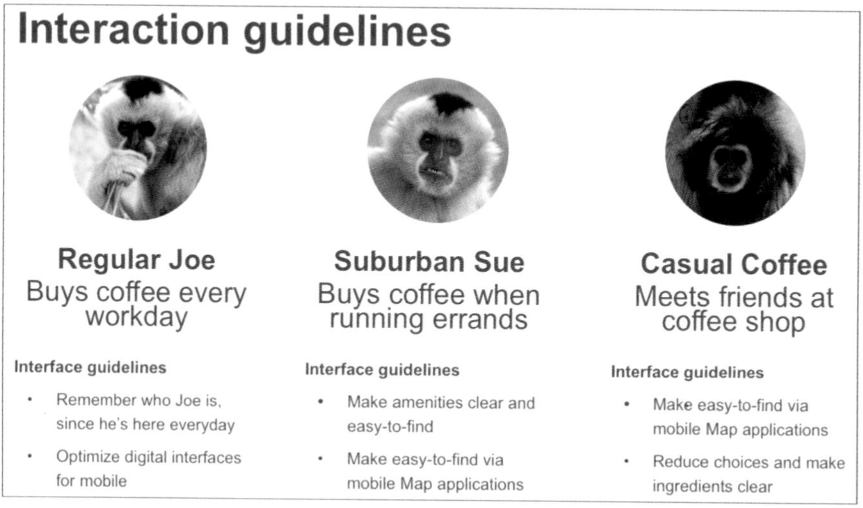

Interaction guidelines

Regular Joe
Buys coffee every workday

Suburban Sue
Buys coffee when running errands

Casual Coffee
Meets friends at coffee shop

Interface guidelines

- Remember who Joe is, since he's here everyday

- Optimize digital interfaces for mobile

Interface guidelines

- Make amenities clear and easy-to-find

- Make easy-to-find via mobile Map applications

Interface guidelines

- Make easy-to-find via mobile Map applications

- Reduce choices and make ingredients clear

FIGURE 13-16

Columns also work well to share high-level design guidelines (photos by Eric Kilby and Jeremy Couture, on Flickr).

Column layouts, loose and friendly, communicate less information by design. If you need to show more information, use a grid.

USE GRIDS TO SHARE DETAILED RESEARCH AND GUIDELINES

Like column layouts, grids set several user models side-by-side on one page or screen. However, where column layouts use whitespace to separate information, grids abandon whitespace in favor of grid lines, so you can squeeze more information into less space (Figure 13-17).

Channels				
Website	None	None	Low	None
App	High	High	Low	None
In-store	High	Low	Low	High
Drive through	Low	High	None	None
Chat	None	None	Low	None
SMS	None	None	None	None
Email	None	None	Low	None
Goals				
Completing ritual	High	High	High	None
Boosting alertness	High	High	None	None
Sipping socially	Low	Low	None	High
Appreciating flavor	Low	Low	High	Low
Tasks/Jobs				
Research coffee	None	None	High	None
Buy coffee	Low	Low	Medium	None
Find a store	Medium	Medium	None	Medium
Try coffee	None	None	Low	None
Work	Low	None	None	Low
Use wifi	Low	None	None	Low
Meet friends	None	None	None	Medium
Take break	Low	None	None	Low
Content and funtionality				
Coffee descriptions	Low	Low	Medium	None
Drink descriptions	Medium	Medium	None	High
Order ahead	High	Low	None	None
Menu	Low	Low	None	High

FIGURE 13-17

Grids trade the column's whitespace for grid lines, so you can squeeze more info into less space

Squeezing makes grids harder to read, something to decipher rather than glance at. However, grids, like any side-by-side format, allow the team to see and compare multiple user models. Although columns and grids squeeze several user models into one screen or page, space limits how much information you can include. To communicate more information about a user, create a one-sheet.

TITLE THE SIDE-BY-SIDE WITH THE DOCUMENT'S PURPOSE

Give the side-by-side a title that explains why someone should look at the document. Are these the five user models the product will target? Is this a collection of design guidelines for each of the user models? A selection of research highlights?

As a general practice, align the side-by-side with one of the two types of user models (page 201) or one of the four questions user models answer (page 200).

MARK EACH COLUMN OR ROW WITH THE USER'S IDENTITY

Based on audience and need, head each column or row with the user's identity. Use good names and visuals to differentiate each user from the others and to communicate who they are. Don't hesitate to change names or visuals based on the audience or your goal. Better communication beats better consistency, every time.

CHOOSE CONTENT THAT MATCHES THE DOCUMENT GOAL

Because of space limitations, side-by-sides only include two to three chunks of content. Choose the content that best fulfills your goal.

Don't worry about running out of space. To show more information, create another side-by-side. For example, you might start with a single side-by-side to show user goals, needs, and design guidelines, titled "User needs and design guidelines."

While creating that side-by-side, you decide you want to include information about user context and journey. Context and journey won't fit onto the first page, so create two side-by-sides. Goals, needs, and journey fit together under the new title, "User goals and needs," and context and design guidelines work well together under a new title, "Design guidelines."

CUSTOMIZE CONTENT DISPLAY

For each content group, customize the display to communicate best. Use lists, binaries, individual values, data visualizations, and text to get the point across. Each content group should answer the question posed by the title.

Focus on a Single User with One-Sheets

When you have more information than fits in a side-by-side, or you need to share more detailed information about a user, create an easy-to-consume, single page—the one-sheet. Use one-sheets to present user data and attributes or to detail design guidelines for a specific user (Figure 13-18).

Regular Joe

Morning coffee is how I start my day

Channels	User goals	Pain points
 Mobile app In-store	• Be comfortable at work because I am there so much • Kickstart my brain to prepare for the morning grind	• Long lines in morning • Jostling crowds risk spilling my drink • Dripping latté foam on my work shirt

Monthly coffee buy

FIGURE 13-18
One-sheet layout and content will always vary by project, team, and user model (gibbon photo by Eric Kilby, on Flickr)

FOCUS ON RESEARCH OR GUIDELINES, NOT BOTH

In the past, I combined research findings and attributes alongside design guidelines on the same one-sheet. However, I think this was an error. Any audience who wants research findings wants to know what they should build. And anyone who wants design guidelines wants to know how to build. Rarely do they want to know what to build and how to build at the same time. If the same person wants to see both, give them multiple documents.

IDENTIFY USERS WITH MULTIPLE NAMES AND IMAGES

One-sheets offer more room for more information. Expand names and imagery to identify each user. A name, role, quote, headshot, icon, context image, and color ensure no matter who sees the one-sheet, they'll know what user it refers to.

MAKE THE MOST IMPORTANT INFORMATION MOST PROMINENT

Most website homepages share a similar structure. A large hero item rules the top of the screen, while three to four content blocks lurk beneath. Posters, brochures, and PowerPoint slides share this layout because it highlights the most important information first and provides access to supplemental information next.

Use the same pattern to lay out the one-sheet. Identify the most important group of attributes or most important group of guidelines. Highlight and place this content prominently in the design.

What information is more or less important will depend on your team and organization. Like any prioritization, ask yourself, what is the one thing they need to know to be successful? Or, what one thing must they know to avoid failure? Every project, team, and organization has that one thing.

INCLUDE SUPPLEMENTAL INFORMATION

Use the rest of the one-sheet to communicate three to four additional pieces of information. Of all the information you have for each user, the supplemental information should include the next most important things the team needs to know.

CUSTOMIZE CONTENT DISPLAY

Like with side-by-sides, customize the display to best communicate the content. Use lists, binaries, individual values, data visualizations, and text to get the point across.

Share User Models in Other Ways

One-sheets and side-by-sides come from a time when one group researched and segmented user models into documents to hand over to another group. Of course, you would never work this way, in silos, like some heathen.

Teams use user models three ways:

- Teams refer to user models when they discuss interfaces and journeys.

- They ingest them to determine what to build.

- They reference user models to make decisions about how to build the product.

You can accomplish these goals and share user models in ways other than one-sheets and side-by-sides.

STICKERS TO MAKE REFERENCES EASY

With teams that do a lot of sketching on paper, stickers make it easy to reference users on a sketch. Sketching interfaces? Paper prototyping? Identify the primary user with a sticker. Print stickers with sheets of adhesive labels.

POSTERS KEEP USER MODELS IN PLAIN SIGHT

If the team works co-located with one another, trade one-sheets and side-by-sides for posters. Layout and content follow the same principles as their smaller brethren. There's more room, and you can make things bigger. Always-visible models allow teams to glance up and check design guidelines or research finding while they work.

CARDS CREATE POCKET REFERENCES

The opposite of posters, cards make user models portable and easy to reference. Think of them like baseball or Pokémon cards, except the team references user stats and design guidelines.

ONLINE HOMES MAKE USER MODELS AVAILABLE TO EVERYONE

Though online tools won't fit in pockets, team members can access them from anywhere at any time. If your team uses online tools like Jira or Azure DevOps to manage user stories and track tasks, publish user models to the same system for easy reference.

If you can't publish user models in the same system, add them to other developer documentation or publish them where everyone has access—like an online document repository or design tool like Mural or InVision.

Where is less important than how easy it is for your team to remember, link to, and view its users. Bonus points if team members can edit and update the models. Nothing is immutable. As the team's understanding changes, the team should update how that understanding is captured in your user models.

SLIDE DECK TEMPLATES INCLUDE USERS IN EVERY REVIEW

Jessica Harllee recommends including the user models as part of your slide deck templates. That way, as you get ready for a review, the user models are already included and ready to set the stage for the review.

Make User Models in the Format You Will Review Them

Without a doubt, anyone can find something more valuable to do than busywork, so limit your busywork. Make user models in the same format you'll use when you check them with the team or other stakeholders. It's no accident that one-sheets and side-by-sides look like PowerPoint slides.

That doesn't mean you should shy away from other methods. There's no reason why you can't check posters, wikis, or other formats. My teams review user attribute grids with stakeholders. If teams can check user models in monster spreadsheets, then other formats will work, too.

Your goal is to review the model you make, not make a model, and then make another version to review. That doesn't mean there's no additional work when you Check a user model, but limit additional work as much as possible and create user models in the same format you will review and use them.

User Models Are Powerful Reference Tools

Pretty personas seem so straightforward. In truth, they culminate a long string of critical decisions about who will consume the information and why they need it. Answer those questions the right way and document the appropriate user models to create useful, powerful tools your team and organization can reference again and again when they make product decisions.

Now that you have condensed user attributes and analysis into easy-to-scan and -read documents, it's time to put them into practice and understand each user's journey.

Interactions

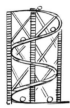

INTERACTIONS

THE EXPERIENCE YOUR ORGANIZATION creates may live in a single product, but users stretch those experiences over time. Better products appear right when the user needs them in exactly the way they need. Interactions describe how users interact with products over time.

This part explores the interactions from both a high level as well as in detail at the task level, so you can Think-Make-Check interactions with your teams and clients.

[14]

Elements of Interactions

MOST OFTEN, TEAMS SHOW each other interfaces. They point at sketches and wireframes and prototypes and describe what the user *sees* or *does*. For everything the user sees, they do something. The user interacts with the interface. See something. Do something.

An interaction model steps away from the interface to map what a user sees and does. Interaction models capture how a user interacts with an interface over time. Because interaction models show the user, what they see, and what they do over a period of time, interaction models answer three questions:

- What are the different parts of the interaction?
- How do the different parts affect each other?
- How do we move the user from one part to another?

Interaction models freeze time, so you can examine individual scenes from any angle and understand how the user moves from scene to scene. Freezing time helps your team understand the full scope of the project. Interaction models also let you identify the highest-value areas of an experience and reveal conversion points that create maximum value.

In this chapter, we'll tear apart interaction models and learn what they're made of. Your team will use interaction models to build better experiences, and you're going to help them.

Three Types of Interaction Models

Interaction models come in many flavors (Figure 14-1):

- Scenarios
- Use cases
- User flows
- Task flows
- Screen flows
- Storyboards
- Prototypes
- Service blueprints
- User journeys
- Experience maps

Teams have created different ways to model interactions. In every case, they illustrate how a user interacts with one or more interfaces over time. As they show how a user moves through a system, each model communicates more or less information and focuses on different parts of the interaction. For example, scenarios describe what the user does with words. A service blueprint documents everything an organization does.

Although interaction models come in many flavors, you can divide them into touchpoints, journeys, and experiences:

- Touchpoints map what users do during a single touchpoint
- Journeys map several touchpoints *inside* a single system
- Experience maps show touchpoints inside *and* outside a system or across several systems

TOUCHPOINTS, THE SIMPLEST INTERACTION MODEL

A touchpoint represents a point in time when your organization and your user "touch" each other. It's literally the point where you touch. The interaction model's simplest form lists the tasks a user completes during a single touchpoint. We can use a flow diagram to show what happens during a single touchpoint (Figure 14-1). The user visits the store, orders coffee, and picks up coffee. When we know what steps a user takes when they enter our coffee store, we can design better interactions.

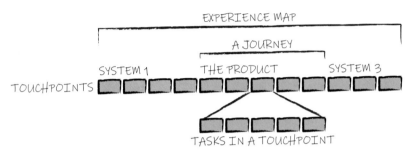

FIGURE 14-1
Touchpoints, journeys, and experience maps fit together like nesting dolls

EXPERIENCE MAPS, THE MOST COMPLEX INTERACTION MODEL

The most complex interaction model lists things a user experiences across different systems. We call this an "experience map" because it maps the user's overall experience with a *thing* (Figure 14-1, again). The user first has coffee in college, drinks socially through their early 20s, adds coffee to their morning routine after having a baby, and continues the daily coffee routine as they get older. When we know how our user experiences coffee throughout their life, we can look for better ways to support our user's coffee habit at each stage.

USER JOURNEYS, THE MEDIUM-SIZED INTERACTION MODEL

In between the touchpoint and the experience map lives what we call a user journey because it maps a specific user's *journey* with your organization (still Figure 14-1). User visits store to buy coffee and sees ad for loyalty card. User uses website to add money to loyalty card. User adds loyalty card to mobile app and uses loyalty app to order coffee for pick-up. The user journey shows how the user interacts with our global coffee company's different products, so we can look for ways to improve how our products work together.

A single experience map should include several user journeys, and a user journey includes multiple touchpoints.

Touchpoints Have Four Building Blocks

Each touchpoint represents an event where your organization and your users interact. "Buy coffee in a store" represents a touchpoint. The user touches you to buy coffee. You touch the user to sell coffee. You come together to exchange coffee for money. "Buy coffee from the website" is another touchpoint. "Sign up for loyalty program on website" is another touchpoint.

All touchpoints start with a scenario.

SCENARIOS, THE STORY YOU TELL

Scenario is a fancy word for the story the interaction model tells. For example, the scenario for how a user buys coffee in a store looks like this:

> The user enters the coffee shop and glances at the menu to select their drink. They move up to the counter to order and pay before moving to the end of the counter to wait for their drink. When the drink is ready, the user accepts the drink from the barista.

Just as interfaces hide assumptions about the user and what they're doing, the scenario hides stuff, too. Every scenario tells a story, and every story has a character and a setting. Product teams cast users as characters, and channels tell us where we've set the story.

USERS, THE CHARACTERS IN OUR STORY

Even if the scenario doesn't mention a specific user, it assumes one. Though scenarios embed the user into the story, it's useful to keep them separate.

If you have more than one user, it's better to specify who the user is rather than using the generic "user." You not only want to tell multiple stories for a single user, you want to tell the same story different ways for different users.

Just as we learn more from more specific stories, we learn more when we think about specific users. Is this a story about how the Coffee Chef buys coffee? The Regular Joe? Or the Casual Coffee drinker? The Buys Coffee scenario changes for each user model (Table 14-1).

TABLE 14-1. Comparison of how different users complete the same scenario

USER	SCENARIO: BUYS COFFEE
Generic user	The user enters the coffee shop and glances at the menu to select their drink. They move up to the counter to order and pay before moving to the end of the counter to wait for their drink. When the drink is ready, the user accepts the drink from the barista.
Coffee Chef	The Coffee Chef enters the coffee shop and *glances at the daily board to see what coffees are brewing*. They move up to the counter to order and pay before moving to the end of the counter to wait for their drink. When the drink is ready, they accept the drink from the barista.
Regular Joe	The Regular Joe enters the coffee shop and moves up to the counter to order and pay. *The barista recognizes them and enters their usual order.* Regular Joe moves to the end of the counter to wait for their drink. When the drink is ready, they accept the drink from the barista.
Casual Coffee	Casual Coffee enters the coffee shop and *studies the menu. They move up to the counter to ask for a recommendation before* they order and pay. They wait at the end of the counter for their drink. When the drink is ready, they accept the drink from the barista.

At a minimum, every interaction model should specify a single scenario and a single user. Examine how different users work through the same scenario to help your team make buying coffee better for every user, or for just one user.

CHANNELS, THE SETTING FOR OUR STORY

The channel is *where* the story happens. Like with users, it's useful to separate the channel from the story. Every touchpoint has a scenario and a channel (Table 14-2).

TABLE 14-2. Sample touchpoint scenarios and channels

SCENARIO	CHANNEL
Buy coffee	In a store
Buy coffee	On the website
Sign up for loyalty program	On the website
Sign up for loyalty program	In a store

Breaking scenarios apart from channels lets us think about how to design a scenario for each. When you buy coffee on the website, how does that compare to buying it in the store?

Breaking the scenario apart from the channel helps teams understand and choose what scenarios they should support for what channels. What scenarios do we need to support on the website? What scenarios do we need to support in the store?

TASKS, BREAKING TOUCHPOINTS INTO PIECES

Breaking the user and the channel out of the scenario helps you think about how different users and different channels might need different designs. But if we want to get granular, we want to break the story into tasks.

For example, to map how a user buys coffee (Figure 14-2), we list the things the user does:

- Choose coffee

- Order coffee

- Pay for coffee

- Wait for coffee

- Pick up coffee

CHOOSE   ORDER   PAY FOR   WAIT FOR   PICK UP
COFFEE   COFFEE   COFFEE   COFFEE   COFFEE

FIGURE 14-2

Break scenarios into a list of steps, or tasks, to optimize the user's experience

This list shows the *tasks* a user completes when they buy coffee. We call it a *task* flow. Most important, this diagrams what happens during a single point where you and your user *touch* each other, this single touchpoint.

Altogether, scenarios, users, channels, and tasks let teams understand a touchpoint, so they can see the parts involved, look for places to improve the experience, and discover new ways to reach the user.

While touchpoints form the basic building block of an interaction model, you can add more touchpoints or more information about each touchpoint to create the more complex interaction models like journeys and experience maps.

Length, Depth, and Point of View

Three perspectives describe what content to include in an interaction model:

Length
> How many touchpoints do you show at one time?

Depth
> How much information do you show about each touchpoint?

Point of view
> From whose perspective do you tell the story?

Length, depth, and point of view act like levers that adjust what questions the interaction model can answer.

LENGTH, HOW MANY TOUCHPOINTS DO YOU SHOW AT ONE TIME?

For Buy Coffee (Figure 14-2), we mapped tasks for one touchpoint: Regular Joe buys coffee in a store. That's enough information to understand and optimize Regular Joe's experience inside the coffee shop.

Regular Joe may also use a mobile app to find the closest store when he wants his caffeine boost. That's a separate touchpoint. If we want to understand how Regular Joe moves from one touchpoint to another—from the mobile app to the coffee shop—we can map two touchpoints instead of one (Figure 14-3).

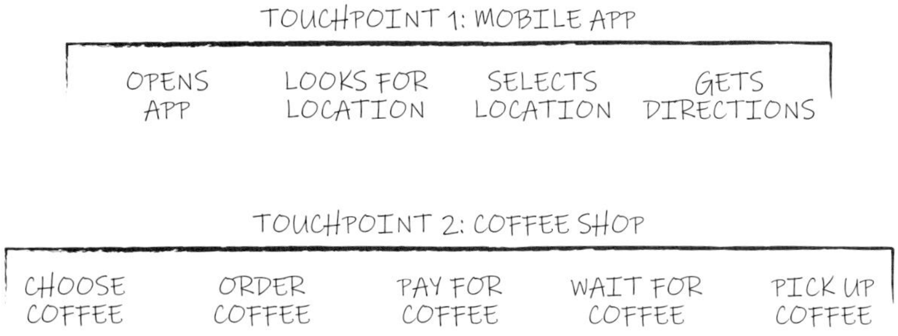

TOUCHPOINT 1: MOBILE APP

| OPENS APP | LOOKS FOR LOCATION | SELECTS LOCATION | GETS DIRECTIONS |

TOUCHPOINT 2: COFFEE SHOP

| CHOOSE COFFEE | ORDER COFFEE | PAY FOR COFFEE | WAIT FOR COFFEE | PICK UP COFFEE |

FIGURE 14-3

Interaction models with more touchpoints have more length

When you add additional length to an interaction model, you reveal more conversion points you can optimize for.

DEPTH, HOW MUCH INFORMATION DO YOU SHOW ABOUT EACH TOUCHPOINT?

For Buy Coffee (Figure 14-2), we listed the steps Regular Joe takes to buy coffee in a store. Those steps help us improve Joe's coffee purchase. We can map other information, too.

What if we wanted to find where we frustrated Joe the most? We can note whether Joe is happy or sad at each step. What if we wanted to make sure we had the right signage for Joe? At each step, we can document what Joe looks at (Figure 14-4).

As we add more information to the interaction model, we add more depth.

SEES MENU	SEES BARISTA	SEES TOTAL	SEES DRINK BEING MADE	SEES DRINK
CHOOSE COFFEE	ORDER COFFEE	PAY FOR COFFEE	WAIT FOR COFFEE	PICKUP COFFEE

FIGURE 14-4

Interaction models with more information have more depth

POINT OF VIEW, WHO OR WHAT SERVES AS YOUR MAIN CHARACTER?

Point of view refers to how you look at the interaction. Most models look at the interaction from the perspective of one user. It doesn't have to be this way. To understand how several people work together, create interaction models with more than one person. For example, you can map the interaction model for both Regular Joe and the coffee store staff (Figure 14-5).

FIGURE 14-5
We can look at interactions from the point of view of a single user or multiple users

You can also map interactions from the point of view of a thing. Model the interaction from the point of view of the coffee bean to make sure Regular Joe gets smooth, easy-to-drink coffee (Figure 14-6). I've mapped interactions for heavy machinery, mattresses, petroleum, and couches, and each one revealed how users and their needs changed over time.

FIGURE 14-6
We can look at interactions from the point of view of a thing

As interaction models become more complex, it's useful to add additional organization.

Phases and Moments of Truth

As you expand the length of the interaction model with more touchpoints, you may notice the touchpoints clump into phases where the user does similar types of things. For example, if you map how Regular

Joe finds a local coffee store and buys coffee, you might group touchpoints into two phases: one for navigating to a store and a second for buying coffee (Figure 14-7).

Navigate to store   **Buy coffee**

Look for store	Find directions	Go to coffee shop	Enter coffee shop	Choose coffee	Order coffee	Pay for coffee	Wait for coffee	Pick up coffee

FIGURE 14-7
Interaction models with multiple touchpoints can sometimes be divided into phases

PHASES MARK DIFFERENT TYPES OF TASKS

For each of these phases, Regular Joe does a different type of activity. When navigating to a store, Regular Joe is most concerned with where he's located and where to go. Once he arrives at the store, he's most concerned with ordering coffee.

When you identify the user's type of activity, you reveal how to optimize the experience at each phase. When Regular Joe wants to find a store, optimize for navigation. When he wants to buy coffee, optimize for selection and ordering.

TRANSITIONS MARK WHEN USERS MOVE FROM ONE PHASE TO ANOTHER

When you add phases, each phase ends with a critical touchpoint that marks when the user moves from the phase they're in to another phase. For example, if Coffee Chef wants a new coffee sensation, they might start with research where they learn about climates and beans, and read tasting reviews. However, at some point, Coffee Chef stops researching and decides to buy. Deciding to buy moves Coffee Chef into a new phase.

That touchpoint, where Coffee Chef ends their research and chooses their new taste sensation, is where the type of activity changes from researching to buying. Instead of thinking about how to choose the right coffee, Coffee Chef thinks about how to pay. The point in time where Coffee Chef chooses their next coffee sensation is the critical step in the interaction that marks when they transition from the research phase to the buy phase. Mess that step up, and Coffee Chef won't buy.

Moments of truth

Some people refer to critical transition touchpoints as moments of truth. I don't like that phrase. It's a moment of truth for the organization, but we're trying to think about the user's experience. It's better to think of them as transitions, so your team can focus on helping the user move through them.

As-Is or To-Be, Looking Forward and Back

Sometimes teams model interactions to identify problem spots in the current product. In these cases, the interaction model may illustrate the system as it exists now. Mapping the as-is experience lets teams see the moving pieces in one glance, so they can optimize how they work together and help the user.

Teams creating new systems want to understand how all the pieces will come together. When creating new systems, teams want to model interactions the way they will be. This "to-be" understanding helps them know what to build and reveals the most important parts of the experience that will need extra attention.

Tailor Interaction Models to Project and Team Needs

There's no limit to how you can tweak length, depth, and point of view in an interaction model. Based on your project, interaction models answer different questions. For projects where the team has a solution, interaction models show teams what to build and how they should build it. For teams that haven't picked a solution or haven't identified the problem to solve, interaction models reveal potential problems and give teams a framework to generate and evaluate possible solutions (Figure 14-8).

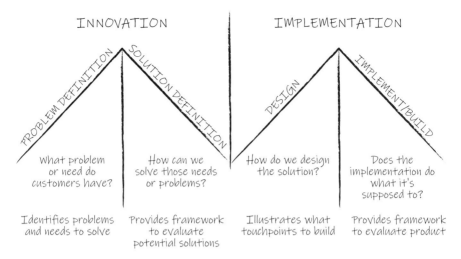

FIGURE 14-8

Based on where the project occurs, interaction models offer different advantages

There's no such thing as *just* a task flow, journey, or experience map. You will create interaction models more *like* flows, journeys, or experience maps. The content you include in the interaction model will make it more like one or the other, and just like user and interface models, include the content that answers the questions your team wants to explore.

In the next three chapters, we'll walk through how to use interaction models to identify new products and services, reveal experience optimizations and improvements, and support product development.

[15]

Identify What to Build with Touchpoint Maps

Iт's tough to make your product easy to use when you don't know how users will use it. Your team builds features without a clear view into how well they work together. You can help teams orchestrate better product experiences when you think about how the user completes individual tasks.

In this chapter, we'll map how a user moves through a series of tasks, so your team can build touchpoints that are easier to use, are more satisfying, and convert better. You can map tasks for a touchpoint as part of sprint planning or formal product discovery. Lightweight versions of this activity help unravel random discussions about improving product flow.

How Touchpoint Maps Work

Before the team maps the tasks for the interaction, step back and specify the story, user, and channel. With everyone aligned on the story, generate and refine the tasks and their order (Figure 15-1):

1. Working together, team discusses and aligns on story, user, and channel.

2. Team generates tasks needed to complete the story.

3. Team refines tasks, task order, and handoffs to other interactions.

4. Team explores task flow to understand relevant information like data, processes, content, analytics, and interfaces.

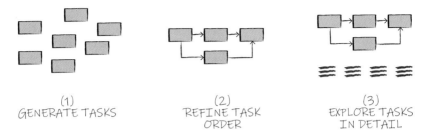

TOUCHPOINT MAPS

(1)
GENERATE TASKS

(2)
REFINE TASK
ORDER

(3)
EXPLORE TASKS
IN DETAIL

FIGURE 15-1

First identify the story, user, and channel, then generate and refine the tasks needed for the story

At the end of the activity, the team will have produced two concrete outcomes:

- A diagram of how the user moves from one task to another

- A list of additional details and requirements

WHEN TO MAP THE USER'S TASK FLOW

Map task flows prior to sketching an interface, such as during formal product discovery. Task flows break user stories into discrete elements that support backlog grooming and sprint planning.

Informal task flows most often occur when the team discusses a specific interface and the team steps back to review the larger picture.

INPUTS AND QUICK STARTS

This exercise assumes a team working on a product or service and requires a user story that includes a specific user and channel. If you explored user attributes with the user profile canvas (Chapter 11), then you have a trove of stories to start with.

To innovate new products and interfaces, map task flows in the abstract: a general "user" does a thing in an unspecified channel (Figure 15-2). Even in these cases, you have assumptions about who the user will be.

MATERIALS YOU'LL USE

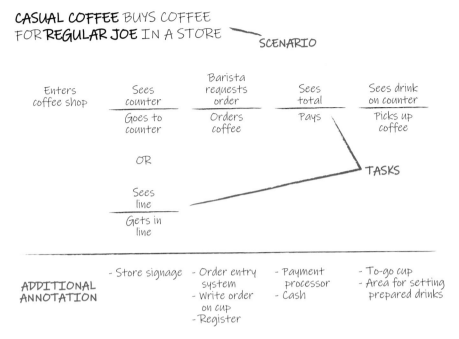

FIGURE 15-2

Task flows have two main parts: the scenario and the tasks. Further discussion may include additional annotation.

Scenario

Text that includes story, user, and channel may change slightly as the team aligns on the purpose of task flow, and most likely remains untouched after that.

Tasks

The team will add, edit, move, and remove tasks throughout the discussion, so make them movable with sticky notes or note cards, or easy to write and erase.

Additional annotation

Sometimes added toward end of discussion. Though these may be edited and moved, it happens less often than with tasks.

Find templates, framing material, and remote resources on the website:

http://pxd.gd/interactions/touchpoint-map

Activity 1: Clarify the Scenario

When you and your team get together and discuss a scenario, it's tempting to jump up and start drawing tasks and arrows. As with most discussions, everyone involved has assumptions about the story, the user, and the channel.

In this activity:

1. You'll identify the scenario

2. You'll clarify the user and the channel

To make sure everyone is mapping the same story, begin every task mapping session by clarifying the scenario. Specifically, what user, what are they doing, and in what channel?

THE FRAME

WHAT WILL YOU DO?	Identify the story, user, and channel
WHAT'S THE OUTCOME?	A clear scenario agreed to by the entire team
WHY IS IT IMPORTANT?	Ensures the team is aligned around and discussing the same user and tasks
HOW WILL YOU DO IT?	Working together

To frame story clarification, say:

> "Before we sketch this scenario, let's write down the user and channel, so we stay on track."

CLARIFY THE STORY

Let's use an example to make this clearer. Let's say Little Red Riding Hood wants to take some coffee to her grandmother, a Regular Joe who's home sick, and you want to map the tasks involved in Little Red buying coffee at the coffee store.

Get to the scenario

Though you might want to map Red's entire journey from home, to the coffee shop, through the woods, and to grandmother's house, we want to focus on a single touchpoint that's controlled by our global coffee company. We map Red's entire journey in the next chapter. For now, let's map what Red does when she goes to the coffee shop.

So, that's our scenario: Red orders coffee for grandma at the coffee shop.

If the team suggests other parts of the story or describes scenarios that are broader than a single touchpoint, capture those as additional touchpoints to map. However, you can only map one touchpoint at a time. For example, a team member may also want to map how Red finds and travels to the coffee shop. Those are fine scenarios to map, but map each one separately.

In this example, we're going to map how Red orders coffee for grandma at the coffee shop.

Specify the user

Chapter 16 shows how even the simple task of ordering coffee might differ for different personas. These differences reveal why it's so important to specify what persona you will focus on. If one team member assumes a Regular Joe who doesn't need a menu and another team member assumes Casual Coffee who always needs a menu, then they will argue about whether or not you need a menu.

In our story, Red doesn't know coffee, so she might need a menu. But she's ordering for grandma who's a Regular Joe, so Red knows exactly what she wants to order.

So, that's our persona: Regular Joe.

If you feel the team isn't aligned, probe to determine if you should map another persona instead of or in addition to the first one. Determine the best approach to take, and then specify the channel.

Specify the channel

Just as the persona changes what tasks you map, the channel changes what tasks the user expects or are possible. Often, the team shares an assumption about the channel that's associated with the product you're working on. However, it's useful to say it out loud and write it on the board, so everyone can see it.

For this example, the channel is in a store.

Like with personas, probe to determine if there is another channel that should be discussed. If team members have alternate channels to map, capture them as well. Touchpoint mapping is a fast exercise, so you can map several in quick succession.

FINISH WITH THE FULL STORY AND MOVE TO GENERATE TASKS

In this activity, we took our story—Little Red Riding Hood wants to take some coffee to her grandmother, a Regular Joe who's home sick—and turned it into a clear scenario to map: Casual Coffee buys coffee for Regular Joe in a store.

Capture the scenario at the top left of the screen, whiteboard, or page, so it will stay visible until you've completed mapping the touchpoint.

You can design, build, and test this kind of specific scenario. And it focuses on a single touchpoint, so you can move from start to finish in a short time with a limited scope. Once you've clarified the scenario's user and channel, it's time to generate tasks:

> "Now that we've captured the scenario's specifics, let's start mapping out the tasks."

Activity 2: Generate Tasks

The beauty of stories is they gather several events in a handy package. How your team thinks about this story determines the tasks they've already assumed will be there. In this activity you'll work through everyone's assumptions and collaborate to identify what tasks should be mapped. It's three straightforward steps:

1. Working together, identify the first task

2. Identify each additional task

3. Identify any decision points

THE FRAME

WHAT WILL YOU DO?	List tasks
WHAT'S THE OUTCOME?	A list of tasks and decision points for a single touchpoint
WHY IS IT IMPORTANT?	Identifies the landscape of tasks from which the team will refine and optimize the experience
HOW WILL YOU DO IT?	Working together

To frame the task generation, say:

> "Now that we know the user and the channel, let's list all the tasks they work through to complete this scenario."

FACILITATE TASK GENERATION

As the team discussed the scenario, user, and channel, they likely also thought about what tasks were involved, so this activity finishes pretty quickly. Start by asking what the first task is. Reference the scenario to prompt discussion. In our example, the scenario is:

Casual Coffee buys coffee for Regular Joe in a store.

Ask the team what is the first thing that Casual Coffee does.

The team may share any number of answers. Casual Coffee walks up to the counter, Casual Coffee orders, or Casual Coffee walks inside the store. At this point, you just want a place to start. It doesn't matter if this is actually the real first step. Capture the first step on the board (Figure 15-3).

CASUAL COFFEE BUYS COFFEE
FOR REGULAR JOE IN A STORE

FIGURE 15-3

All task flows start somewhere. Capture an idea for the first thing on the board.

Enters
coffee shop

If the team offers multiple options for the first step, capture the one that seems earliest in the process and work through the additional ideas in the next step.

Probe for what the user sees

You can continue by asking what's next and so on until you get to the end of the scenario. However, you have a specific user and channel that limit how the scenario can be completed. Hidden in everything the user does is something they saw.

The user sees something, so the user does something. Ultimately, your team's job is to show the user the right thing, so the user can do the next thing, and move through the scenario.

Instead of asking what the user does, after the first step, ask what the user sees (Figure 15-4). What does Casual Coffee see when she walks into the coffee shop? She sees the menu and the counter. Capture what she sees as the next step and draw a line underneath. For now, just capture what the user sees. Shortly, though, the team will optimize the task flow by making sure the user sees what they need or expect to see.

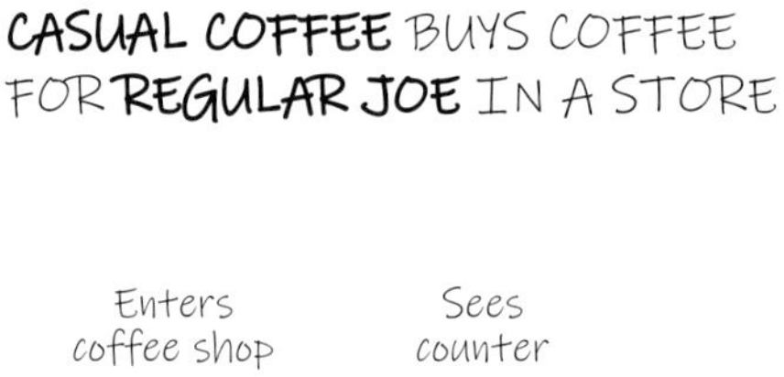

CASUAL COFFEE BUYS COFFEE FOR REGULAR JOE IN A STORE

FIGURE 15-4

Capture what the user sees after the first step

Enters coffee shop	Sees counter

Probe for what the user does in response to what they see

When you first identify what the user sees, it helps frame the team's response to the next question: what does the user do next? Casual Coffee sees the menu and counter. What does she do next? Does she walk to the counter? Capture what she does beneath the line and what she saw (Figure 15-5).

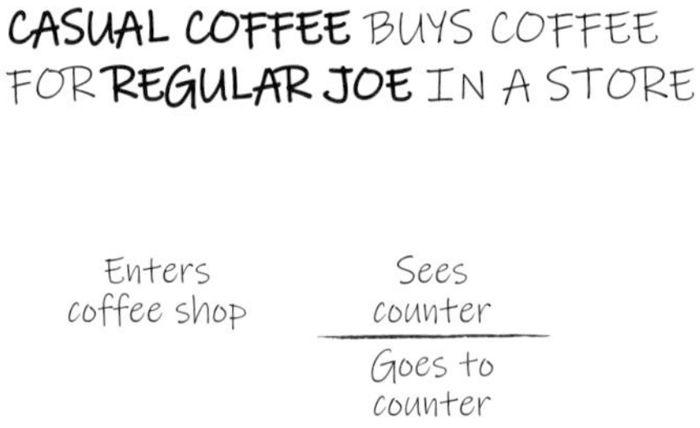

CASUAL COFFEE BUYS COFFEE FOR REGULAR JOE IN A STORE

FIGURE 15-5

Capture what the user does in response to what they see

Enters coffee shop	Sees counter
	Goes to counter

Watch for multiple paths and decision points

Rare occasions let you map a process where the user follows one step after the other in a clean line. Frequently, the user reaches a fork in their path where what they do changes based on some circumstance or decision. We refer to these splits as *decision points*.

Watch for decision points as the team generates tasks. In the example above, does Casual Coffee always go to the counter? What if there's a line? Capture additional sees/does pairs above and below the line (Figure 15-6).

CASUAL COFFEE BUYS COFFEE
FOR REGULAR JOE IN A STORE

FIGURE 15-6

Capture decision points with additional sees or does information above and below the line where it makes the most sense

Structurally, stories assume a single ending, and scenarios are no different. Because each scenario will have one ending, decision points end in one of two ways. First, the decision point may lead the user to a separate touchpoint. Or, the decision point will lead the user back to the scenario's main path.

In our example, if Red does not see a line, she goes to the counter. Otherwise, if Red sees a line, she gets in line. However, after moving through the line, Red arrives at the counter. No matter how she gets to the counter, Red will order coffee.

In contrast, if Red heads to the bathroom before she goes to the counter, then that would lead to a separate touchpoint (Figure 15-7). When decision points lead to a separate touchpoint, it's like saying you want to remember there's another path over here, but right now you're focused on this other story.

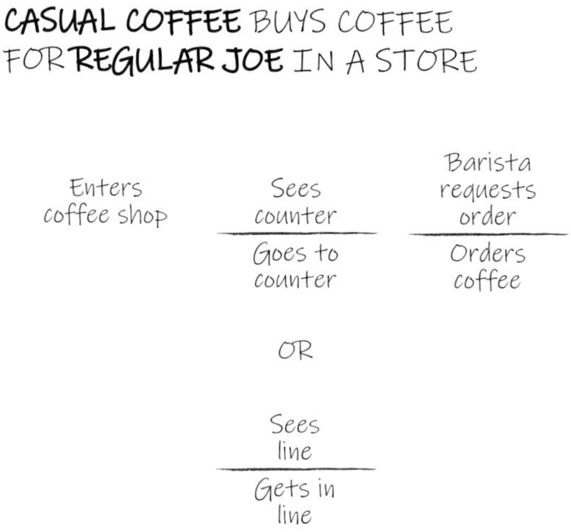

CASUAL COFFEE BUYS COFFEE
FOR REGULAR JOE IN A STORE

FIGURE 15-7

Decision points lead
back to the main story
or off to another story

Enters coffee shop	Sees counter	Barista requests order
	Goes to counter	Orders coffee

OR

Sees line
Gets in line

Continue to generate what the user sees and does

Continue to capture the next thing the user sees and does until you
reach the end of the scenario. In the example scenario, Casual Coffee
ordered coffee for Regular Joe. The scenario contains an implicit end
state—that Casual Coffee picks up the coffee order—so continue with
tasks until you reach the end state (Figure 15-8).

CASUAL COFFEE BUYS COFFEE
FOR REGULAR JOE IN A STORE

Enters coffee shop	Sees counter	Barista requests order	Sees total	Sees drink on counter
	Goes to counter	Orders coffee	Pays	Picks up coffee

OR

Sees line
Gets in line

FIGURE 15-8

Continue to capture each next step until you arrive at the scenario's end state

The team may have different ideas about where the scenario ends. Like with the first step, capture everything that makes sense as part of the diagram. For steps that don't fit so easily, capture them off to the side, so you don't forget them. You may be able to work them in during the next activity where you refine the task sequence. Or, they might be included in further task flow diagrams.

FINISH GENERATING STEPS AND MOVE TO REFINE THEM

Continue asking what the user sees and what they do until the user gets to the end of the scenario or discussion slows. It's OK if the team doesn't generate every task or decision point. In the next activity, the team will refine these steps and add and remove additional tasks. To move to refinement, highlight the need to optimize the task flow:

> "Now that we've identified how the user completes their tasks, let's look for a way to make it easier, smoother, and more delightful."

Activity 3: Refine Tasks and Sequence

When you generate tasks, you provide the ingredients your team needs to improve the task flow. How can the team make it easier, simpler, more delightful? Or if designing a hunger game, how can the team make it more difficult, dangerous, and deadly?

In this activity, the team will:

1. Look for ways to change the sequence of tasks to make the interaction easier

2. Look for ways to remove tasks

3. Look for ways to automate tasks, so the user doesn't need to do them

4. Look for ways to introduce decision points to make the main scenario easier

This refinement of the task flow creates better products for your team to build.

THE FRAME

WHAT WILL YOU DO?	Refine task sequence
WHAT'S THE OUTCOME?	A finalized task sequence
WHY IS IT IMPORTANT?	Designs an optimized task flow for the team to build and test
HOW WILL YOU DO IT?	Working together

To frame the sequence refinement, say:

"Let's look for ways to make this sequence of tasks easier to complete."

FACILITATE TASK SEQUENCE IMPROVEMENT

Review the task flow diagram and look for places to reorder the tasks. Ask the team if it would be easier for the user to complete the tasks in a different order. Often, existing processes were designed to accommodate how the organization did things in the past. Or they were built without much thought to making it easier for users. Probe the team for why the tasks appear in the order they do and whether or not the scenario would be better if the team reordered them.

Probe for steps to remove

Removing steps makes scenarios easier for users to complete. Fewer steps means fewer things to do and fewer opportunities to change minds or make mistakes. Probe the team to identify any steps they can remove.

Probe for steps to automate

Sometimes, although you can't remove steps, you can automate a step, so the product does the step automatically for the user. From the user's perspective, the process is still easier. From the team's perspective, the process probably requires more work.

Probe for steps to combine

Often automation allows the team to combine two or more steps into one step. The user experiences the same result: an easier process with fewer opportunities to abandon or face an error. In addition to automation, look for other opportunities to combine steps. Existing processes represent fertile opportunities to combine. New thinking, technologies, and business processes may allow the team to combine steps that needed to be separate in the past.

Probe for steps to move to another scenario

Task flow diagrams that become too busy or are too long with too many decision points indicate you have mapped more than one touchpoint in the same diagram. If this is useful, keep the diagram this way. Usually, it's more useful to identify the separate touchpoints and move them to separate diagrams.

Separate diagrams for each touchpoint allow the team to focus on a specific interaction, so they can build it better. Look for opportunities to divide large touchpoint diagrams into several smaller diagrams. This reflects a clarity of thinking about how users interact with the product.

FINISH REFINEMENT AND MOVE TO UNDERSTAND DETAILS

After the team refines the task flow, you would think you're done. However, the task flow precludes discussion around the interaction's specific details. Edit the diagram to capture the final sequence of tasks. The conversations that follow will vary widely.

Conversations Around Touchpoint Diagrams

Touchpoint diagrams allow teams to see an entire interaction at one glance, so they can identify and look for issues that hamper the user. The discrete tasks in the diagram allow the team to zoom in and understand specific steps. The ability to zoom in and out lets the team freeze time and look at the interaction from multiple perspectives. These multiple perspectives help teams plan how to build new interactions as well as optimize and improve existing ones.

Touchpoint diagrams support five common team conversations around an interaction:

1. Interfaces

2. Data

3. Business processes

4. Content

5. Analytics

INTERFACES: HOW USERS COMPLETE THE TASK

The interface, often the most concrete part of a product, takes up a large mindshare in most teams. At its simplest, touchpoint diagrams let you assume an individual interface for every sees/does combination. However, in the digital realm, it's easy to combine multiple steps onto one screen. To indicate multiple steps will occur in the same screen, draw a rectangle around those steps to tie them together.

Although most touchpoint diagrams focus on a single channel, you can indicate handoffs to other channels right on the diagram. For example, some interactions kick off a single SMS or email message (Figure 15-9).

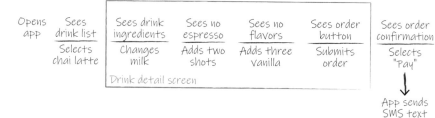

REGULAR JOE BUYS COFFEE
WITH THE MOBILE APP 1ST TIME

FIGURE 15-9
Draw a rectangle around multiple steps that occur on the same screen and identify when short interactions kick off in other channels

DATA, BUSINESS PROCESSES, AND CONTENT: WHAT YOU NEED TO SUPPORT THE TASK

Data constitutes some of the biggest constraints and most difficult development tasks facing product teams. Touchpoint diagrams allow teams to view an entire interaction and identify the data they have, need, and want to support the scenario.

To discuss data requirements, capture the data you have or need in columns below the touchpoint diagram. Columns tie data annotations to the discrete steps above without obscuring the diagram with too much visual noise (Figure 15-10).

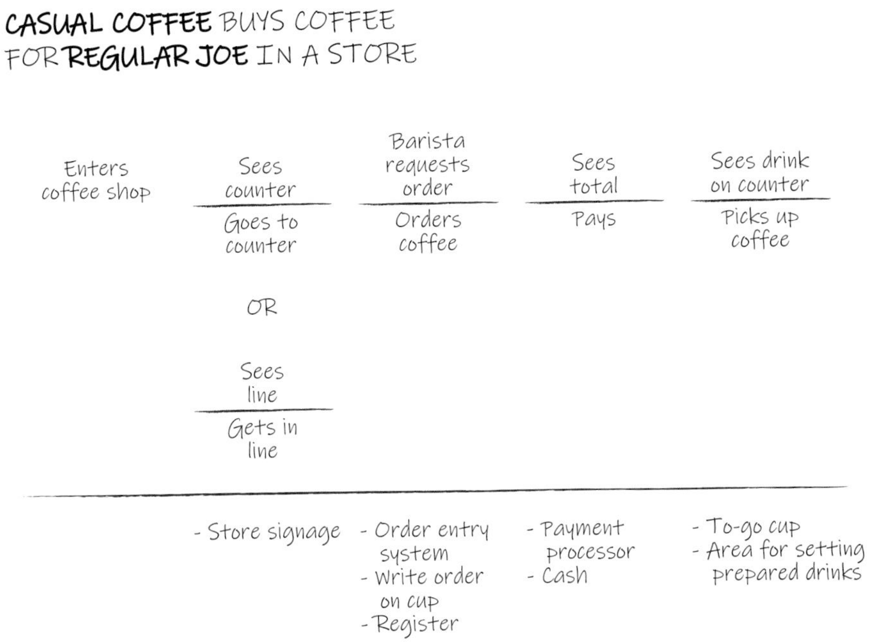

CASUAL COFFEE BUYS COFFEE
FOR REGULAR JOE IN A STORE

Enters coffee shop	Sees counter	Barista requests order	Sees total	Sees drink on counter
	Goes to counter	Orders coffee	Pays	Picks up coffee

OR

Sees
line

Gets in
line

- Store signage	- Order entry system	- Payment processor	- To-go cup
	- Write order on cup	- Cash	- Area for setting prepared drinks
	- Register		

FIGURE 15-10
Annotate the touchpoint diagram with data needs and wants

Some tasks may entangle with business processes like approvals, limits, or reporting. Like data, capture business processes that affect or are affected by the task in the column beneath.

Likewise, interfaces require content. To build or support the interaction, will you need text, images, video, audio, smells, people? Capture all of this information in the area below each task. If you have formal business requirements or user stories, requirement or story IDs help teams and approvers trace how requirements and stories tie into the overall product.

Unfortunately, teams focus so readily on interfaces, data, and processes, they miss what to track to measure success. The task flow's sequence provides an easy look at an entire interaction to identify where to apply analytics.

It might be tempting to measure every step in a scenario, but too much data is worse than no data. Focus on the right data. What steps in the interaction are the most critical? Do you want to know how many users finish to identify whether people use the feature at all? Do you need to compare how many start against how many finish to identify usability problems?

Think about what you need to measure and note those analytics. Key interactions need more measurement than less important interactions. If it's not as important, it's OK to measure less, or even not at all.

Touchpoint Maps Reveal Discrete Parts of the Experience

As organizations design more and more touchpoints, the touchpoint diagram helps teams work through conversations about interface, data, process, content, and measurement. Document touchpoints to support user story definition or sketch them in support of as-needed project conversations.

Just as touchpoint diagrams let teams zoom in and out of individual interactions, products stretch across entire ecosystems, and teams need to zoom in and out of these landscapes as well. In the next chapter, we'll apply these same techniques to diagram user journeys and experience maps that let teams design products that fit with their users' lives and needs.

Understand How Products Fit Together with Journey Maps

Optimized touchpoints won't help if users never come across your product in the first place. User journeys and experience maps show teams the broader landscape where the product lives, so they can make sure the product fulfills user needs in a useful way.

In this chapter, we'll learn how teams can map user journeys into and out of your product landscape. While we'll learn how to map the user's journey as a series of activities, the journey unlocks its real value when it serves as a continuous touchstone for the team.

How Journey and Experience Maps Work

User journey workshops are messy, illustrated discussions that begin with a false start and iterate until everyone gets tired or satisfied with what you've mapped. Journey mapping combines touchpoint generation with an analysis of the different channels and phases to create a high-level view into how a user moves into and out of your product ecosystem (Figure 16-1). That's a lot, but teams work through mapping in three steps:

1. Working together, generate touchpoints

2. Analyze the journey to understand the context

3. Explore touchpoints in detail

At the end of the activity, the team will have created a list of touchpoints and identified when the user moves from one phase to another.

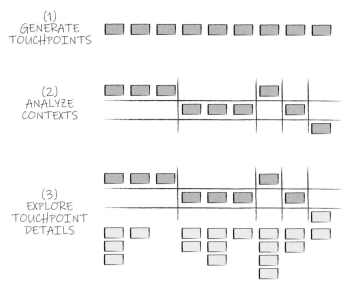

JOURNEY/EXPERIENCE MAPS

(1)
GENERATE
TOUCHPOINTS

(2)
ANALYZE
CONTEXTS

(3)
EXPLORE
TOUCHPOINT
DETAILS

FIGURE 16-1

Generate touchpoints and group into channels and phases to create journey maps

WHEN TO MAP USER JOURNEYS

Map user journeys during project kickoff and project discovery to help teams understand how the product fits into the user's landscape. For mature products, it's worthwhile to create journey maps when the team needs to improve conversions, adoption, and retention.

INPUTS AND QUICK STARTS

Journeys require a user and a goal. If the team completed the user profile canvas (Chapter 12), use one of those goals for the journey map. Tasks identified at the bottom of the user profile canvas likely translate into touchpoints on the journey map (Figure 16-2).

If you don't have an explicit user goal or touchpoints, ask participants to generate them during the first two activities.

MATERIALS YOU'LL USE

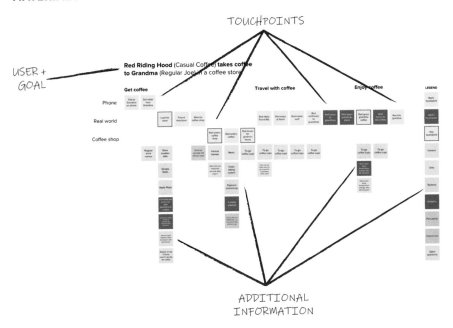

FIGURE 16-2
Journey maps have four parts: the user and goal, touchpoints, channels, and phases

User and goal
The user and goal will almost certainly not change, so will not need to be moved or edited.

Touchpoints
Once identified, touchpoints will be moved. Capture each on movable sticky notes or pieces of paper, or make them easy to erase and rewrite.

Additional information
As with touchpoint maps, teams can capture additional information about data, content, analytics, business processes, and even research. Capture these on movable sticky notes or pieces of paper or make them easy to erase and rewrite, so they can be moved when their associated touchpoints are moved.

Find templates, framing material, and remote resources on the website:

http://pxd.gd/interactions/journey-map

Activity 1: Generate Touchpoints

Where touchpoint flows map the user's tasks, journeys live one level higher and map the user's touchpoints. Some teams choose to limit the journey to touchpoints controlled by their organization. When teams look at touchpoints inside and outside of their product's ecosystem, they can identify more and better opportunities to improve conversion and retention.

In this activity, the team will:

1. Identify a false start to begin the journey

2. Identify previous touchpoints

3. Identify next touchpoints

If you identified touchpoints as part of the user profile canvas (Chapter 12), use those to kickstart the discussion.

THE FRAME

WHAT WILL YOU DO?	List touchpoints
WHAT'S THE OUTCOME?	A list of touchpoints both inside and outside the product ecosystem
WHY IS IT IMPORTANT?	Helps the team identify opportunities to improve conversion and retention
HOW WILL YOU DO IT?	Working together or in groups

To frame touchpoint generation, say:

> "Let's map the user's journey, so we can look for opportunities to make the product more appealing. Let's start by listing the touchpoints the user has with the product as well as related to the product."

FACILITATE TOUCHPOINT GENERATION

All journeys begin with a single step.

If you already have a list of touchpoints, place them on the board in roughly chronological order. For example, if you created lists of tasks with a user profile canvas (Chapter 12), position these on the board. If you don't have touchpoints, ask the team when users first come in contact with the product.

Let's whip up an example. Say we want to improve how Red buys coffee and delivers it to her grandmother. In the last chapter, we mapped Red's interaction as a Casual Coffee persona who bought coffee in a store. Now we want to map Red's entire journey with grandmother's coffee.

Where does Red first encounter the global coffee company? As with touchpoint diagrams, there is no right answer to this question, and the first answer is just a starting point for the rest of the conversation. Let's say the team suggests Red's journey starts when she enters the coffee shop. Capture the touchpoint on the board.

Choose current state or future state

Activity participants often ask whether they should generate touchpoints for how things work now, or for how they want them to work. Map the current state journey when you want to look for places to improve it. Map the future state when you want to understand how it may look or change after you build your product.

Regardless of whether you focus on the current or the future state, participants will use, reference, and default to the current state whenever possible because that's what they're used to. It's the most comfortable way for people to describe the journey. If participants illustrate the current state when you want the future state, probe to understand how they want the current state to *change* in the future and correct any touchpoints that will be different. Or, leave them. Some things will stay the same even when you're building a new product.

Probe for previous touchpoints

With a touchpoint on the board, explore what happens before. What happens before the user comes in contact with the product? What leads the user to think of the product? How does the user get to the starting point?

What did Red do before she entered the coffee shop? She found the location on her phone and followed directions there. What prompted her to look for a location? She just finished talking to grandma on the phone.

Capture each prior touchpoint on the board (Figure 16-3). Continue to ask why and what happened until you have enough information about prior events. Don't travel all the way back in time to when grandma was born, but go back far enough to be useful.

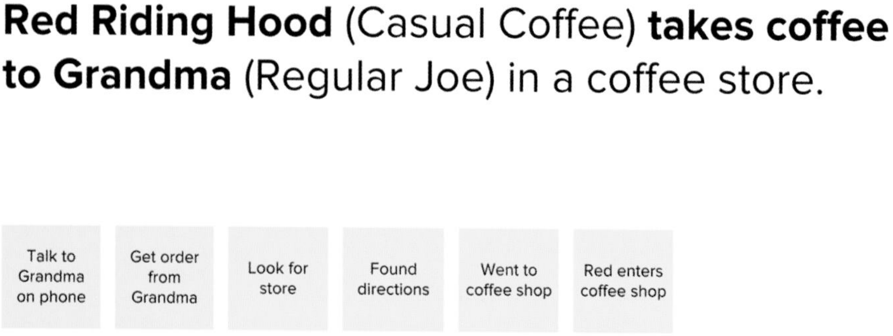

Red Riding Hood (Casual Coffee) takes coffee to Grandma (Regular Joe) in a coffee store.

Talk to Grandma on phone	Get order from Grandma	Look for store	Found directions	Went to coffee shop	Red enters coffee shop

FIGURE 16-3

Ask what happened before and map what the user was doing why and where to understand how the product fits into the user's full context

Probe for the next touchpoint

Just as you move backward in the journey, move forward. From the last touchpoint on the board, ask what the user does next. What happens after that? Where is the user going? What's the user doing? Continue to ask what happens next until it feels like you have enough information.

What happens after Red enters the coffee shop? She orders coffee. We know what that looks like. We mapped that touchpoint in Chapter 15, from when Red orders coffee to when she picks it up. What happens next? Red leaves for grandma's house and takes the forest road. Red stops at a florist to pick up flowers. Red meets a wolf. Red arrives at grandma's house and gives grandma coffee. Grandma doesn't like the coffee. Red kills grandma.

Capture each following task on the board (Figure 16-4). Continue to ask why and what happened until you have enough information about the events that follow.

Red Riding Hood (Casual Coffee) **takes coffee
to Grandma** (Regular Joe) in a coffee store.

FIGURE 16-4

Ask what happened next and map what the user does and why to understand
how the user interacts with the product over time

Probe to understand what you don't

When you include multiple perspectives and diverse teams, you learn
new things. To you, the new thing seems strange. For them, it seems
obvious, old hat. If you don't know the story of Little Red Riding Hood,
you'd wonder why Red kills grandma. Perhaps, even, why grandma
didn't like her coffee.

When you encounter a touchpoint you don't understand, ask why the
user does that. Why does Red kill grandma? It's not really grandma. It's
the wolf dressed like grandma. Why is the wolf dressed like grandma?

As you ask questions to understand, capture new touchpoints on the
board (Figure 16-5).

Red Riding Hood (Casual Coffee) **takes coffee
to Grandma** (Regular Joe) in a coffee store.

FIGURE 16-5

Ask about touchpoints you don't understand to learn more about the context

Probe for missing steps

As the journey begins to fill up with more and more touchpoints, step
back and look for places that seem emptier than others. Explore those
areas. Ask what else happens and why. Look for touchpoints the team
may have overlooked.

Split into groups to cover more ground

If you have more than about four or five participants, break into groups to probe different parts of the journey at the same time. As groups probe, exchange group members every so often to focus fresh eyes on each part of the journey and identify new touchpoints.

Linearize the journey

When you organize things by time, people imagine a process flow. They might branch touchpoints in different directions and create parallel paths. Encourage alternate paths. They help team members explore a process and generate additional touchpoints. However, in the next activity, you'll need each touchpoint in its own column. Once the team tires or becomes satisfied with what you've documented, move touchpoints so they are all in one line (Figure 16-6).

Red Riding Hood (Casual Coffee) **takes coffee to Grandma** (Regular Joe) in a coffee store.

FIGURE 16-6

When touchpoint generation subsides, move touchpoints, so they form one line

When you place parallel touchpoints in a single line, they no longer accurately reflect the process or flow of time. However, they still suggest chronological time, and that's enough. If you want accurate diagrams of the process, make task flows (Chapter 15). For our journey map, one touchpoint per column pays big rewards as we examine each touchpoint in detail.

FINISH AND MOVE TO ANALYZE THE JOURNEY STRUCTURE

Touchpoint generation slows as everyone tires out or runs out of new ways to think about the journey. You won't have all touchpoints, and that's OK. You have enough to begin to understand big ideas about the journey:

> "Now that we have a good idea about the touchpoints in the journey, let's step back and look at the journey's structure."

Activity 2: Analyze the Journey's Structure

A long line of touchpoints gives the team a sense of what's happening, but it doesn't highlight what's important. Useful journeys highlight useful information that teams can use to make the product more beneficial for users.

To carve useful information out of a line of touchpoints, use the grid to make vertical and horizontal slices that correspond to something interesting.

In this activity, the team will:

1. Analyze the journey by time

2. Analyze the journey by interaction

3. Analyze patterns in the journey

THE FRAME

WHAT WILL YOU DO?	Add additional structure to the journey
WHAT'S THE OUTCOME?	Interesting ways to organize touchpoints
WHY IS IT IMPORTANT?	Helps the team identify and understand how to make the product more relevant
HOW WILL YOU DO IT?	Working all together

To frame analysis of the journey, you might say:

> "Now that we have a good sense of the touchpoints the user moves through, let's understand the journey's different phases and systems involved."

ANALYZE THE JOURNEY BY TIME

With touchpoints in a line, time moves in one direction. In our example, it moves from left to right because that's how we map time in the United States. You can also map touchpoints in other directions: right to left, top to bottom, bottom to top, and so on.

To analyze the journey by time, look for reasons and ways to segment the timeline. How can you break your line into pieces? Every journey differs and every team needs different information, so there is no single right way. However, work through a list of common questions that may apply to your situation.

Break time into parts

Timelines frequently break time into smaller pieces. If you had a time-line of the economy in the twenty-first century, you might break it into before the Great Recession, the Great Recession, and after the Great Recession. More important than how you break the timeline into parts is why. You break timelines into parts so you can analyze events in each part of the timeline in isolation to reveal useful insights.

Looking at Red's journey, can you carve the timeline into parts? You could organize the timeline into three parts: before Red buys coffee, when Red buys coffee, and after Red buys coffee (Figure 16-7).

Red Riding Hood (Casual Coffee) **takes coffee to Grandma** (Regular Joe) in a coffee store.

FIGURE 16-7

Split the journey into segments of time that provide insight into how to improve the user's experience

Break time into phases

As you break the timeline into parts, you will notice the user does different kinds of activities at different times. In our example, Red interacts with the global coffee company in different ways. At the beginning, she talks about coffee orders with grandma. Next, she finds and navigates to a store. Then, she orders coffee to go. Finally, she transports the coffee to grandma.

For each of these phases, Red does a different type of task. Look for places on the timeline where the user completes different types of tasks. Table 16-1 shows several examples of how different teams have broken their journeys into phases.

TABLE 16-1. Common phases for user journeys

JOURNEY	PHASES USED
Product/service selection	Discover
	Evaluate
	Select
	Consume

JOURNEY	PHASES USED
Service experience[1]	Before—Before user buys service
	Begin—User buys service and uses for first time
	During—Regular use of service
	After—When user leaves the service
Travel	Research and planning
	Shopping
	Booking
	Post-booking, pre-travel
	Travel
	Post-travel
Gaming[2]	Awareness
	Choose
	Purchase
	Play
	Share
Furniture shopping	Inspired by something they see
	Explore similar looks
	Evaluate
	Purchase
Capital projects	Identify opportunity
	Validate
	Plan
	Execute

---

1   Miller, Megan Erin. "Understanding the Lifecycle of Service Experiences." *Practical Service Design*, Practical Service Design, 22 Sept. 2016, *blog.practicalservicedesign.com/ understanding-the-lifecycle-of-service-experiences-33b29257f401*.

2   From a user journey created by nForm (*https://www.nform.com*) for a Comcast gaming site.

Break time into systems

Journeys show how users move into and out of different systems as they interact with the product. If the user moves from one system to another, break the timeline into sections based on the system in use at that time.

For example, Red interacts with three separate systems in her journey to take coffee to grandma. First, she maps the closest location to find directions and navigate to a store. Second, she interacts with the store to choose and order coffee. Lastly, she interacts with the coffee packaging to transport the coffee.

Break time up by users

Just as different systems may figure more prominently at different points, different users may figure more prominently at different points in the journey. In our example, coffee store staff and the wolf figure prominently in different places. Identify prominent actors at different stages to help teams understand how to make the product more useful.

Try different ways and don't settle for just one

There's no one way to break the journey into horizontal segments. Your team will find a way that makes the most sense for them. Don't be afraid to try different approaches or even apply two at once. There is no right journey, only the one that provides useful information.

ANALYZE THE JOURNEY BY INTERACTION

Analyzing the journey by time splits our timeline into horizontal segments. Analyzing by interaction lets the team use vertical space to reveal more information about the journey (Figure 16-8). Useful ways to think about the journey's touchpoints include:

- Owned or unowned? Who controls where the touchpoint occurs?

- Online or offline? Does the touchpoint happen digitally or in real life?

- Location, channel, or device? Does the touchpoint occur over email, text, chat, web, phone, conversation?

As the team identifies ways to group the interactions, move the applicable touchpoints up and down in their columns. For example, if you identify owned and unowned interactions, perhaps owned interactions are at the top and unowned interactions are at the bottom (Figure 16-8).

FIGURE 16-8
Move touchpoints up and down to group them by interaction type

Identify owned and unowned channels
Every journey should map how the user moves around the product, both inside your organization's systems and outside of them. Highlight who owns the channel at every stage to understand whether you can control the interactions or merely influence them.

In our example, Red's journey takes her through several systems. First, she uses the coffee company's app to find a store, her phone's map to get directions and navigate to the coffee shop, and her phone's map again to get to grandma's house.

When the team wants to improve the product for Red, they have some sense of the available options. They don't control the phone's map application. However, they can try to influence its data, so coffee shop locations appear there. The company controls coffee shops and can make it easy to order and pick up coffee. And, even though the team has no control over the forest road, they can create coffee cups and drink holders that make it easier to transport coffee by foot or in the car.

Identify online and offline interactions
In this digital age, interactions occur both online and offline. In fact, if your journey has no offline interactions, it's most likely missing key touchpoints. Just like with owned and unowned channels, noting online and offline interactions provides additional information for the team on how to improve the experience at that touchpoint. Can they control the experience? Or can they only influence it?

When Red moves through her journey, she has several online and offline interactions. Finding a location and getting directions is online. Navigating to the store combines online and offline. Store interactions all occur offline. Navigating to grandma combines online and offline again, and visiting grandma happens offline.

Identify location, device, or channel

The touchpoint's location can offer additional insight for product teams. Location can suggest important details about context like what's going on around the user and what types of information or interfaces might be useful.

With Red, is she at home or walking around when she looks for a store location? Finding a location is different in spin class than sitting on the couch at home.

Sometimes, for online or mixed interactions, teams can identify the specific device or channel where the interaction occurs. To find a location, does Red use a phone, tablet, or laptop? Does she use an app or website; ask Siri; ask by SMS, chat, or phone?

Like when you analyzed by time, try different approaches or apply more than one. Help the team identify the information that's most useful for them.

ANALYZE PATTERNS ACROSS THE JOURNEY

So far, the team has sliced the journey into horizontal and vertical pieces, creating a grid that provides additional useful information. However, at some point, you run out of horizontal and vertical space to use. When this happens, mark touchpoints to reveal patterns across the journey.

Look for the same kinds of information you've already examined:

- Systems
- Users
- Owned or unowned
- Online or offline
- Location, channel, or device

Without the ability to move cards up or down, left or right, use visual indicators to highlight touchpoints. Colors, dots, and icons can signify a given touchpoint belongs to a given group. For example, all the touchpoints where Red uses her phone could have a phone icon. Color the wolf's touchpoints red. Anywhere coffee is in play, add a black dot. Add a legend, so everyone knows what the indicators mean (Figure 16-9).

FIGURE 16-9
Mark touchpoints to reveal patterns across the journey

FINISH AND MOVE TO UNDERSTAND SPECIFIC TOUCHPOINTS

This analysis slices the journey into broad swaths of touchpoints and provides a wealth of additional information and context the team can use to build better products. Stop here, or dive into specific touchpoints to learn more:

> "With this view of the journey's structure, let's dive in and understand more about each touchpoint."

Activity 3: Explore Touchpoints in Detail

When you analyze the journey's structure, you understand, think about, and gain insight from groups of touchpoints. Now, with each activity isolated into its own column, you can analyze individual touchpoints in more depth.

To analyze individual touchpoints, take each touchpoint in turn, and add additional information in the column below.

In this activity, work in groups to discuss and analyze each touchpoint.

THE FRAME

WHAT WILL YOU DO?	Analyze individual touchpoints
WHAT'S THE OUTCOME?	Additional information about each touchpoint
WHY IS IT IMPORTANT?	Reveals additional patterns across the journey and specific constraints and requirements for each touchpoint
HOW WILL YOU DO IT?	Working in groups, review each touchpoint in turn

To frame the touchpoint exploration, say:

"Let's dive deeper and explore each touchpoint in detail."

FACILITATE TOUCHPOINT EXPLORATION

Across a journey packed with touchpoints, some touchpoints represent critical interactions. Others reveal difficult constraints or complex business requirements. Working in teams of 2–5, examine each touchpoint to identify critical information about the interaction.

The team will not need to probe for everything described here. Pick and choose the topics most important for your product. As you capture information, use each touchpoint's column to collect everything you know about a single interaction (Figure 16-10).

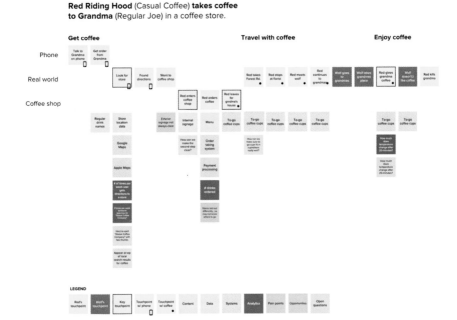

FIGURE 16-10

Capture additional information in each touchpoint's individual column

Probe for key interactions

Look for touchpoints where users move from one type of interaction to another. For example, the user moves from online to offline, from one system to another, or from one channel to another. These touchpoints may require extra care during design to ensure the user can move easily from one interaction to the other.

Similarly, look for touchpoints where the user moves from one phase to another. Often, these shifts indicate where the user makes a decision to move on in the journey.

Probe for business processes

For any touchpoint your organization controls, identify any relevant business processes. For example, when Red enters the store, the global coffee company has processes for taking customer orders and making drinks.

For other types of products, business processes may require approvals, notifications, or other requirements. For these touchpoints, the team needs to make sure the product supports the completion of these processes.

Probe for data requirements

Especially critical for digital products, for each touchpoint, identify whether the product needs to display, collect, or reference any data. For example, when Red looks for a store in the app, the app needs data about each store. When Red orders coffee in the store, the barista needs to provide accurate drink prices.

Probe for system integrations

Like with data, for each touchpoint, identify any systems needed to support that interaction. Systems pass data back and forth, so the touchpoint needs systems for all the data it uses. Business processes may also require systems. For example, a system may process approvals or send a notification.

Probe for content needs

For any touchpoint your organization controls, identify any content required. Data the user sees counts as content, and touchpoints often need other kinds of content like instructions, help information, and, for multilingual systems, content translations.

Probe for analytic needs

Based on project goals, identify touchpoints where you can or should measure key metrics. For example, you may want to measure how many users view stores in the app and link out to get directions. Or you may want to compare how many users enter a store to how many orders a store receives. Identify useful analytics. Note the analytics you can get now and the ones that require more work to track.

Probe for pain points and opportunities

For each touchpoint, discuss specific pain points or barriers the user faces. If you identified pain points on the user profile canvas, map those to the journey where applicable. How can the team help the user overcome pain points?

Similarly, teams can explicitly identify opportunities for each touch-point. Capture any new ideas for improving the interaction or overcoming a user pain.

Probe for open questions
The team possesses uneven information about each touchpoint. For the most part, missing information is OK. You don't need to fill in everything for every touchpoint. Sometimes, though, you run into an important question the team can't answer. Capture these open questions in the column for each touchpoint.

Journey Maps Reveal Secrets to Better Products

When you capture the user's journey with the product, the team can make the product more relevant, useful, and usable for each user. When the product offers what the user needs right when they need it, you create happy users and moments of delight.

So far, we've only talked about how the team should build the product and why it needs different features. All this talk wastes your time if the team can't translate these ideas into something real. In the next section, we'll explore how teams can think about and make the interfaces their product needs.

[V]

Interfaces

As an experience machine, your organization produces experiences for both employees and customers (Figure V-1). To have these experiences, employees and customers engage with interfaces. The interface enables, facilitates, and drives these experiences.

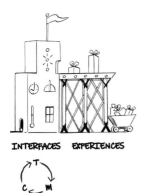

INTERFACES EXPERIENCES

FIGURE V-1

Your organization is a user experience factory. Ideas go in, everybody does their part, and interfaces comes out that create experiences for employees and customers

Because they drive the experience, projects require a lot of time and work to be spent on the interface. Whether you want to design a wireframe, get the frontend CSS to work, or look at analytics to see how users behave, teams focus on interfaces. Screens are a concrete thing everyone can point to.

This part explores the parts of an interface, the different types of interfaces, and how to control interface fidelity, so you can Think-Make-Check interfaces with your teams and clients.

To help your organization create better experiences, change how your teammates think about and make interfaces. You work better together to create better user experiences. Ideas go in, everyone does their part, and better interfaces comes out.

[17]

The Visible and Invisible Parts of an Interface

FOR ANY SYSTEM, ASK yourself: "How does the end user interact with the product?" Do they call in? Send an email? Browse a website? Mail in a form? Talk with an associate?

When you ask how an end user interacts with your product, the answer is an interface. The interface is the one object many organizations think about more than any other. Interfaces are concrete, the last bit of the experience that the experience machine controls. But interfaces are so much more.

In this chapter, we'll learn about the visible and invisible parts of the interface. When you focus on the visible elements of an interface, like the screen, it's easy to overlook the invisible elements, the scene. Every interface screen is just one step in an overall scene, one step in the user's journey (Figure 17-1).

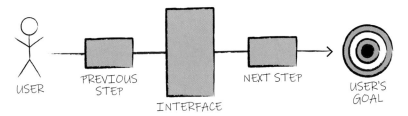

FIGURE 17-1
An interface is just one step in the user's overall journey toward a goal.

ACTUAL INTERFACES

You can talk about the *actual* interface, or a *model* of the interface.

When you browse a website and notice hard-to-use widgets and unclear instructions, you're Checking the *actual* interface. Analytics measure how customers interact with the *actual* interface (Figure 17-2).

INTERFACE MODELS

Each design profession focuses on a different kind of interface. Architects design buildings. Interior designers design rooms. Service designers create services. User interface designers craft screens. Regardless of your design flavor, when you Think-Make-Check a design, you probably review a *picture* of some kind of interface. You don't look at the *actual* interface. You review a *model* of the interface.

When we talk about interface models, we could talk about buildings, emails, chats, phone trees, scripts, websites, applications, cars, or anything, really. For this book, most examples will reference screens for digital products and services.

 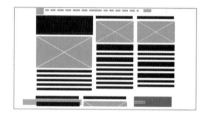

FIGURE 17-2

The actual interface on the left is the actual product or service. The interface model on the right is a picture of the interface.

The Four Visible Parts of an Interface

Whether you're talking about at an actual interface or an interface model, you probably talk about one of the four, visible parts of an interface:

- Content, what the interface communicates to you
- Functionality, what the interface lets you do
- Layout, how the interface is organized
- Design, how the interface appears

CONTENT

Content covers anything the interface explicitly communicates to the user. Content does not include what a user might infer from the interface. On a website, content includes text and images (Figure 17-3). In a movie, content includes text, images, and sound (Figure 17-4). For hardware like Amazon's Echo Dot, content includes the Amazon logo, icons, and what Alexa says (Figure 17-5). A wooden spoon has no content (Figure 17-6).

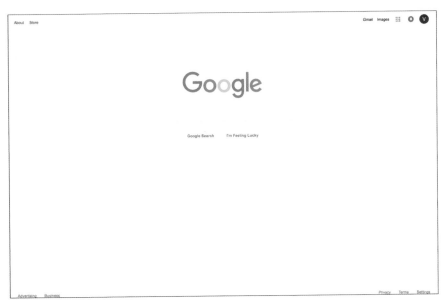

FIGURE 17-3
On websites, content includes text and images.

FIGURE 17-4

In a movie, content includes text, images, and audio.

FIGURE 17-5

On Amazon's Echo Dot, content includes the Amazon logo, icons (images), and anything Alexa says.

FIGURE 17-6

On some interfaces, like a wooden spoon, there is no content (photo by Marco Verch, *www.flickr.com/ photos/30478819@ N08/38273620312*).

FUNCTIONALITY

Functionality is what an interface lets you do. The Google home screen lets you enter a search query and press Search (Figure 17-7).

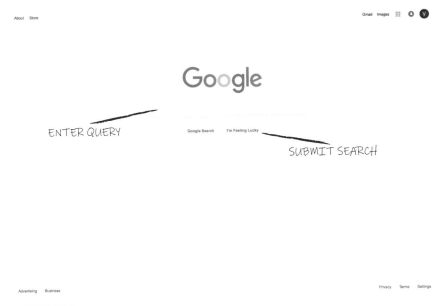

ENTER QUERY

SUBMIT SEARCH

FIGURE 17-7

The Google home screen functionality lets you type in a search query and submit the search.

Affordances

Sometimes, designers refer to functionality as an *affordance*. Design thinker Don Norman described affordances as "properties that determine just how a thing could be used."[1]

Functionality isn't limited to how you *intend* an interface to be used. Functionality is however someone might use it. A wooden spoon is also Hermione's wand (Figure 17-8).[2]

---

1 Norman, Donald A. *The Design of Everyday Things*. New York, NY: Doubleday, 1990.

2 Norman now recommends referring to "signifiers" instead of affordances when you create a design. In terms of an object's properties, we still talk about affordances. See: Norman, Don. "Signifiers, Not Affordances." Jnd.org, 17 Nov. 2008, *jnd.org/signifiers_not_affordances/*.

FIGURE 17-8
A wooden spoon is also
a wand.

LAYOUT

Layout describes how the interface is organized. On their home screen, Google centered search in the middle of the screen and pushed secondary functions to the edges (Figure 17-9). Amazon nested icons, the speaker, and buttons on top of the Echo Dot and wrapped branding around the sides (Figure 17-10).

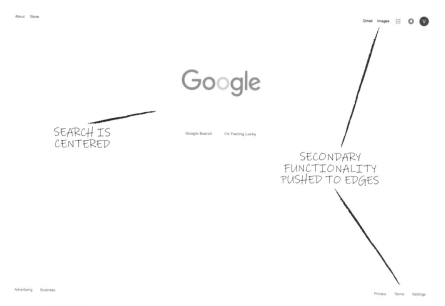

FIGURE 17-9
Google centers search in the middle of the screen and pushes secondary functionality to the edges.

FUNCTIONALITY
ON TOP

BRANDING
ON THE SIDE

FIGURE 17-10

Amazon organized the Echo Dot with functionality on the top and branding around the sides.

DESIGN

Design is how the interface appears. Although Google and Bing both help users search the web, their home screens look different (Figure 17-11). Shop for spoons, and you enter a universe of spoon designs (Figure 17-12).

FIGURE 17-11

Google and Bing gave their search screens different designs.

FIGURE 17-12

Even wooden spoons come in a wide range of designs (photo by Marco Verch, *www.flickr.com/photos/30478819@N08/38273620312*).

Form versus function

The cliché "form follows function" suggests a designer should link an object's design to its functionality. This is an *opinion* about how to make good design. But form and function have nothing to do with one another.

The designer chooses the form. Functionality emerges from both the designer's intent and the user's imagination. The designer controls the form. The designer and the user share control of the function.

The Invisible Parts of an Interface

When anyone imagines a screen, they picture content, functionality, layout, and design, the visible parts of an interface. However, they also make assumptions about who will use the screen, why, what happened previously, and what will happen next, the invisible parts of an interface. Even though you draft a wireframe of a screen, that wireframe catches a snapshot from an entire scene.

Every interface has four hidden parts (Figure 17-13):

- The user

- The task the user wants to complete

- The previous step

- The next step

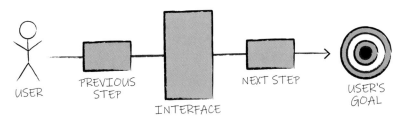

FIGURE 17-13
An interface has four invisible parts: the user, their goal, the previous step, and the next step.

THE USER

When you and your team talk about an interface, you imagine a user. Even if you haven't talked about the user, everyone imagines a user. You can't think about functionality unless you imagine someone who uses it. The affordances you build into an interface must be usable by the user.[3] Hands hold spoons. Fingers poke buttons.

THE USER'S GOAL

An interface assumes someone will use it to complete a goal. When you design an interface, you help the user reach that goal. You build the interface for a reason.

THE PREVIOUS STEP

For any interface, your user did something or looked at something *before* they saw your interface. When your team talks about a single screen, they make assumptions about what happened just before. Your team imagines an entire scene.

3 Hinton, Andrew. "Perception, Cognition, and Affordance." *Understanding Context Environment, Language, and Information Architecture.* Sebastopol: O'Reilly Media, 2014.

THE NEXT STEP

Just like you imagine the previous step when you think about an interface, you also imagine the next step. You imagine what happens *after* the user picks up the spoon or pokes the Search button.

Whenever you discuss an *actual* interface or a *model* of an interface, the interface's visible and invisible parts come into play. To design an interface, you design the visible and the invisible interface.

The Invisible Parts of the Interface Are Most Important

While teams focus on the visible parts of the interface, the most important parts are invisible. As you work on interfaces, you need a way to keep the invisible, visible, so your team makes the right decisions. In the next chapter, we'll look at a way to think about the visible and invisible parts of an interface.

Design Interfaces with 4-Corners

FOUR WEEKS INTO A website redesign, I ran a workshop that included both my team and the client. I asked each of the 15 participants to take two minutes and sketch a wireframe of the website's homepage. When the timer went off, we collected all 15 sketches and taped them to the conference room's beige walls.

Across the length of the conference room hung 15 different versions of the website's homepage. Common elements appeared in several sketches. Many included a large image at the top of the screen. For some, the large image was a carousel. Others featured lists of products or news items. Some featured prominent links that spoke directly to different types of users.

After four weeks, why would 15 people on the same project have so many different visions of the homepage?

When anyone thinks about a screen, in their head, they picture content, functionality, and a layout. And they make assumptions about who will use the screen, why, where they came from, and where they'll go next.

Even though wireframes seem like they are about screens, they really catch a snapshot from an entire scene. In my workshop, the participants sketched 15 different versions of the homepage because each participant imagined a different invisible interface.

Good interfaces need thinking. The 4-corners method helps you think with your team or clients, so you can make better interfaces. Your team will start building better screens, and you're going to help them.

How 4-Corners Works

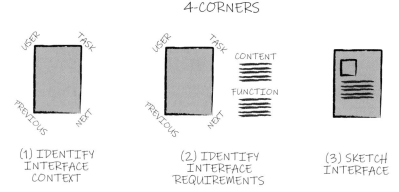

4-CORNERS

(1) IDENTIFY INTERFACE CONTEXT

(2) IDENTIFY INTERFACE REQUIREMENTS

(3) SKETCH INTERFACE

FIGURE 18-1

First, identify the invisible parts of the interface. Then, identify the required contents and functionality. Finally, sketch the interface.

4-corners helps teams think about the visible and invisible parts of an interface. 4-corners uses a canvas, so teams have a place to see the invisible parts of an interface before they work on the visible parts. 4-corners helps teams think about the design behind the design with six activities:

1. Identify the user

2. Identify tasks

3. Identify next and previous steps

4. Generate list of content

5. Generate list of functionality

6. Sketch the screen

4-corners creates a visual checklist teams use to think about the visible and invisible parts of an interface (Figure 18-1). When teams think about the user's journey, they design better interfaces that create more value for both end users and the organization.

At the end of this activity, the team will have created:

• One or more sketches of the interface

• A description of the interface's content and functionality

When you work through the 4-corners, the team agrees on the screen's most important user, goal, and the previous and next steps, the invisible parts of the interface. The team also aligns on what content and functionality should appear, the visible parts of the interface.

WHEN TO SKETCH INTERFACES WITH 4-CORNERS

Use 4-corners any time you need to sketch or review an interface. I've used 4-corners with designers, developers, and clients to design successful screens for business-to-business (B2B) and business-to-consumer (B2C) websites and applications on all kinds of platforms. It works anywhere, any time.

INPUTS AND QUICK STARTS

Before using 4-corners, the team should have a sense of the product's users as well as a vision about the product's end state. This shared vision about the users and the end state helps focus your 4-corners discussions. (Learn how to create a future state vision in Chapter 7. We cover system users in Part III.)

MATERIALS YOU'LL USE

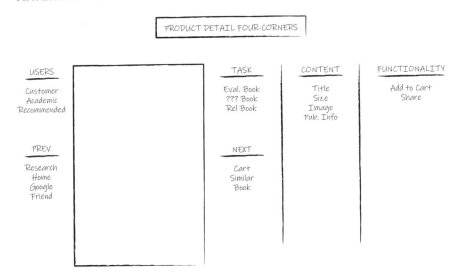

FIGURE 18-2

4-corners uses five lists to think about what to sketch.

4-corners canvas

To use 4-corners with your team, you need a way to visualize the 4-corners canvas (Figure 18-2). Use a pre-printed worksheet, or sketch the canvas on a whiteboard, flip chart, or piece of paper.

Users, Tasks, Previous/Next Steps, Content, and Functionality

These may be edited or moved during discussion. Use sticky notes or write and erase, as there aren't that many individual items.

Find templates, framing material, and remote resources on the website:

http://pxd.gd/interfaces/4-corners

Activity 1: Identify the Interface User

Every interface helps a user do something. Identifying that user leads to useful interfaces that create value for your organization and the end user. To think about the user, the team will:

- identify people they think will use the interface
- prioritize those users to identify the most important one

If there's only one user, or you already know the most important user, skip this and jump to the next activity to talk about the user's task.

THE FRAME

WHAT WILL YOU DO?	Identify primary users
WHAT'S THE OUTCOME?	The screen's most important user
WHY IS IT IMPORTANT?	Helps you optimize the screen for the most important user
HOW WILL YOU DO IT?	Work together to discuss the interface's different users

To frame discussion around users, say:

> "Let's identify the screen's most important user, so we make sure we optimize the screen the right way. First, let's list the possible users, and then choose the most important one."

FACILITATE DISCUSSION ABOUT POSSIBLE USERS

Talking about a screen's users is as easy as asking the team, "who will use this screen?" As the team talks, write possible users on the 4-corners canvas where everyone can see them (Figure 18-3).

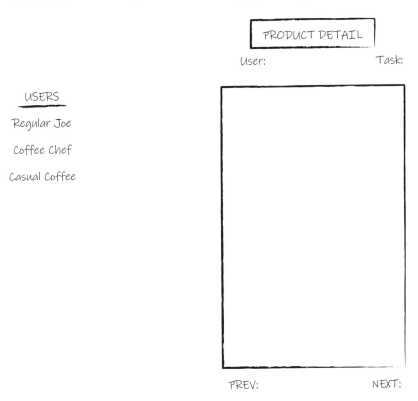

FIGURE 18-3
List users at the top left of the canvas

When you feel the team missed a few users, probe with questions or statements. Open-ended questions help the team expand their thinking. For example, you might ask, "Are there other users who might use this screen?" If you think the team overlooked a specific user, say something like, "Mobile workers might use this screen to pick a coffee shop."

Users who work together

It's also useful to think about how users work with others. We designed a Product Detail screen for a furniture site. Research indicated online shoppers made purchase decisions with their family. Discuss with the team whether users share information with other users.

When you don't know the user

If the team doesn't know possible users, you've skipped an important step. Pivot to discuss users (see Chapter 10).

Prioritize multiple users

The end goal is to identify the most important user for this screen. If the team identifies only one user, then you're done and can move on to the user's task.

More likely, the team needs to prioritize a list of several users, so they can identify the most important ones. Rank users from most to least important (Figure 18-4). If the team has trouble ranking, ask questions to help prioritize:

- If we could only design this screen for one person, who would it be?

- Who will use this screen most frequently?

- What user cannot afford to fail on this screen?

- What user creates the most value for the organization when they use this screen?

- What user needs this screen the most?

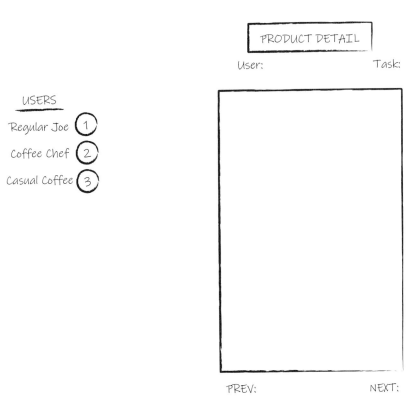

FIGURE 18-4
Rank the list of possible users

Once the team agrees on the most important user, note the user at the top left of the screen and tell the team you're ready to focus on what the user is trying to do.

But this screen is for all users!

It can be scary to choose one, most important user for a screen. Reassure clients and team members you won't disregard other possible users. Often, an interface will have two important users. As long as you capture and prioritize both users in the list, you can design the interface to support both of them.

During discussion, you captured all the possible users on the 4-corners canvas. This reassures everyone that you heard them. If the team can't rank users from most to least important, try other prioritization techniques. Knowing the most important user helps you decide what content and functionality to include and how to organize the layout.

FINISH AND SHIFT TO DISCUSS THE USER'S TASK

The team assumes the users will use the interface to complete one or more tasks. Once the team has identified and prioritized the interface's users, shift the discussion to clarify each user's task.

> "Based on the interface's primary users, let's identify the task they want to complete."

Activity 2: Identify the User's Task

When I ran that workshop where 15 participants sketched 15 different versions of the homepage, all 15 participants had slightly different ideas of what the homepage would help users do. Each design helped the user accomplish a slightly different set of tasks.

Every interface helps users do something. To think about the user's task, the team will identify the tasks the users complete in the interface and then prioritize those tasks to identify the most important one.

If there is only one task for this screen, or you already know the most important task, skip this and jump to the next part of the interface and talk about the user's next step.

THE FRAME

WHAT WILL YOU DO?	Identify prioritized list of tasks
WHAT'S THE OUTCOME?	The screen's primary task
WHY IS IT IMPORTANT?	Helps you optimize the interface for the right user and task
HOW WILL YOU DO IT?	Identify and prioritize the interface's tasks

To frame discussion around tasks, say:

> "Let's identify the screen's primary task, so we make sure we optimize the screen the right way. First, let's identify possible tasks, and then choose the most important one."

FACILITATE DISCUSSION ABOUT POSSIBLE TASKS

To generate a list of tasks, ask the team: "What tasks do users need to complete on this screen?" As the team lists tasks, write them on the canvas (Figure 18-5).

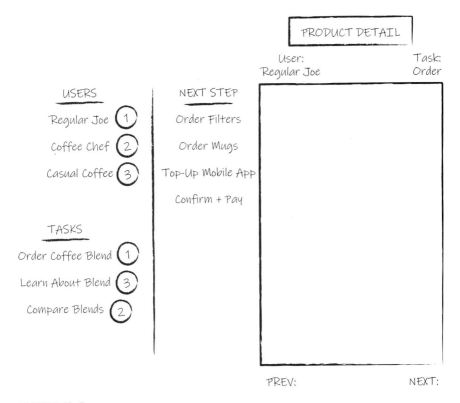

FIGURE 18-5
List tasks on the canvas

Even though the team will generate several tasks, probe the team to think of other possibilities. Just like with users, probe with questions or statements:

- A question: "What else might the user want to do on this screen?"
- A statement: "The shopper may want to share this coffee blend with a friend."

Tasks that are too broad

To make sure a task isn't too broad, ask: Will the user accomplish that task on this screen? Or will they complete the task across several screens?

On the Product Detail screen, you say the primary task is to buy the product, but the user can't buy the product on the detail screen. You *want* the user to buy the product, so how does the Product Detail screen help them buy? In this case, the Product Detail screen helps users *decide* to buy the product.

Tasks that are too narrow

Some tasks *support* the primary task. For the Product Detail screen, users may want to see the price or tasting notes or evaluate ratings and reviews. These tasks help the user complete the primary task, to decide to buy the coffee.

When you identify tasks that are too narrow, capture them under functionality to the right of the canvas. Talk about them more when you talk about functionality.

PRIORITIZE TASKS

There's a trick to interaction design. If you design an interface to support two tasks, neither task is as successful as if it was the only task you designed for. For every additional task you add to an interface, the overall effectiveness of the design for each task goes down. When the team identifies the most important task, you learn what task to prioritize in the final design.

Rank tasks from most to least important. Use questions like the ones you used to choose the most important user:

- What task will be completed most frequently on this screen?
- If we could only design this screen for one task, what would it be?
- What task can we not afford to mess up on this screen?
- What task creates the most value for users on this screen?
- What task creates the most value for the organization?

FINISH AND FOCUS ON WHERE THE INTERFACE LIVES IN THE USER'S JOURNEY

Note the primary task at the top right of the screen. With the primary users and tasks identified, the team knows why someone will use an interface. However, every interface leads to another, and you want to make sure the handoff is as smooth as possible.

> "Now that we know the user and task, we want to make sure the interface supports their journey. Let's look at where the user goes next."

Activity 3: Identify the Next Step

You talk about the user's next step, so you can design *this* interface to help the user get there. Reinforce how every interface leads to another, and your team will build better, more useful experiences that help users get where they want to go.

To think about the user's next step, the team will discuss and prioritize possible next steps and identify the most important one.

THE FRAME

WHAT WILL YOU DO?	Identify next steps
WHAT'S THE OUTCOME?	Identify the screen's primary, most important next step
WHY IS IT IMPORTANT?	Helps optimize the screen layout and design
HOW WILL YOU DO IT?	Identify and prioritize next steps and safety nets

To frame discussion around the next step, say:

> "Let's identify where the user will go next, so we make sure we optimize the screen the right way. First, let's identify possible next steps, and then we'll choose the most important one."

FACILITATE DISCUSSION ABOUT NEXT STEPS

As you discuss the user's next step, help your team explore all possible options. Ask your team: "What happens after the user completes their task on this screen? Where should the user go next?" Write next steps down on the canvas (Figure 18-6). Reassure everyone that you're listening and including their perspective.

The primary task should make the next step obvious. If our Product Detail screen helps the user decide to buy the product, and they click "Add to cart," what happens next? What do they see?

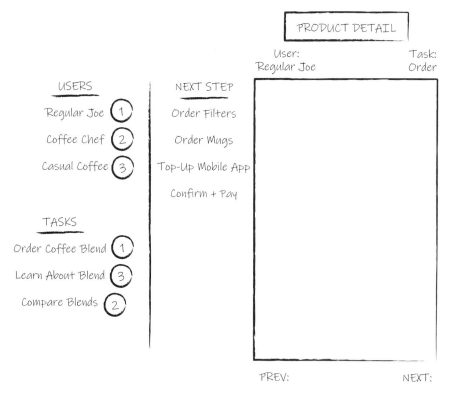

FIGURE 18-6
Every interface you design is just one step in the user's journey

Probe for conflicting next steps

Sometimes your organization's interest competes with the user's interest. Probe the team for conflicts between what *you* want the user to do and what the *user* wants to do:

- What does the user want to do?

- What does your organization want the user to do?

With the Product Detail screen, you may want the user to "Add to cart." Meanwhile, the user may want to Google the product and buy it from someone who sells it for less. If you're lucky, the organization and the user want the same next step. If not, capture these conflicting next steps on the canvas.

PRIORITIZE NEXT STEPS

Faced with more than one next step, work through the prioritization questions to rank next steps from most to least important (Figure 18-7):

- What next step will the user visit most frequently?

- If you can design this screen to drive users to only one next step, where would you send users?

- What next screen *must* users be able to get to?

- What next screen creates the most value for your users?

- What next screen creates the most value for your organization?

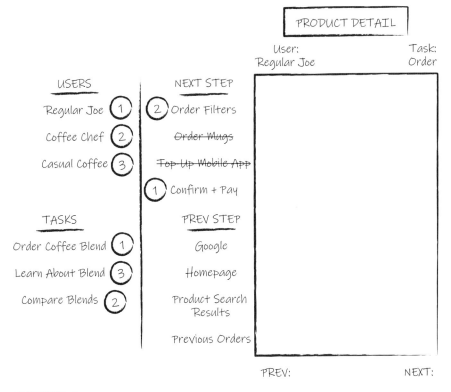

FIGURE 18-7

Rank next steps from most to least important

FINISH AND DISCUSS THE PREVIOUS STEP

Note the primary next step at the bottom right of the canvas and tell the team you're ready to focus on the user's previous step:

> "Let's talk about where the user came from."

Activity 4: Identify the Previous Step

You ask where the user came from, so that when they arrive on the screen, you make sure everything makes sense. You want to make sure the user doesn't get lost, they're appropriately welcomed, and they can get to the next step in their journey.

If users arrive at the Product Detail screen and don't see what they expect or what they're looking for, they'll hit the back button. To get the user to the next step, keep the user on this screen. To optimize this screen to maximize conversions, you need a strong link between where they came from and where they're going.

To think about the previous step, the team will discuss and prioritize possible previous steps and identify the most important ones.

THE FRAME

WHAT WILL YOU DO?	Discuss all the ways the user may arrive at this screen
WHAT'S THE OUTCOME?	The most important previous step
WHY IS IT IMPORTANT?	Helps optimize the screen layout and design
HOW WILL YOU DO IT?	List and prioritize all the ways a user can arrive at this screen.

To frame discussion around previous steps, say:

> "Let's figure out where users will come from, so we make sure the screen reflects what the users expect. Let's list the possible previous steps, and then choose the most important."

FACILITATE DISCUSSION ABOUT PREVIOUS STEPS

In the digital world, multiple paths bring your user to any given screen. For the Product Detail screen, the user might see the product featured on the homepage and click the link (Figure 18-8).

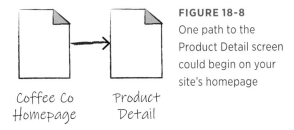

FIGURE 18-8
One path to the Product Detail screen could begin on your site's homepage

Coffee Co Homepage   Product Detail

Alternative paths also bring users to the Product Detail screen. Perhaps the user searches for the product by name in an external search engine like Google or Yandex or Baidu. They see the product in the search results and click the link to arrive at the Product Detail screen (Figure 18-9).

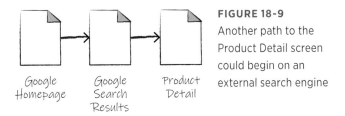

FIGURE 18-9
Another path to the Product Detail screen could begin on an external search engine

Google Homepage   Google Search Results   Product Detail

To generate a list of possible previous steps, ask the team: "Where did the user come from? What path did they take to arrive at this screen?" Since you almost always have multiple entry points for a given screen, the team will generate several options. Write the options down on the canvas (Figure 18-10).

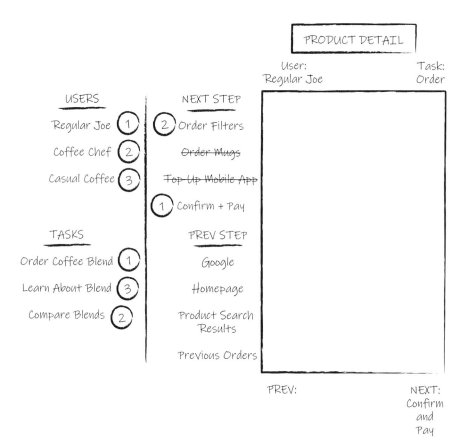

FIGURE 18-10
Capture previous steps on the canvas

Probe for paths from other sites and channels

Some teams are so focused on their product, they overlook external paths. Ask about paths from other channels. Did they see a URL on a billboard? Click a link in an email? Hear about your site from a friend?

Think about where the user is and how they get to the screen. If they're in a store, they're on a mobile phone. If they're talking to a salesperson, they're probably in an office on a desktop. Did they click a link? Scan a QR code? Type in a URL? How did they get to the screen you're designing?

For brick-and-mortar retailers, it's common for customers to search for information about a product they see in the store. If your organization's sales force drives most purchases, maybe your customer types a URL they see on a brochure.

PRIORITIZE THE PREVIOUS STEPS

How do you identify what path to prioritize? Four questions help identify the most important paths:

- What path occurs most frequently?
- If you design this screen to support users arriving on only one path, what would it be?
- What previous step can you support that will create the most value for your organization?
- What previous step can you support that will create the most value for your users?

Rank the previous steps from most to least important. Capture the most important previous step at the bottom left of the canvas.

FINISH AND SHIFT TO DISCUSS CONTENT

Now it's time to talk about the screen's content:

"Let's talk about what content should appear on the screen."

Activity 5: Identify Interface Content

Content is how you communicate with your users and help them reach their goal. Before you can design a screen, you need to know what content should appear.

At the end of this discussion, your team will have listed and prioritized content to include in the design. To help the team focus content on user needs, use the 4-corners to describe the user's story.

THE FRAME

WHAT WILL YOU DO?	Identify content the user needs to complete their task
WHAT'S THE OUTCOME?	A prioritized list of content
WHY IS IT IMPORTANT?	Identifies elements that need to be included in the screen design
HOW WILL YOU DO IT?	List and prioritize the different content elements

To frame the content discussion, say:

> "Now that we know what users are trying to do, let's identify the content, so we make sure the screen includes everything they need. Let's list the different types of content, and then prioritize the content to understand what's most important."

FACILITATE CONTENT DISCUSSION WITH THE USER'S STORY

4-corners helps teams think about the invisible parts of an interface: the user, their task, and the previous and next steps. Without the 4-corners, you design screens by asking: what content do we need? By working the corners, the team frames the design as a *story*. The interface shifts from a single *screen* into a *scene* in the user's journey.

For the Product Detail screen, the story might be: The user sees the product listed in Google, clicks the link to see the Product Detail screen where they decide to buy, and clicks "Add to cart."

When you focus on the user's story, you transform the team's thinking. Instead of designing a Product Detail screen, the team designs a screen that helps users decide. The user's story reflects the team's shared vision of how the interface can be useful and successful.

Stories make vision easier to share

Stories knit together complex details into a self-contained, easy-to-understand package. It's difficult to keep a list of requirements in your head and remember what requirements are important. Stories explain what details are most important and why.

When you communicate with stories instead of requirements, it's easier for your team to share the same vision. The story makes it easy to internalize and remember the user's journey. This also makes stories easier to share with clients and other audiences.

Working with stories changes how the team thinks and talks about the interface. Instead of designing a Product Detail screen with a list of features, the team adopts a user-centered approach they'll begin to use on every interface they produce.

Stories counteract design paralysis

Good collaboration includes everyone, generates more ideas, and provides more perspective for evaluating those ideas. These broad perspectives include a wide range of reasons for why one idea is better or worse than another. In the book *Switch*, Dan and Chip Heath note our analytical selves love to poke holes and debate ideas. The "'analyzing' phase is often more satisfying than the 'doing' phase, and that's dangerous..."[1]

When you focus on the story, the team directs their energy to help the user complete the task. The story identifies an end goal, a destination. For our Product Detail screen, the destination is no longer product information. Now the destination is a decision. In the Heaths' words, when you focus on the user's story, the team can sidestep analysis paralysis and navigate toward the destination.

With the user's story in mind, the team has a frame for thinking about the visible interface, the content and functionality. To open the discussion, use the 4-corners to generate the user's story:

> When [the user] arrives from [previous step], what content do they need to [task], so they can move on to the [next step]?

For the Product Detail screen, your story would sound like this:

> When [the customer] arrives from [Google search results], what content do they need to [decide to buy], so they can move on to the [shopping cart]?

As the team lists content, write it down to the right of the 4-corners canvas (Figure 18-11).

---

1   Heath, Chip, and Dan Heath. *Switch: How to Change Things When Change Is Hard.* New York: Broadway, 2010.

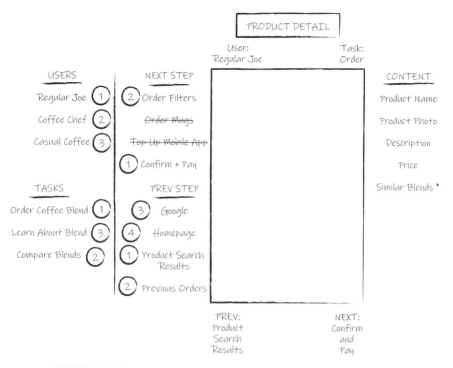

FIGURE 18-11

List content the user needs to the right of the canvas

For our Product Detail screen, the customer needs four pieces of information to decide to buy this coffee:

- The coffee blend's name
- A picture of the coffee package
- A description of the coffee
- The coffee's price

Because you've chosen the most important user and task and identified previous and next steps, the team can easily generate necessary and appropriate content.

The difference between content and functionality

When you generate content, you want to know about text, images, and multimedia (like audio, video, and animation). Content's different from functionality. Content is consumed. Functionality lets users to do something. During content generation, people will also call out functionality.

Content and functionality intertwine. For example, for the Product Detail screen, someone might suggest the user can download a tasting guide. The tasting guide is content. Downloading the tasting guide is functionality.

Try to separate content from functionality. Of course, to reinforce that you're listening, capture both content and functionality on the canvas. If someone suggests downloading a tasting guide, capture "tasting guide" under content and "download tasting guide" in the functionality column (Figure 18-12).

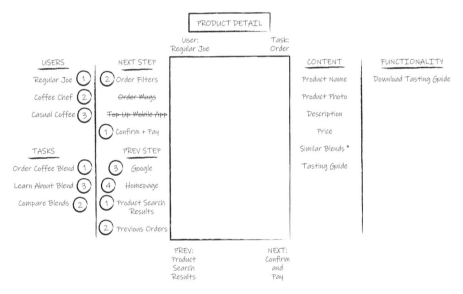

FIGURE 18-12

When your team combines content and functionality, write both ideas on the 4-corners canvas

Probe for additional content

When 4-corners focuses on a single user and task, it helps the team create an interface targeted toward a single scenario. This advantage is also a disadvantage. Most screens support multiple users and scenarios.

Five questions help probe for additional content:

- What other content would be useful?
- What content will other users need?
- How else could this screen be used?
- What kinds of content do competitors offer?
- What kinds of content appear in similar types of screens?

Refer to the user's story: what other content will help the user complete their task? For our Product Detail screen, you would ask: "What other content will help our customer decide to buy this product?"

For the Product Detail screen, what other content helps the customer decide to buy this coffee? All kinds of things come to mind:

- The region
- The blend
- Available formats like ground, unground, or K-cups

Ask about other ways the screen may be used. For example, will your customer refer to the Product Detail screen *after* they've purchased the coffee? Will other users use the screen to support other tasks?

For example, on many B2B sites, customers reference product information to locate product specs.

Steal from the best

Ask about content competitors use or content that appears in similar interfaces. What should you copy from your competitors? Buying a car is nothing like buying coffee, but maybe there's something interesting about the content car dealers surface that makes your Product Detail screen more useful.

PROBE FOR CONTENT THAT'S OUT OF SCOPE

A project's scope of work (SOW) refers to assumptions and agreements the team makes about what will and won't work within the timeline and budget. The scope creates a shared vision for what the project will and won't be. Even on projects with no specific scope, like an agile team, the team has an unspoken assumption about the project's scope.

Although you can't and won't build everything, probe past assumptions about scope. You'll help the team identify content they think is out of scope but really isn't.

It's possible the team's assumption is wrong. When I collaborate with teams, it's not uncommon for a developer to know of additional, useful content hidden in an API or database somewhere. You never uncover these possibilities unless you probe beyond what the team *assumes* is in scope.

Focus on ideation, instead of scope

To probe beyond scope, focus the discussion on *ideation*. The question isn't "what content *that's in scope* would help the user with their task?" The question is "what content will help the user complete their task?" At this stage, you want to generate ideas.

Product owners, developers, and project managers get twitchy when you talk about anything that's out of scope. "Out of scope" means missed deadlines, budget creep, and lots of late nights. Reassure the team you're looking for ideas and no one's committed to delivering anything.

Out of scope identifies a roadmap

At worst, out-of-scope content can be added in later phases. Understanding what you may build later helps the team architect the product to accommodate future builds. It ensures you don't build yourself into a corner that requires future rework.

Scope may need to change

Probing helps teams check assumptions around scope. For a Product Detail screen, you may have agreed that ratings and reviews were out of scope. When you probe beyond scope, you open the conversation to revisit some of these early assumptions.

Scope is like any rule. Rules are less about what to do and more about the consequences when they're broken. Project scope is less a guideline for what to build and more about what needs to happen when you cross the line.

Perhaps for the Product Detail screen, the team decides rating and reviews are critical for the project's success. With that realization, the team learns it should renegotiate the scope to include ratings and reviews.

You may need to reassess what's in scope. Maybe something gets bumped, so you can include ratings and reviews. Maybe the timeline gets extended, more team members added, more money added to the budget. For now, ideating content that helps users doesn't require difficult conversations about timeline, budget, and features. However, ideation can surface difficult conversations the team should have.

Reassure team members that you haven't committed to anything. Mark out-of-scope items when they're captured. This can be as simple as an asterisk next to out-of-scope ideas (Figure 18-13).

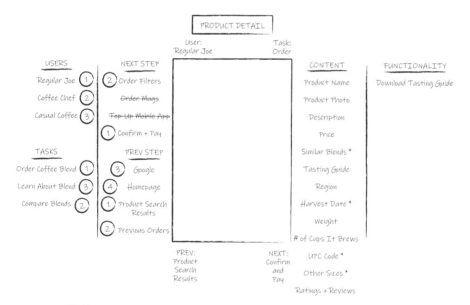

FIGURE 18-13

Mark out-of-scope items to reassure the team that you heard their concern and aren't trying to add scope to the project.

PRIORITIZE THE CONTENT

Once you've explored possible content, prioritize what's most important. Identify what content is more and less important and write a number next to each content item (Figure 18-14).

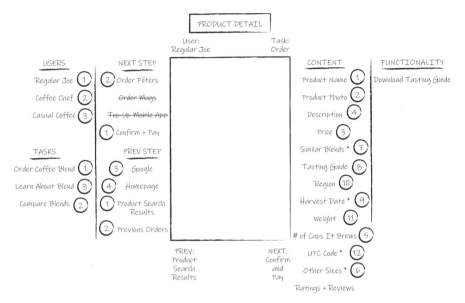

FIGURE 18-14

Number content items to record priorities.

Begin with the first prioritization question:

- If we could deliver only one piece of content on this screen, what would it be?

Refer to the user's story to help the team prioritize. If you have an idea for how content should be prioritized, number several of the most important content items. This offers the team something to react and respond to.

Use the other standard prioritization questions to help the team rank each content item:

- What content will be used most frequently on this screen?

- What content provides the most value for users on this screen?

In the age of responsive design, you can use the mobile screen to help prioritize:

- In what order should content appear when viewed on a mobile phone?

The prioritized content list becomes a checklist for what to include when you design the screen. The priority reveals the content's layout.

FINISH AND SHIFT TO FUNCTIONALITY

After the team prioritizes the content, move on to talk about functionality:

> "Now that we've nailed down the content, let's talk about what functionality we should include on the screen."

Activity 6: Identify Functionality

Content gives users information they need to complete their task. It's possible the user's next step will be outside of your control. A user may use the Product Detail screen to decide to buy a book, and buy the book somewhere else. Functionality helps the user to complete their task within your experience.

In this last conversation, the team will generate and prioritize functionality. Focus the team on the user's story and capture a prioritized list of functionality.

THE FRAME

WHAT WILL YOU DO?	Discuss the functionality that the user needs to complete their task
WHAT'S THE OUTCOME?	A prioritized list of functionality
WHY IS IT IMPORTANT?	Identifies elements that need to be included
HOW WILL YOU DO IT?	List and prioritize the different functionality elements

To frame discussion around functionality, say:

> "Now that we know what users are trying to do and what content they have, let's identify the functionality, so we make sure the screen includes everything they need. Let's list the different types of functionality, and then prioritize them to understand what is most important."

FACILITATE THE FUNCTIONALITY DISCUSSION

To open the conversation and generate functionality, include the user's story in your question like you did for the content discussion:

> When [the customer] arrives from [Google search results], what functionality do they need to [decide to buy], so they can move on to the [shopping cart]?

For the Product Detail screen, your story would sound like this:

> When [the customer] arrives from [Google search results], what functionality do they need to [decide to buy], so they can move on to the [shopping cart]?

List any functionality the team generates to the right of the screen on the 4-corners canvas (Figure 18-15).

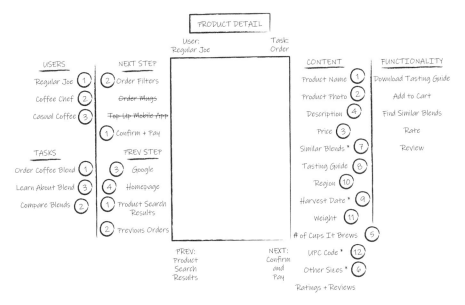

FIGURE 18-15

List functionality the user needs to the right of the canvas

Focus on the primary next step

Help the team focus on the singular most important piece of functionality. One piece of functionality will relate to the user's most important task. For the Product Detail screen, if the user decides to buy the book, then they need an "Add to cart" button.

This principle is at work in applications and websites you use every day. There's usually one piece of functionality that is more prominent than all the others. Sometimes the most important piece of functionality is called the *primary call to action*.

If the team is unsure of where to start, refer back to any flows or journeys they've completed.

Probe for functionality related to each user task

Although you identified the user's most important task, you also identified additional tasks. Use the prioritized list of user tasks to probe for additional functionality. If the user wants to recommend a coffee, should the Product Detail screen include tools to share the coffee with other people?

Probe for functionality related to content

Each piece of content offers opportunities for additional functionality.

First, although the user may need to *access* each piece of content, that doesn't mean they need to *consume* the content on this screen. The user may want to see a tasting guide. That doesn't mean you display the tasting guide on the Product Detail screen. (But what if you did?) You can provide functionality that allows users to access content.

Second, functionality may enhance content. For example, perhaps the user would like to see a larger map of the growing region. You could offer functionality that allows the user to zoom in on a map or to view a larger version of the map.

If you offer product reviews, you may offer ways to filter what reviews appear. Users could look at only the good reviews or view only one-star reviews.

Probe for out-of-scope functionality

Like with content, don't limit discussion to what everyone assumes is in scope. Although you can't and won't build everything, probe past assumptions about scope to help the team identify functionality they *think* is out of scope but really isn't. While you may end up with functionality that is out of scope, you'll likely discover useful functionality you can implement that isn't.

Probe for safety nets

There is no perfect design. Sometimes we fail our users. If a user comes to this screen and it's not what they were expecting or doesn't give them the content or functionality they need, how can you help them? How can you provide a safety net that catches these users and helps them on their way?

For the Product Detail screen, maybe they're looking for a different version. Can you provide a link to whole bean or K-cups? Maybe this isn't the coffee they want. Can you provide links to similar blends?

PRIORITIZE THE FUNCTIONALITY

After generating functionality, write a number next to each piece of functionality to represent what's most and least important (Figure 18-16). The most important functionality is the primary call to action.

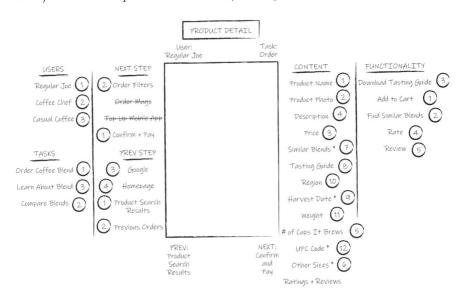

FIGURE 18-16

Rank each piece of functionality from most to least important

To kickstart prioritization, ask:

- If we could deliver only one piece of functionality on this screen, what would it be?

Refer to the user's story to help the team prioritize. Use the standard prioritization questions to help prioritize functionality:

- What functionality will be used most frequently on this screen?
- What functionality provides the most value for users on this screen?
- What functionality provides the most value for the organization?

With prioritization complete, you know what functionality needs to appear on the screen and what should be most prominent.

FINISH AND MOVE TO SKETCH THE INTERFACE

Now that the team has explored the invisible and visible parts of the interface, it's time to start sketching.

4-Corners for Wireframes, Mockups, and Prototypes

Before you sit down to create wireframes, mockups, or prototypes, use 4-corners to think about the primary user and context and to prioritize content and functionality.

You can also use 4-corners to annotate wireframes, mockups, and prototypes with the story behind the interface (Figure 18-17). Stitch the 4-corners information together to describe the scenario you used to create the screen. For the Product Detail screen, you might note:

> "The customer wants to decide whether to buy this coffee. They see the coffee listed on the Product Search results and click the link to come to the Product Detail screen. If they decide to buy the coffee, the customer clicks the 'Add to cart' button."

Product Detail Screen

User:
Regular Joe

Others:
Coffee Chef
Casual Coffee

[Product Name]

[Product Price] ($x/ounce)

Add to cart

Excepteur sint occaecat cupidatat non proident, sunt in culpa qui officia deserunt mollit anim id est eopksio laborum. Sed ut perspiciatis unde omnis istpoe natus error sit voluptatem accusantium doloremque eopsloi laudantium, totam rem aperiam, eaque ipsa quae ab illo inventore veritatis et quasi architecto beatae vitae dicta sunot explicabo.

Other blends you may like

18 ounces brews ~64 cups of fresh, delicious coffee.
Recommended if you drink more than 2-cups of coffee per day.

Also available in these sizes:

[Product Size]	[Product Size]	[Product Size] for the office
~y cups	~y cups	~y cups
~1 cup per day	~few cups on	~400 cups

Task:
Select and Order Coffee

Others:
Compare blends
Learn about this blend

Previous step:
Organic search

Next step:
Confirm and pay

FIGURE 18-17
You can annotate wireframes, mockups, and prototypes with the 4-corners story to describe the why behind the interface

Documenting a screen's 4-corners helps the team remember the decisions they made when they created the screen.

4-Corners for More Than Just Screens

4-corners is a method for thinking and making any kind of interface. While I've used screens as examples so far, that doesn't mean you shouldn't use the 4-corners approach to think about the visible and invisible parts of an interface in other contexts.

4-CORNERS FOR AGILE USER STORIES

When you're working on agile development teams with user stories, the 4-corners checklist helps the team think through how to implement a user story. Like with wireframes, mockups, and prototypes, documenting the 4-corners along with the user story helps the team remember key decisions and context around how to implement the user story.

4-CORNERS FOR CROSS-CHANNEL DESIGN

Although the examples use screen-based interfaces, the 4-corners method works for any kind of interface and any kind of touchpoint. Use 4-corners when designing emails, hardware, augmented reality, and voice systems. The 4-corners provide a checklist for thinking about any kind of interface, not just screens.

Similarly, the previous and next step in your 4-corners don't need to be in the same channel. The previous step could be an email, and the next step could be a physical store. 4-corners helps you think about an interaction's context regardless of the user's current, previous, or next channel.

4-CORNERS FOR SERVICE DESIGN

The flexibility of 4-corners extends to service design as well. The primary user becomes the actor and can apply to any front- or back-stage actor when designing a service. When mapping services, annotate each touchpoint with its 4-corners story to record the context around the service interaction.

4-Corners Creates a Shared, Holistic Vision of the Interface

We won't cover how to sketch an interface here. How you sketch an interface varies based on the type of interface you want to sketch, styles and trends at the time, and the type of interactions you want to support. You know how to sketch. After working through the 4-corners, you've created a shared vision about what and why, and have improved the odds that the product will really do what you need it to do.

In the next chapter, we'll look at a few ways you can apply 4-corners and sketching to bring teams together and generate lots of ideas.

[19]

Strategies for Sketching Interfaces

BEFORE YOU START TO Make an interface, a ton of thinking goes on. The 4-corners canvas provides a way for you to think with your team *before* you make the interface. 4-corners embeds user-centered thinking into the design process. With the thinking done, you can move on to making the interface.

Different sketching activities offer teams unique advantages. We'll look at three specific activities:

- Group sketching to create a single, shared vision

- Individual sketching to reveal multiple perspectives within a group

- 6-8-5 sketching to generate multiple variations for individual screens

Each of these activities helps your team or clients sketch a model of an interface. When you use 4-corners and collaborate on a sketch, your team learns how to make better interfaces. If this sketching continues your thinking with the 4-corners (from the previous chapter), refer to the topics you and the team just discussed.

Activity: Group Sketching to Create a Single, Shared Vision

When you sketch with a group, the team collaborates to draft a single version of a screen. This is useful when you believe the primary problem is not what the interface should look like, but getting everyone to agree. Group sketching creates a shared vision of what the interface should look like. Use the collaboration roadmap to keep the team focused. Start with the frame, facilitate sketching, and finish with a final version of the sketch.

THE FRAME

WHAT WILL YOU DO?	Sketch an interface
WHAT'S THE OUTCOME?	A single sketch of the interface
WHY IS IT IMPORTANT?	Provides a sketch we can check with other stakeholders and build off of
HOW WILL YOU DO IT?	Sketch the interface's layout, including content and functionality

To frame group sketching, say:

> "Let's sketch the interface together, so we have a first draft of what we want to build. Keeping our 4-corners in mind, let's take our prioritized lists of content and functionality and lay out the screen."

FACILITATE GROUP SKETCHING

Blank canvases daunt timid teams. Seed participation by adding the first piece. Sketch the most prominent piece of content or functionality to get collaboration rolling. Adding the first piece shows the team what to do, demonstrates how easy it is, and provides a straw man your team can react to.

For our Product Detail screen, you might draw the product image at the top left of the screen (Figure 19-1). Narrate what you are doing. Ask the team:

> "What if we put the product image at the top left?"

When you describe where you put the image as a question instead of as statement, you signal to the team that the idea is open for discussion.

Avoid closing down options

In *Fast Company*, Leigh Thompson, a management professor at the Kellogg School, warns how the first idea risks closing off alternatives.[1] As a facilitator, don't force your ideas on the group. Successful collaboration reveals consensus around the group's idea, not your idea.

---

1 Greenfield, Rebecca. "Brainstorming Doesn't Work; Try This Technique Instead." *Fast Company*, 20 Jan. 2017. Web. 01 Mar. 2017.

Narrating with questions keeps discussion open, but it's not enough. People, eager to please, will agree with your reasonable suggestion rather than suggest a conflicting idea. Generate alternative, conflicting ideas with direct questions. For the product image, you could ask probing questions, like:

- Where else could we put the image?

- Where do our competitors place the product image? Should we do the same or choose to be different?

- What problems does the product image cause if it's at the top left?

- What if we don't have a product image?

- Will different products have different size images? What if there's a video? Will we ever want to display a product a different way?

Probing questions will be different for every screen. Each interface solves a different user problem with different sets of content and functionality. Push the team to think of other options.

A room full of quiet participants is like an empty canvas. People hesitate to talk first. Successful collaboration requires that you include everyone. If the room is too quiet, direct questions to specific team members. When questioned directly, the team member should respond. This changes the activity from you leading to two people talking.

If the first participant agrees too quickly, direct the same question to another participant. However, if everyone is well-aligned, it's possible there's no useful discussion to be had. Continue to sketch the rest of the interface.

Encourage participation by being wrong

A coworker likes to hide a bad idea in a list of good ideas. The bad idea provides something that's easy and safe for participants to react to and disagree with.

For the Product Detail screen, place things where they typically wouldn't go or suggest that something like a button should be in an uncommon place. You could sketch the "Add to cart" button at the very bottom of a very long screen and hope someone pushes to display the button higher on the screen. You can also place a secondary or tertiary call to action more prominently than the primary call to action. This will trigger team members to speak up.

Hand sketching duties to active participants

When discussion goes well, the ideas, comments, and feedback flow fast and furious. When a participant offers a more involved idea or comment, hand them the marker so they can sketch. You can say:

"I'm not sure what that looks like. Can you draw it for me?"

In teams where everyone feels included and trusted, team members will jump up to sketch. Encourage others to sketch as often as possible. If teammates decline to take the marker, ask them again more forcefully. Say:

"Here. Draw what you're talking about."

Get help sketching because you're busy

If you still can't get participants to contribute to the sketch, have them take over by necessity. In a sketching exercise, someone has to sketch. If you're at the board with the marker, then your team has no obligation to sketch anything. Make yourself unable to sketch to place the obligation on them.

To hand off sketching duties, invent a reason to get away from the board. Decide to look up something that's relevant to the current discussion. Find the person closest to the board and ask them to cover for you while you're busy. You can say:

"Can you take the marker for a second? I need to look something up."

Hand them the marker. Socially, it's difficult not to accept something that's handed to you. Your team member will take the marker, and you can move to the back of the room. Continue to facilitate the discussion, so the marker holder only needs to sketch.

Iterate frequently

Some people have no problem tossing their first draft and starting again. Others cling to that first, precious idea. Encourage the team to iterate by starting over again and again.

When you iterate, draw an "x" over the first sketch and start another next to it. Sketching's speed means you can start and finish a new sketch in a matter of seconds. Model frequent iteration, so your team learns how fast and easy it is.

If someone else is sketching, encourage them to sketch alternate versions and iterate.

THE FINISH

After you have sketched, discussed, and iterated on the interface layout, and the team has reached a consensus, close the conversation around the final sketch.

If necessary, create a neat, clean version of the sketch, so the content, functionality, and layout are clear. Name or describe critical boxes or squiggles, so the team doesn't forget. If you're using the 4-corners canvas, make sure the user, task, and other information are clear, and double-check that the sketch has a clear title. Take a photo or save the document, and share the sketch with everyone as soon as possible.

Remind the team you will share the sketch, so they know what to expect:

> "I'll save this and share the sketch with everyone as soon as we're done here."

If you're sketching several screens in one session, move on to frame the next screen. You can sketch, discuss, and iterate a screen in as little as 10 minutes. More complex screens may take as long as 30 minutes. Most teams can sketch several screens in a user's journey in as little as 30 minutes.

Group sketching aligns the team around a single, shared vision of the interface. Shared vision allows the team to work together and apart and creates a shared language and understanding for how the team talks about and works through the experience, from concept all the way through launch. The shared vision helps your team build better experiences, and you help them learn how when you facilitate group sketching activities.

Sometimes, the team's not ready to create a shared vision. The team may have several disparate, competing visions floating around in their heads, or may have chosen a direction without evaluating all the options. This is what happened in my workshop where participants sketched 15 different versions of the homepage.

Activity: Individual Sketching to Reveal Competing Perspectives

Although a single direction for your interface will align the team, you might not be ready for a single vision. Team members may have competing ideas that need to be discussed before you align on a single direction. Individual sketching helps teams reveal and discuss *competing* visions. If you believe the team has prematurely decided on a direction, individual sketching helps teams generate multiple options. Individual sketching is especially useful on contentious screens like homepages and landing screens where competing groups have different priorities.

To generate multiple, competing versions, everyone will sketch the screen on their own before sharing with the group.

THE FRAME

WHAT WILL YOU DO?	Identify multiple alternatives for an interface
WHAT'S THE OUTCOME?	An individual sketch from each participant
WHY IS IT IMPORTANT?	Helps identify competing ideas to make the interface better
HOW WILL YOU DO IT?	Each participant will sketch a version of the screen

With individual sketching, you want to generate many different options. In keeping with this goal, frame the activity with as little direction as possible. Don't close down options by directing participants toward a specific solution.

To encourage options from each team member's perspective, frame individual sketching around their individual perspective. For the Product Detail screen, you might say:

> "Let's sketch the Product Detail screen. Everyone grab a piece of paper and a pen and sketch what *you* think the Product Detail screen should look like."

When you focus on individual perspectives, you encourage diverse groups of stakeholders to focus on their unique perspective.

If you want to generate multiple options and your team has similar perspectives, frame the activity to focus on generating alternate versions. For the Product Detail screen, you could say:

> "Let's sketch as many *different* variations of a Product Detail screen as we can. This will help us think of different ways to improve the interface. Everyone take 3 minutes to sketch a different way we could build the Product Detail screen."

FACILITATE INDIVIDUAL SKETCHING

Regardless of how you frame individual sketching, run the exercise the same way.

Pass out materials and start sketching

Pass out 1 or 2 blank sheets of paper and a pen or marker to each participant. Make sure everyone has the supplies they need to participate. Say:

> "Does everyone have some paper and something to write with?"

Once everyone is ready, repeat the instructions from the frame, tell the team how much time they have, and start the timer. For the Product Detail screen, you could say:

> "We will take 3 minutes, so everyone can sketch the Product Detail screen. I will start the timer now."

Keep participants on track

As everyone starts to sketch, move around and check on each participant. Look at each person's sketch. Some people start right away. Others sit and think before they start. Some team members will need clarification. Check on everyone so unsure participants have the chance to ask a question in private. If you find someone who looks perplexed, ask if they have a question and help get them started.

Some participants will be unsure about what's allowed. They're afraid of the blank canvas or sketching the wrong thing. Reassure them that they can sketch anything as long as it's a Product Detail screen.

Some participants will want to clarify things like whether they should sketch for mobile or desktop. Again, anything goes. Reassure them that they can sketch anything. Help them make a choice by asking: "What do you want to sketch? The mobile version or the desktop version?"

Count down the time

An impending deadline gives the team the push they need to get started. Announce each minute as it passes. Tell the room when there are 2 minutes left, 1 minute, 30 seconds, and 10 seconds.

The countdown also helps participants bring their individual sketches to a point of completion, so the activity ends with a sketch from everyone. When everyone contributes a sketch, you include everyone and build trust that supports later collaboration.

Collect and share individual sketches

When time has ended, announce that time is up and collect everyone's sketches. Say:

> "Time's up. Finish what you're working on and let's share what we did."

Ideally, tape each sketch on a wall or place them on a table where everyone can see the different versions side-by-side. Have each participant tape their sketch on the wall to get everyone out of their seats and moving around to help fight the collaboration doldrums.

Highlight and discuss the range of variations

Although several sketches will look similar, rarely will two look the same. Individual sketching generates alternative ideas for the screen and reinforces the idea that everyone on the team has a unique perspective and picture in their head. Learning that everyone has a different idea in their head illustrates the value of collaboration and a shared vision.

Ask team members to present their sketch to the group. Identify common features. Highlight differences. Usually a few sketches are totally unlike the others. Ask sketch owners why they sketched the screen the way they did. Make sure to timebox each presentation to two or three minutes.

THE FINISH

The ultimate goal is a single sketch of the screen that everyone agrees on. After you discuss the different versions, lead a group sketching exercise (from earlier in this chapter) to create a single, shared vision.

Activity: 6-8-5 Sketching to Generate Multiple Directions

Individual sketching explores a wide range of options. This helps teams avoid choosing a direction before they've considered alternatives. However, each participant may have individually settled on a direction before thinking about possible variations.

To help individual participants expand their thinking, each participant sketches multiple versions. Adaptive Path, Todd Warfel, and Russ Unger each popularized this method, sometimes called 6-8-5 sketching. In 6-8-5 sketching, each participant creates 6–8 variations of a screen in 5 minutes. Focus less on the 5-minute time limit and more on each participant sketching multiple variations.

While individual sketching works great with diverse groups of stakeholders, 6-8-5 sketching offers the opportunity to explore a wide range of variations even in homogenous groups.

You can use 6-8-5 sketching in lots of situations because it only needs two things:

- Some paper
- Something to write with

PREPARE THE MATERIALS

In addition to something to write with, there's a bit of preparation involved. Either use a sketching worksheet with 6–8 areas for users to sketch in, or have participants fold a blank piece of paper to create 8 subdivided sections where they can sketch:

1. Fold the paper in half. This divides the paper into two parts.

2. Fold the paper in half again to divide it into four sections.

3. Fold the paper in half one more time to divide it into eight sections.

When participants have a worksheet or have folded their paper to create the sections, you can facilitate the 6-8-5 exercise:

1. At the top left of the page, write the name of the screen you will sketch.

2. Start the timer and give everyone 5 minutes to sketch 6–8 versions of the screen.

3. Participants sketch a version of the screen in each section of the paper.

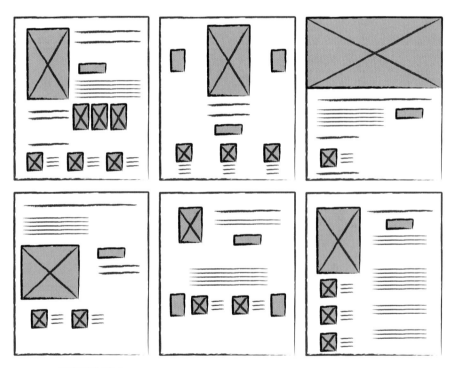

FIGURE 19-1
You can facilitate 6-8-5 sketching with pre-prepared worksheets or fold any blank sheet of paper to create your own sketching worksheet

THE FRAME

Like with other sketching exercises, the team should already have a sense of the product's users as well as a vision about the product's end state. The shared vision constrains the sketches. Set a frame similar to when the team does individual sketching.

WHAT WILL YOU DO?	Identify multiple alternatives for an interface
WHAT'S THE OUTCOME?	6–8 sketches from each participant
WHY IS IT IMPORTANT?	Helps identify multiple ideas to make the interface better
HOW WILL YOU DO IT?	Each participant will sketch 6–8 versions of the screen

To encourage each team member to provide their viewpoint, frame 6-8-5 sketching around their perspective. For the Product Detail screen, you might say:

> "Let's sketch the Product Detail screen. Everyone should grab a piece of paper and a pen, so you can each sketch six different versions of what you think the Product Detail screen should look like. When I start the timer, sketch at least six versions of the Product Detail screen on your page. Try and sketch as many different versions as possible."

If someone asks what you mean by different versions, explain that a different version can have different content, layout, organization, strategy, or approach.

FACILITATE 6-8-5 SKETCHING

Count down time, share, and discuss

Like with individual sketching, count down the time to keep everyone on track, then have everyone share and discuss their sketches.

To share and discuss, have each participant present their 6–8 variations to the rest of the group. Highlight similarities and differences. Help the group find unique ideas that offer content or functionality the user would find especially useful.

Use groups to limit share time

Because each participant should share, 6-8-5 sketching works best with 5–7 participants. If there are more participants than that, sharing may take so long that some participants will lose interest. If you have 8 or more participants, break the room into groups of 4–5 people. Participants can share and discuss their sketches with their group.

After everyone has shared their 6–8 variations with their group, have the group sketch the screen together, so the group finishes with one screen that combines the group's best thinking. When each group is down to a single screen, you can have each group share their screen with the broader group. Highlight and discuss the range of variations just as you would with individual sketching.

THE FINISH

Like individual sketching, follow 6-8-5 sketching with group sketching to create a single, shared vision of the screen.

Additional Things to Think About When Sketching

UNFRAMED SKETCHING

Both individual sketching and 6-8-5 sketching reveal alternative approaches to an interface. To encourage as much diversity as possible, frame the screen as generally as possible. For example, you would ask everyone to sketch a Product Detail screen without describing the content or functionality that should appear on the screen.

Without explicit framing, it's easier for team members to rely on their preconceived notions about what content and functionality should appear, how the screen should be laid out, and how users will interact with the functionality. Give the team wide latitude to envision how the interface will function to allow a broader set of variations to emerge.

Without explicit framing, individual and 6-8-5 sketching identify a wide range of possible content, functionality, layouts, and interaction models. A lack of explicit framing provides an alternative method for generating lists of content and functionality that's different from the generation you do as a group with the 4-corners model.

FRAMED SKETCHING

Individual generation answers the question: what should the interface include? However, if you have already aligned on what the interface should include, you may only want to answer the question: how should the interface appear?

If you only want to generate variations in how the interface appears and not what it should include, then frame sketching activities using the 4-corners. Aligned on content and functionality, your team will focus on generating variations in the layout and how users interact with the content and functionality.

Before sketching, ask yourself if the team needs to align on layout and interaction, or if they also need to align on content and functionality.

SYNTHESIZE MULTIPLE VARIATIONS

At the end of the day, the team will only build one version of the Product Detail screen, so they need to synthesize several variations into one model of the interface. Both individual and 6-8-5 sketching create several variations for an individual interface. Group sketching aligns the team on a single sketch for the interface.

WHAT IF THE GROUP CAN'T DECIDE ON A SINGLE VARIATION?

Sometimes, the group is ready to align on a single version of the interface. Sometimes, team members disagree on how the interface should function. Knowing you don't agree is just as valuable as knowing you do. When teams can't decide to proceed with a single version, sketch competing versions you can check and test. Competing variations will differ in either layout, interaction, or both.

When a team can't choose a single approach, that means they lack a shared understanding of an underlying assumption. When you create competing variations to Check, the team can evaluate competing assumptions and align on a specific direction.

Layout variations

With layout variations, the team can't decide where content and functionality should appear. With a Product Detail screen, the team might split on whether the product image appears at the top right or the top left of the screen. Or maybe they disagree on whether the "Add to cart" button appears closer to the top or the bottom of the screen.

In both cases, the team wants to understand what layout best helps users achieve their task and move to the next step. What layout best helps the user to decide to buy the product? What layout best helps the user add the product to their cart? What layout is most useful to the user?

When you create alternative layouts, you can evaluate which layout is most useful.

Interaction variations

With interaction variations, the team can't decide how to make the interface most usable. If the user chooses from multiple options, is it more usable to have the user select an option from a drop-down? Or is it more usable for the user to choose from one of several radio buttons? Even if both variations have similar layouts, you can check each interaction—select box or radio buttons—to determine what method is most usable.

Trust Others to Make Interfaces on Their Own

When you work through the 4-corners a few times with your team, your team starts to think like designers. When they approach screens, they'll think about the user, the task, and the previous and next steps. They'll list and prioritize content and functionality before they start to design the screen. They'll design better experiences, and you helped them do it.

Introducing your team to 4-corners changes the way they think. The team shares a vision about what goes into good screen design, so trust your team to create their own sketches and wireframes without you. Trust the decisions they make, the designs they create, and that they will reach out when they need expertise or feedback.

Instead of designing every screen, help the team create better screens. Help the team design better. A couple of tactics help your teams design better without you.

MAKE 4-CORNERS EASILY ACCESSIBLE

It's easier to fill out a worksheet than think about something in the abstract. Make 4-corners materials easy to find and use. Leave stacks of worksheets in common areas. Link to templates on team wikis and project sites. Attach the 4-corners worksheet to tasks in tracking systems like TFS and JIRA. When 4-corners worksheets and checklists are easier to find and use, more people will find and use them.

CREATE A RITUAL

For 10 years, every night before bed, I brushed my teeth with the kids. We all go into the bathroom, put toothpaste on our toothbrushes, count to three, say go, and then brush our teeth while we hum the ABCs twice. Every night. A couple of years ago, we added mouthwash and flossing to our nightly ritual.

Now, if the kids brush their teeth on their own, they follow the same ritual. They count, say go, brush while they say the ABCs twice, floss, and use mouthwash.

To make 4-corners part of your team's ritual, observe the ritual yourself where everyone can see. When you model behavior, yourself, others learn how to do it and how easy it is to get the benefits.

SOLVE TEAM PROBLEMS, NOT DESIGN PROBLEMS

When you collaborate on an interface, your team works through one of two, basic problems:

- How can the team align multiple visions into one, shared vision?
- How can the team evaluate the success of a screen?

When you collaborate on interfaces, you help teams work through these problems. When you make an interface with your team, collaboration identifies and solves specific questions the team doesn't even know they have. When you reveal and answer these questions, you improve the final interface. And your team members take those learnings with them throughout the experience machine.

With 4-corners and sketching, the low-fidelity sketch includes content, functionality, and layout. However, as an interface model, the limited fidelity of the sketches restricts how well you can model content, functionality, visual design, and context.

Sketches only let you model and test so much. When you make an interface, what if the sketch won't let you check what you want to check? 4-corners and sketching provide one way to think about and make an interface at a specific fidelity to answer specific questions. How do you know when to create a sketch versus a wireframe or prototype? How do you make the right interface? We'll find out in the next chapter.

[20]

Choose the Right Interface Model: Wireframes, Comps, or Prototypes?

UNTIL NOW, WE'VE USED sketches to make interface models. You make a model, so you can Check it. Another way to say that is: you make interface models to answer a question. And since sketching helps teams think about three visible parts of the interface—the content, functionality, and layout—another way to say this is: you make sketches to answer questions about content, functionality, and layout.

A sketch is *one* type of interface model that lets you ask certain questions, but it isn't the only way. You can model interfaces five ways. To answer the right questions, choose the model that offers the right fidelity to answer the right question.

Five Types of Interface Models (and the Actual Product)

Whenever you talk about an interface, you talk about either an *actual* interface, like the actual product, or an interface *model*, like a wireframe. The actual product is always the actual product. However, you can model an interface in other ways. In all, you have six ways to Check an interface:

- Text descriptions
- Sketches
- Wireframes
- Mockups (or visual comps/compositions)
- Prototypes
- The actual product

Each interface model offers a different level of fidelity. Knowing how the five types of interface models compare to the actual product helps you choose what model to Think-Make-Check when you collaborate with your client and team.

TEXT DESCRIPTIONS

Text descriptions are the fastest way to describe an interface.

Think about the best developer you've ever worked with. Now imagine you both want to build a Product Detail screen for your ecommerce site. Imagine you bump into your favorite developer in the hallway and talk about the new Product Detail screen. You talk about having the product name, a description, and a product image. And of course, you talk about an "Add to cart" button.

With only that information, you know everything you need to design the interface, and the developer has everything they need to start coding. For any interface, talking about the content and the functionality is the quickest, easiest way to describe the interface. In the case of the Product Detail screen, you and your developer friend walk away with two lists.

For content, you identified three items:

- Product name
- Product description
- Product image

For functionality, you identified one item:

- "Add to cart" button

Although a text description lets you describe the content and functionality, you and your favorite developer each make assumptions about the visual design and the layout.

SKETCHES

With a text description, you can describe content and functionality. Sketches expand a text description's content and functionality to include layout (Figure 20-1).

FIGURE 20-1
A sketch shows content, functionality, and layout

Imagine the Product Detail screen you talked about with your favorite developer. Step up to a gleaming whiteboard and draw the screen in blue marker. Squiggles for text, a box with an X for the product image, and a rectangle for the "Add to cart" button. By sketching the screen, you've now discussed the content, functionality, and the layout.

Although a sketch offers more information, it's only a general idea about the layout, and you still have to imagine the visual design.

WIREFRAMES

Wireframes add more detail than when you describe the interface (Figure 20-2). In addition to content, functionality, and general layout, you start to replace unspoken assumptions about format with real specifics.

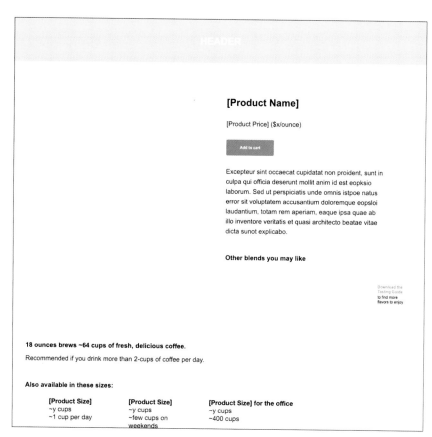

FIGURE 20-2

A wireframe adds content format and quantity to the functionality and layout

The additional detail in a wireframe reveals how much content can appear, the length and format of content strings, the size of images, and other details. Wireframes also include more accurate information about the layout and clearer detail about affordances for functionality. Is "Add to cart" a big button or a small button?

MOCKUPS

Mockups, or visual comps, show what the actual product would look like to the user (Figure 20-3). The mockup isn't the actual product, but it *looks* like the actual product. Mockups show a "comprehensive layout"[1] that includes exact color, spacing, typography, and photo and illustration styles.

---

1 "Comprehensive Layout." Wikipedia. Wikimedia Foundation, 2 Feb. 2005. Web. 31 Dec. 2016.

FIGURE 20-3
A mockup shows what the product could look like

Usually, a mockup shows how the wireframe will appear in its final state. However, like the wireframe, the mockup only suggests screen behavior. You can't see actually what happens when the user clicks on the "Add to cart" button.

SCREENSHOTS

Unlike the other types of interface models, a screenshot is an image of the actual product, not a model of the interface. However, because it's just an image, it provides the same kinds of information you see in a mockup. Screenshots show actual content, its format, fonts, color, and layout.

Although screenshots seem exactly like mockups, there's one important difference. A mockup is a model of an interface. A screenshot is a picture of the actual interface.[2]

PROTOTYPES

Prototypes add real functionality. In addition to knowing the content, functionality, layout, and design for the screen, the prototype can show what happens when the user clicks the "Add to cart" button (Figure 20-4). Does the user stay on the Product Detail screen and see a message that says the product was added to the cart? Does the user click through to another screen where they see their shopping cart?

FIGURE 20-4

A prototype allows you to show what happens when users interact with the screen

---

2   On every project I've ever been on, a screenshot of the actual interface never looks exactly like the mockup that is a model of the interface. Funny thing, yeah?

THE ACTUAL PRODUCT

The actual product isn't a model of the interface. It's the actual interface. For the Product Detail screen, you see real content and the functionality really works. You see the Product Detail's actual visual design, and you can look at the screen in a real web browser.

Each of these ways for discussing interfaces illustrates the interface at a different level of fidelity. These different fidelities let your team answer different questions.

How do you know what interface model to use? You choose the model that provides the right fidelity.

Five Kinds of Interface Fidelity

When you design interfaces with your team and clients, you want to have the right kinds of conversations about the right things. The right fidelity maintains your team's shared vision. The more fidelity, the more you ensure the shared vision, but the longer it takes to Make something before you can Check it. Less fidelity and you iterate faster, but the team shares less vision.

Adjust the fidelity of your model in five ways:

- Content fidelity
- Functional fidelity
- Layout fidelity
- Visual fidelity
- Contextual fidelity

CONTENT FIDELITY

When you create an interface model, content fidelity describes how accurate the content is. When you show a Product Detail sketch, do you have a squiggle for the Product Name? Did you write, "Product Name," or did you write the name of a real product?

Visual designers often use "greeked text," like "Lorem ipsum...," in mockups. Greeked text has less content fidelity than real, sample content (Figure 20-5). When visual designers use greeked text, they want to see how well a typeface works in a visual design, and any letters will do.

What if you wanted to Check that your labels were clear? Can you evaluate labels in an interface with greeked text? Probably not.

Oluptam ut officab orestios ditem nonsequi beruptat. Vidio corem. Et quam faccaborem volecest, od et ulliquos ducil maximagnimus magnitiis quasi quatur simus re occus, quodit magnam aligenimaio quae numquias eaque et ullendit et que alignit lanimus modit landam .

From seven to twelve per cent, of the supply of coffee received in the United States comes from the northern part of South America, and is known as Maracaibo, Laguarya, or Porto Cabello coffee. It is grown either in Venezuela or the United States of Colomboa.

Content fidelity exists at three levels:

- Content type
- Content format
- Actual or sample content

Let's say you sketch a Product Detail screen with your team. If you scrawl "Product Name" at the top of the sketch, then you've identified the *type* of content that will appear.

If you note the Product Name will be "text" that is no longer than 150 characters, then you have defined the content format.

If instead you wrote, "Guatemalan French Roast," then you've used actual or sample content.

LEVEL OF CONTENT FIDELITY	EXAMPLE
Content type (low)	Product Name
Content format	Text, 150 characters max
Actual or sample content (high)	Guatemalan French Roast

The fidelity lets you Check different questions about the content. Do you want to ask about what content? The content format? Or make sure the interface works with real content?

FUNCTIONAL FIDELITY

Functional fidelity describes how well functionality works in your interface model (Figure 20-6). Do links work? Or are they just blue text with underlines? You can gesticulate wildly to describe how something moves, or you can just show an animation.

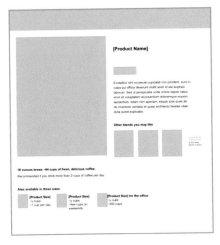

FIGURE 20-6
Functional fidelity refers to how accurately functionality appears in your interface model

Like content, functional fidelity works at three levels:

- Functionality type
- Functionality format
- Actual or sample functionality

Let's say you sketch a Product Detail screen with your team. If you scrawl "Add to cart," then you've identified the type of functionality you want available.

If instead you make a wireframe and include a button that says, "Add to cart," then you have defined the functionality's format as a button. (You could have used a link instead.)

If you create a prototype that shows a lightbox appears when you click the "Add to cart" button, then you've illustrated the actual or sample functionality.

LEVEL OF FUNCTIONAL FIDELITY	EXAMPLE
Functionality type (low)	Add to cart
Functionality format	"Add to cart" button
Actual or sample content (high)	Lightbox appears

LAYOUT FIDELITY

Layout fidelity describes how well your model demonstrates the interface's layout (Figure 20-7). Do you have a sketch with a general layout? Or are you looking at a mockup with exact spacing and positioning?

FIGURE 20-7

Layout fidelity refers to how accurately the layout appears in your interface model

Layout fidelity also works at three levels:

- Prominence or priority

- Relative position

- Actual position

When you use 4-corners to prioritize a list of the Product Detail's content, you identify the importance of each element, or how prominently it should appear in the interface.

When you sketch the Product Detail screen with your team, you placed the content on the screen. Your layout describes how each piece of content will appear relative to other content.

If instead you create a pixel-perfect mockup, you illustrate the actual position of each piece of content.

LEVEL OF LAYOUT FIDELITY	EXAMPLE
Prominence or priority (low)	Prioritized list of content
Relative position	Sketch of content layout
Actual position (high)	Mockup of content layout

VISUAL FIDELITY

Visual fidelity describes how closely the interface model resembles the actual product (Figure 20-8). Like all fidelity, the higher the visual fidelity, the easier it is for someone to understand. You can see this in action in your career: some clients just don't "get it" when they see a wireframe. They have to see a mockup.

FIGURE 20-8
Visual fidelity describes how closely the interface model resembles the actual product

Like content, functionality, and layout, visual fidelity also works at three levels:

- Suggested visual design

- Relative visual design

- Actual visual design

If you describe the Product Detail screen in an email and mention it will include your logo, then you suggest the visual design.

If you make a wireframe and use the company logo and brand colors, you use the relative visual design.

If you create a mockup and use the company typeface, colors, logo, and spacing, then you show the actual visual design.

LEVEL OF VISUAL FIDELITY	EXAMPLE
Suggested design (low)	Description to include the logo
Relative design	Logo and brand colors
Actual design (high)	Logo, colors, typeface, and spacing

Each of these visual fidelities provides answers to different questions about the visual design.

CONTEXTUAL FIDELITY

Contextual fidelity refers to the context where people will see and use the interface (Figure 20-9).

Let's say you want to test the usability of a web application. Do you show users paper printouts of each screen? Or do you have them click through screens in a web browser?

If you show your interface model in the context where end users will actually interact with it, your interface model has more contextual fidelity than if you showed a bunch of printouts.

FIGURE 20-9
When you show an interface model to someone, how accurate is the context? Are they looking at a mobile app on paper or on their smartphone?

You can describe contextual fidelity in three levels:

- Suggested context
- Relative context
- Actual context

If you say customers will use the Product Detail screen in their web browser, then you have suggested the screen's context. If you make a wireframe the same size of a web browser, then you illustrate the relative context. If you show the Product Detail screen in an actual web browser, then you show the screen's actual context. If you install a hardware prototype in a place similar to where it will live in the real world, then you're displaying the device's context.

LEVEL OF CONTEXTUAL FIDELITY	EXAMPLE
Suggested context (low)	Description of screen in a web browser
Relative context	Product Detail wireframe with web browser dimensions
Actual context (high)	Product Detail screen in an actual web browser

Contextual fidelity affects the types of questions you can ask about how an interface will be used.

Three Ways to Make Interface Models

The tools you use to make the model also control the fidelity of your interface model.

Text descriptions and sketches can be made by hand. You use software to create wireframes and mockups. Prototypes and actual products require operable code that receives and responds to user interaction.

TOOLS YOU USE	MODELS YOU CAN MAKE
Hands	Text descriptions and sketches
Software	Wireframes and mockups
Code	Prototypes and products

That doesn't mean you can't use software to write a text description or sketch an interface. You can, but you can't create a wireframe or mockup without software, and you can't build a prototype or product without code.

Different Models Support Different Interface Fidelity

To Think-Make-Check an interface with your team or your client, you work through two steps:

1. Know what question you want the audience to answer.

2. Show a model or actual interface that includes the information your audience needs to answer that question.

Different types of interface models support different types of fidelity at different levels (Table 20-1).

TABLE 20-1. Five types of interface fidelity at three levels

	CONTENT FIDELITY	FUNCTIONAL FIDELITY	LAYOUT FIDELITY	VISUAL FIDELITY	CONTEXTUAL FIDELITY
Low	Content type	Functionality type	Priority or prominence	Suggested design	Suggested context
Medium	Content format	Functionality format	Relative layout	Relative design	Relative context
High	Actual or sample content	Actual functionality	Actual layout	Actual design	Actual context

FIDELITY OF PROTOTYPES AND THE ACTUAL PRODUCT

Of all the ways you can Check an interface, prototypes and products display the highest possible fidelity and take the longest to produce. Prototypes and products also provide the greatest flexibility since they can also display fidelity at any range from low to high (Table 20-2).

TABLE 20-2. Prototypes and products provide the maximum amount of fidelity (area shaded in orange) and take longer to produce

	CONTENT FIDELITY	FUNCTIONAL FIDELITY	LAYOUT FIDELITY	VISUAL FIDELITY	CONTEXTUAL FIDELITY
Low	Content type	Functionality type	Priority or prominence	Suggested design	Suggested context
Medium	Content format	Functionality format	Relative layout	Relative design	Relative context
High	Actual or sample content	Actual functionality	Actual layout	Actual design	Actual context

FIDELITY OF SKETCHES AND TEXT DESCRIPTIONS

Prototypes and products take much longer to create than other interface models. In contrast, you can create interface models like text descriptions and sketches by hand much more quickly than you can create prototypes or products. In exchange for that speed, your model has much less fidelity and you can answer a more limited set of questions (Table 20-3).

TABLE 20-3. Text descriptions and sketches provide low levels of fidelity (area shaded in green) in a short amount of time

	CONTENT FIDELITY	FUNCTIONAL FIDELITY	LAYOUT FIDELITY	VISUAL FIDELITY	CONTEXTUAL FIDELITY
Low	Content type	Functionality type	Priority or prominence	Suggested design	Suggested context
Medium	Content format	Functionality format	Relative layout	Relative design	Relative context
High	Actual or sample content	Actual functionality	Actual layout	Actual design	Actual context

FIDELITY OF WIREFRAMES AND MOCKUPS

Wireframes and mockups live in a sweet spot between how long they take to create and how much fidelity they provide. Wireframes and mockups let you answer more questions and evaluate more assumptions in less time. This flexibility and usefulness explain why wireframes and mockups continue to be used despite periodic trends for prototypes or sketches (Table 20-4).

TABLE 20-4. Wireframes and mockups provide almost as much fidelity (area shaded in blue) as prototypes and products in a fraction of the time

	CONTENT FIDELITY	FUNCTIONAL FIDELITY	LAYOUT FIDELITY	VISUAL FIDELITY	CONTEXTUAL FIDELITY
Low	Content type	Functionality type	Priority or prominence	Suggested design	Suggested context
Medium	Content format	Functionality format	Relative layout	Relative design	Relative context
High	Actual or sample content	Actual functionality	Actual layout	Actual design	Actual context

Use the Lowest Fidelity Possible to Reduce Iteration Time

With each type of model, trade how long it takes to create with what kind of question you can answer. To help the experience machine learn as quickly as possible, choose the model you can make in the least amount of time that answers your team's specific question.

The interface model you choose must include the information you need to Think-Make-Check. If you want to check content and functionality, don't spend a bunch of time creating a mockup. If you want to see if an animation makes sense, then a wireframe won't do. You have to use a prototype.

When you choose how much fidelity to include, use the highest fidelity for the question you want to check. At the same time, use the lowest fidelity possible for everything else. Optimizing fidelity makes the model quick to produce, so you can iterate quickly.

Also, if you show too much fidelity too soon, you can trigger disagreements that distract from the question at hand. If you want to check functionality, and someone gets hung up on color, you lose what they might have had to say about functionality.

So, it all comes down to the question you want to answer.

QUESTIONS DIFFERENT INTERFACE MODELS CAN ANSWER

The question you want to answer drives the fidelity you need and the interface model you can use. Your team can evaluate an almost infinite number of questions about any given interface.

The following table of common questions (Table 20-5) can help you decide what interface model to choose. Although a list of questions is never complete, the table includes many common questions that face product teams. Select the question you want answered, and the color of the cell indicates the model that supports the fastest iteration time for that question: green for sketches and text descriptions, blue for wireframes and mockups, and orange for prototypes and products.

TABLE 20-5. Different interface models can answer different types of product questions. Sketches and text answer many questions (area shaded in green) while other questions require wireframes or mockups (area in blue) or prototypes and products (area in orange)

	CONTENT FIDELITY	FUNCTIONAL FIDELITY	LAYOUT FIDELITY	VISUAL FIDELITY	CONTEXTUAL FIDELITY
	What content should we have?	What functionality should we have?	What layout should we have?	What design should we have?	What interface will it be in?
Usefulness and usability questions	Does the content support organizational goals?	Does the functionality support organizational goals?	Does the layout support organizational goals?	Does the design support organizational goals?	Does the interface support organizational goals?
	Is this content useful? Does it support user goals?	Is this functionality useful? Does it support user goals?	Is the layout useful to users? Does it support user goals?	Is the visual design useful to users? Does it support user goals?	Is the interface useful to users? Does it support user goals?
	What format should content be in?	What type of interaction should we use?		What format should the visual design be in?	
	What content variations should/will we have?	What functionality variations should/will we have?	What layout variations should we have?	What design variations should/will we have?	What interface variations should we have?
	How should we lay out content?	How should we lay out functionality?		How should the design affect the layout?	How should the interface affect the layout?
	Will this type of/sample/actual content work in this layout?	Will functionality work in this layout?		Will design work in this layout?	

	CONTENT FIDELITY	FUNCTIONAL FIDELITY	LAYOUT FIDELITY	VISUAL FIDELITY	CONTEXTUAL FIDELITY
	Will content work in this interface?	Will functionality work in this interface?	Will layout work in this interface?	Will design work in this interface?	
	Is this content usable?	Is this functionality usable?	Is this layout usable?	Is this design usable?	Is this interface usable?
Feasibility to create questions	Where will this content come from?	Who can build this functionality?	Who can build this layout?	Who can build/create this design?	
	What integrations are needed for this layout?	What integrations are needed for this functionality?		What process integrations are needed for this design?	
Feasibility to maintain questions	Who will maintain this content?	Who will maintain this functionality?	Who will maintain this layout?	Who will maintain this design?	
Feasibility for learning and optimization questions	What content should we measure?	What functionality should we measure?			
	What content should we personalize?	What functionality should we personalize?	Should we personalize the layout?	Should we personalize the design?	
	Do customers consume content as expected?	Do customers use functionality as expected?		Does visual design match the brand?	
UAT/Test questions	Does the content appear correctly in the interface?	Does the functionality perform correctly in the interface?	Does the layout appear correct in the interface?	Does the visual design appear correctly in the interface?	

Adjust Fidelity for Your Audience

Way back in Chapter 2, we talked about how your audience and channel affect the fidelity of the models you make. Generally, the farther away the audience, the more fidelity you need to include in your model (Figure 20-10).

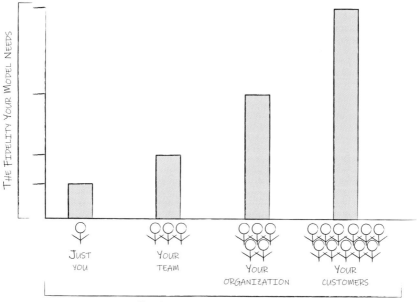

FIGURE 20-10

The farther away your audience, the more fidelity you need to include in your interface model

Audiences that are farther away need more fidelity because they share less of the team's vision. Your team shares more vision with itself than with the CEO because you and your team talk every day, while you communicate with the CEO less frequently.

TACIT, IMPLICIT, AND EXPLICIT INFORMATION

As a rule of thumb, you can share interface models at low fidelity with yourself and your team. When you share with your organization, the models need to be at medium fidelity, and when you share with users, you should aim for high fidelity (Table 20-6).

	YOURSELF OR YOUR TEAM	YOUR ORGANIZATION	USERS
Low fidelity	Yes	No	No
Medium fidelity		Yes	No
High fidelity			Yes

In practice, you can reduce the amount of fidelity you show a given audience if the audience already has the information they need to answer the question you want to ask.

Let's say you want to ask if someone agrees with the content on the Product Detail screen. If that person is on your team, and you've worked through the 4-corners together, then they know what content you want to include. Let's say you ask the CEO about the content. How would they know what content you wanted to include? When you adjust the fidelity for your audience, you make sure the CEO knows enough about the content on the Product Detail screen to agree or disagree with your design.

There are three kinds of information your audience may or may not have:

Tacit information
    Information that is understood without being suggested

Implicit information
    Information that is implied, though not stated

Explicit information
    Information that is specifically stated

Explicit information

Explicit information is the easiest to understand because it's anything that is specifically stated. If you see text on a screen that says, "View my profile page," the text is telling you exactly what happens when you click it (Figure 20-11).

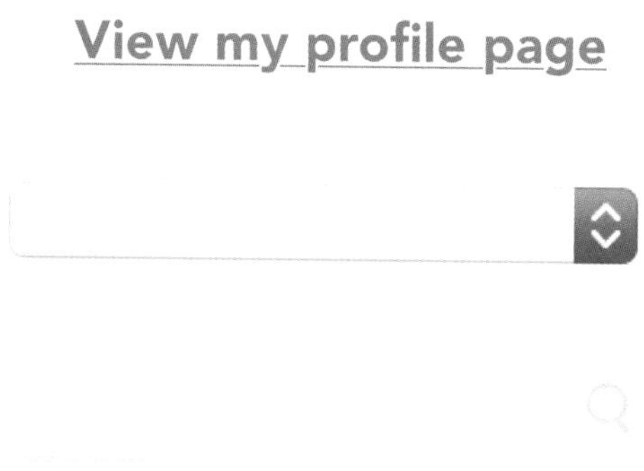

View my profile page

FIGURE 20-11
Explicit information is
anything that's clearly
stated in the interface

Implicit information

Implicit information refers to anything your audience can figure out from looking at your interface model. If you have a wireframe with a drop-down, most people will know that when they select the drop-down, they'll see a list of options to choose from.

Tacit information

Teams live off of tacit information. This is all of the things you and your team members know because you've been working together. Tacit understanding is about your team culture. When you see a magnifying glass next to a text input, you probably know that's a search field. Nothing in the interface model tells you it's a search field, and a magnifying glass by itself doesn't say "search."

You can check the content in your sketch with the CEO if they understand that the squiggle at the top is the product name and the lines are the product description. However, if they might not understand the squiggle and lines, then you need to make the interface more clear.

CLARIFY FIDELITY TO SET EXPECTATIONS

For an ecommerce website, I presented a wireframe to a room full of C-level executives. The room got quiet, and then the CTO spoke. "This is terrible. The website can't be all gray." I wanted to check content, functionality, and layout, and my audience wanted to check visual design.

Either spend more time to create interface models with more fidelity, or set expectations about what the model includes and—just as importantly—what it doesn't (Figure 20-12). For the CTO, I should have clarified that I wanted him to Check the content, functionality, and layout and that the wireframe would not show the final visual design.

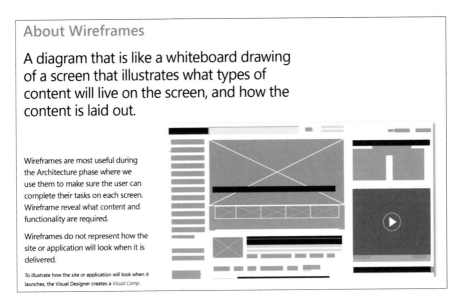

About Wireframes

A diagram that is like a whiteboard drawing of a screen that illustrates what types of content will live on the screen, and how the content is laid out.

Wireframes are most useful during the Architecture phase where we use them to make sure the user can complete their tasks on each screen. Wireframe reveal what content and functionality are required.

Wireframes do not represent how the site or application will look when it is delivered.

To illustrate how the site or application will look when it launches, the Visual Designer creates a *Visual Comp.*

FIGURE 20-12

Set expectations to share tacit information with your audience so they can answer the question you want

When you set expectations, it creates a tacit understanding about the model that gives your audience the additional information they need to answer your question.

USE ANNOTATION TO OFFSET LOW FIDELITY

You can provide more information about an interface without improving fidelity. Annotations provide explicit information without any changes to a model. If you want to ask the CEO about the content on your Product Detail sketch, and you're worried she won't know what the squiggle is, you can add an annotation that says, "Product Name."

Annotations can add explicit information to any part of a model. Annotate content, functionality, layout, visual design, or context. Designers pack wireframe specifications with annotations to describe information you'd only otherwise see in a prototype or actual product (Figure 20-13).

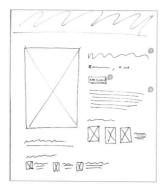

FIGURE 20-13

Wireframe specs use annotation to describe functionality that would not otherwise be clear without a prototype or the actual product

SET EXPECTATIONS AND USE ANNOTATIONS TO CONQUER DISTANCE, TIME, AND REACH

Set expectations and add annotation to counter the effects of distance, time, and reach. Team members separated by distance and time will never have the same tacit understanding as colocated team members, so set expectations and add annotations to collaborate better.

Add clarifying notes to your interface model to reduce misunderstandings and unnecessary churn that slows iteration. Ultimately, it's your responsibility to make sure your audience understands what they're looking at and has the information they need to answer your question.

As always, balance your need for speed with your need to communicate clearly. Get the balance right,[3] and you'll help your team learn more and faster,[4] and your experience machine will release better products.

---

3   I love Depeche Mode.

4   And KMFDM.

[*VI*]

Checks

THE CHECK SEEMS LIKE it lives at the end, but it's really just the beginning. The Check lets you and your team evaluate your thinking and making, so that you can do more and better thinking and making. This part examines the Check in Think-Make-Check and how to structure and facilitate checks with teammates, coworkers, and clients, so that you can generate good, useful feedback to fold into your Think-Make-Check process.

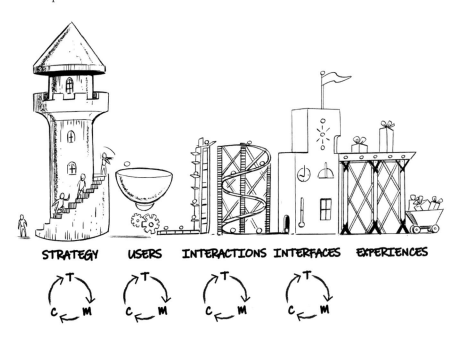

[21]

Checks (and Balances)

I LEFT THIS CHAPTER for last. I almost didn't finish it. I spent all my time and energy thinking and making the rest of the book, and now I don't have the proper amount of time to give this chapter its due.

How ironic that this mirrors real life. You spend your time thinking about stuff and making stuff and spend much less time checking stuff.

If you survey the literature—or even flip through this book—the bulk of the job is thinking about stuff and making stuff. But remember the model: Think-Make-Check (Figure 21-1). Check is just as important as Think and Make. And the model is a cycle. You Think so you know what to Make. You Make so have something to Check. You Check so you get feedback to Think about. Think-Make-Check creates a virtuous cycle where Check provides fuel to Think about and Make better things.

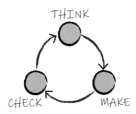

FIGURE 21-1

Think-Make-Check create a virtuous cycle where each iteration teaches you more and more about the product and its users

Thinking and making vary more than checking. How you Think about users differs from how you Think about interactions. How you Make interactions differs from how you Make interfaces. In contrast, you always Check everything the same way. Checks follow the same pattern regardless of what you want to Check.

In this chapter, you'll learn how to receive and manage feedback, how to handle jerks, and most importantly, how to think about Checks, so you and your team learn about your product and its users more and faster. You'll also learn how Frame-Facilitate-Finish structures your Checks, so you answer the questions you need to answer and receive the right feedback at the right time.

Checks Start with the Finish

Every collaborative activity works through the same three stages: Frame-Facilitate-Finish. Checks follow this same pattern, and to plan your Check, you want to begin with the end in mind and start with the finish. So, to plan a good Check, you need to identify the question you want the audience to answer. What's the question?

Often, teams request feedback on something they've made. That's the common scenario when you say Think-Make-Check. However, there are lots of other things you can Check.

CHECK EACH STEP IN THINK-MAKE-CHECK

Think-Make-Check suggests you Check the model you Make. That is, you Think about users, Make a user model, and then Check that model with your team. Yet Think-Make-Check hides opportunities for teams to collaborate more closely with each other and others. You can Check at every step. Check after you Think, Check after you Make, and Check after you Check (Figure 21-2).

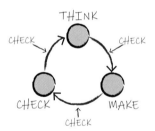

FIGURE 21-2
You can Check at every step of the Think-Make-Check process

You can Check after each step of the Think-Make-Check model because each step has its own inputs and outputs (Table 21-1). Before you can Think, you need observations, something to think about. You Think about them to create analysis. You use the analysis about the user, interaction, or interface to Make the model, and you Check the model to gather observations (Figure 21-3).

TABLE 21-1. The Think-Make-Check cycle and the inputs and outputs for each stage

	THINK	**MAKE**	**CHECK**
Inputs	Observations	Analysis	Model
Transformation	Think about observations	Make a model	Check a model
Outputs	Analysis *for a model*	A model *to check*	Observations *to think about*

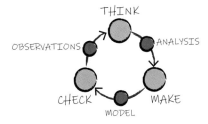

FIGURE 21-3

In Think-Make-Check, each stage creates an output used by the next stage as an input

This process plays out when you design an interface. You Think about your observations about users and their needs. Your analysis suggests a certain kind of interface. You can Check that analysis, or you can Make the interface. So, you open your favorite software and create a screen. You want to Check that screen with your users, but before you do, you can Check it with your team to make sure everyone is on board.

CHECK WHAT YOU DID AND HOW YOU DID IT

Each step of the Think-Make-Check process creates its own output, and you can Check that output before you move to the next step. You don't need to check every step of the Think-Make-Check process, but when you need to, you can.

To make it more convoluted, you can Check two things for each of those outputs. First, you can Check what you did. Second, you can check how you did it. Imagine a math problem. You have the problem, you show your work, and write the answer. Of course, you can Check whether you have the right answer, and you can also check whether you used the right method to get to the answer (Table 21-2).

TABLE 21-2. The Think-Make-Check cycle and Checks for the outputs from each stage

	THINK	MAKE	CHECK
Outputs	Analysis *for a model*	A model *to check*	Observations *to think about*
Check what you did	Is the analysis right?	Is the model right?	Are the observations right?
Check how you did it	Did we do the right kind of analysis?	Did we make the right kind of model?	Did we check the right model with the right people?

It turns out there's a whole lot you can Check, from the most critical outcomes of the team's work to the most minor or trivial ideas.

So, zoom out for a moment. The important takeaway: Check as often as is possible and useful with yourself, your team, your organization, and your users. And you don't have to Check just the user, interaction, or interface model. You can Check the inputs or the outputs for any step.

Identify what you want to Check, so you know what you want the Check to finish with, and then it's time to frame the Check, so your audience has the context they need to give you the feedback you need.

Frame the Check

For a Check, the Frame works the same as it does any other time we collaborate. For each Check, answer the four questions:

- What are we doing?
- Why are we doing it?
- How will we do it?
- Why is it important?

So, if you wanted to Check a user journey with your team, you might frame it this way:

WHAT WILL YOU DO?	Check a user model
WHAT'S THE OUTCOME?	A list of changes to make to the model
WHY IS IT IMPORTANT?	Ensures the team is aligned around a single vision of the user
HOW WILL YOU DO IT?	Review key user attributes

If you wanted to frame a Check of a user model, you might say:

> "Let's review the persona to make sure we agree on how we've described the user. We'll review key user attributes and collect any feedback and changes."

When you frame the Check in this way, your audience understands what they're doing, why it's important, and what the outcome will be. However, people who Check things need some additional context. They may not be familiar with how you got to where you are. Checks invite two additional questions:

- Where are we in the process?
- How did we get to where we are?

WHERE ARE WE IN THE PROCESS?

Participants want to know where you are in the process, so they understand both what they're looking at as well as what kind of feedback to provide. When you tell participants where you are in the process, you help explain why you want the feedback. Are you at the beginning of the process and reviewing something rough and unfinished? Or are you at the end of the process and reviewing something that's about to be shipped to five million customers?

When participants understand where you are in the process, they can adjust between more directional feedback and more specific feedback. If you're about to launch a new app, you don't want feedback on whether to include core functionality. You're looking for feedback on fit and finish. In contrast, if you show early sketches, critiques on spelling and layout are useless, while discussion around core concepts offers real value.

HOW DID YOU GET WHERE YOU ARE?

If you don't tell participants where you are in the process, much of their feedback may be around who you've talked to and what activities you've done. For example, when you show your persona, participants might say to go do user research. If you haven't done any research, that's good feedback. But if you're showing a persona, you've probably already addressed the idea of user research.

Save yourself some back and forth during the Check and tell participants how you got to where you are. Explain the steps you've gone through to get to where you are. Who did you talk to? What did you do? What inputs did you use? What background information have you reviewed? Who else has seen this material? What have you taken into account? Or what have you not considered and why?

When you provide this additional context to your participants, you answer common questions ahead of time and help make the most of your time with your participants and increase the likelihood you will receive the feedback you're looking for.

INFORMAL CHECKS CAN USE VERBAL FRAMING

A Check shouldn't need to be a formal affair. Checks should be easy, so you do them all the time, out of habit, reflexively whenever you have the opportunity. If a team member comes by, grab them to Check whatever you're working on. In these situations, frame the Check verbally.

Provide the complete frame: what do you want them to do, what's the outcome, why is it important, and how will you do it? Then share additional context around where you are in the process and how you got there before collecting feedback.

FORMAL CHECKS NEED SUPPORTING DOCUMENTATION

For formal reviews, document the Check's framing and context, so you can share it with participants before they see what you want to Check. In common scenarios, you share the frame and context as slides in a presentation. For example, if you review an early draft of a persona, you might share the frame in two slides:

- One slide with the frame (Figure 21-4)

- One slide with where you are in the process and how you got there (Figure 21-5)

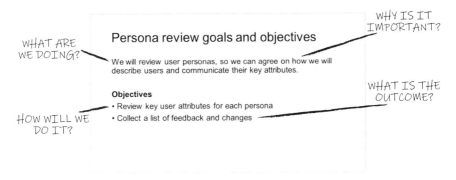

FIGURE 21-4
You can share the frame for a formal Check in a single presentation slide

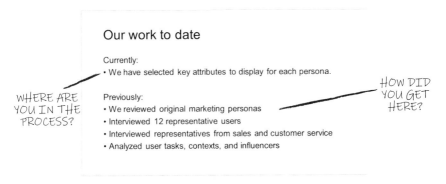

FIGURE 21-5
Where you are in the process and how you got there will fit on one slide

Those two slides give the audience and participants the context they need to give you good feedback. If you share material asynchronously, share the frame, context, and the material for the Check as part of a single package.

MAKE IT EASY TO PREPARE FOR CHECKS

Even though teams focus on the thinking and making, the Check is just as important and requires intentional preparation. However, it's tough to make sure your team prepares if the preparation takes too long or is too difficult. Make preparation easy. A good Check is the difference between a waste of time and a successful iteration through Think-Make-Check.

Add the frame and context slides to the beginning of your presentation template. If you share long-form documents, add pages for the frame and context at the beginning of the document.

 Find templates, framing material, and remote resources on the website:

http://pxd.gd/check

Facilitate the Check

After you have properly framed the check and provided additional context, it's time to facilitate the Check. Show the thing you want to Check and restate the question you want to answer. In our example, you'd show the persona.

Don't forget to restate the question. If you show a persona, people can comment on the attribute groups, the individual attributes, the attribute values, the design, the persona's name, imagery, layout, color, or typography. What do you want participants to comment on? If you want them to comment on the attributes and their values, then restate the question, so they remember:

> "On this persona, did we communicate the right attributes to help the team design the product?"

After you restate the question, dive into the thing you want to check. Describe it, show it, demo it, whatever. Dive in.

Some teams may want some additional information. Feel free to provide more background. For example, if you're showing a model, talk about the analysis that led you to the model. If you show observations collected from another Check (like a usability test), talk about the model you used for the Check. If you're reviewing analysis, talk about the observations that formed the basis.

And then restate the question. And keep restating the question. There's a lot to talk about and a lot of things you can get feedback on. Continue to focus the discussion on the question at hand, so you make sure to get the feedback you need.

CAPTURE FEEDBACK

Collecting feedback is about more than just writing down a list of things to change or taking notes. Good feedback collection demonstrates good collaborative behavior, so you want to demonstrate that you trust everyone's feedback and include everyone.

Ask questions, especially when you disagree

When someone offers feedback, ask question to clarify what they mean. Clarifying questions help you understand exactly how the feedback applies and demonstrates that you're listening and trust the participants' feedback enough to really engage with and understand it. For example, if someone suggests changing the name when reviewing the persona, ask why. What's wrong with the current name? What are you trying to achieve by changing the name? Your goal is to understand the why behind the feedback.

Most important, never say you disagree unless you've probed to understand the why behind the feedback. Most likely, you will agree with the why, so you can work toward a shared understanding about what should change. If, after you discuss the why, you disagree, then you have the opportunity to help get both parties on the same page or to agree to disagree.

Repeat the feedback back to the participant

When you understand the feedback, repeat it back to the provider, so they can verify that you understand it correctly. For example, after working through why the name should change, you might repeat the feedback as: "Change the name to something less generic, so the persona seems more real."

Collect feedback visibly

If you want the team to invest the time in providing feedback, collect feedback in a way that's visible, so they can see clearly that you're listening. This can take the form of visible notes or making edits in real time while the team watches.

For in-person Checks, write feedback on a whiteboard or easel pad where everyone can see. For remote Checks, you can swap your screenshare from the item being checked to a document where you type feedback, so everyone can see the collected feedback.

Collect the feedback in the same way you repeat it back to the participants.

Affirm and repeat feedback when you agree

When someone says something you don't agree with or don't understand, repeat it back and ask a question to understand. When someone says something you do agree with, make sure you say so. If you don't take the time to tell them you agree before you talk about something else, they will think you don't agree or don't understand and keep giving you the same feedback. They want to make sure you're listening.

You can't just say, "yes." In my experience, "yes" doesn't communicate that you heard the feedback and you agree. You need to be more explicit and say something like, "yes, I agree." You can't say, "yes, I agree" to everything without sounding robotic, so you should vary a bit. You've likely heard other people use these common variations:

- Yes, I agree

- I agree 100%

- That is a really good point

- I'm totally with you on that

- We're on the same page

- Let me "plus one" that

When you explicitly indicate your agreement, it reassures the speaker that you agree, and when you restate the feedback, it shows you understand what they said.

Affirm and extend when you almost agree

Sometimes you almost agree with someone. In those cases, focus on where you agree and try to extend the discussion to address where you disagree. The easiest way to affirm and extend is the phrase, "yes, and…" This affirms what the speaker said and lets you extend the discussion to explore an area where you don't agree.

As with, "yes, I agree," there are several useful variations you can use to affirm and extend:

- Yes, and let's explore that more
- Yes, and let's dive in a little deeper
- Yes, and let's double-click into that

When you want to affirm and extend, phrase the request as a statement instead of a question. A question invites others to stop the conversation exactly when you want to dive in a little deeper.

No buts

These strategies rely on affirmation to cement trust between team members. In keeping with our focus on affirmation, avoid the word "but." "But" signals disagreement, the opposite of affirmation. Instead of saying "but," create the habit of saying "yes, and" or "and," or if you must be contrary, just start a new sentence. Never say "but."

Talk to everyone in the Check

Good collaboration includes everyone, so make sure you ask each participant for feedback during the Check. The shared discussion should raise any and all issues the team has with the item being checked. Toward the end of the Check, ask the room if there is any other feedback or anything missed.

If anyone has been too quiet, ask them directly. If someone's buried in their laptop, address them by name. You want explicit assent from everyone in the room that you've discussed all feedback for now. Verbal alignment now will reduce churn later.

Reassure everyone that this isn't the last word and explain how to provide additional feedback they identify later. Usually, this is direction to send you an email or submit an issue.

Table discussion when it's not productive

Anytime a Check stops being productive, table further discussion, so you can correct the issue and reconvene when you can use everyone's time wisely. Three chief causes discussion may not be productive include:

- You don't have the people or perspective you need

- What you want to Check is not what the audience expected

- What you want to Check is obviously wrong

If the right people didn't attend the Check, end as quickly as possible and reschedule for another time. Continuing without the people you need wastes time. Ending the meeting so you can reschedule respects everyone else's time.

You also want to reschedule if you have the wrong thing to Check. For example, if you wanted to Check high-level functionality in sketches and your team expected to Check layout and content in wireframes, you may want to end the meeting and reschedule. If you still want to Check something in the sketches, continue. However, if the team trusts you at that level and is ready to Check something with higher fidelity, end early and reschedule for when you have the right thing to Check.

Similarly, when you have the right thing but it's wrong, you should table the discussion and reschedule. For example, let's say you want to Check a user profile built from survey data. At the beginning of the meeting, you learn the survey data isn't any good. It's no use to continue to Check a bad profile. It's probably wrong. Stop the Check and come back after you've adjusted.

In each case, you want to be respectful of your team's time. Checks are an important part of collaboration, but respect, especially of people's time, is foundational. When the Check stops being productive, stop the Check.

Transform Feedback into Gold

Checks feel scary because your team might disagree with you. They might think you're wrong, that your analysis is bad, that your idea is no good. Negative feedback can feel like rejection. But on a collaborative team, it's no longer about you. On a collaborative team, feedback is all about learning. With modern products, there is no done, there's always another version, the team is always just working through another iteration, and the team only moves forward when it learns new things about its users or the product.

On collaborative teams, on modern teams, the Check is always about the team. When you think about the Check, don't think about "me," think about "we."

MOVE FROM "ME" TO "WE"

In "Teaching Smart People How to Learn,"[1] Chris Argyris introduces the concept of a "defensive learner." Argyris argues that many people approach feedback from the perspective of a defensive learner. When defensive learners receive feedback, they respond with four strategies:

- To remain in control
- To maximize "winning" and minimize "losing"
- To suppress negative feelings
- To define clear objectives and evaluate whether or not they achieved those objectives

Defensive learners spend more effort avoiding the embarrassment or threat of being wrong or feeling incompetent than the effort they spend on learning. As Argyris explains, "defensive reasoning encourages individuals to keep private the premises, inferences, and conclusions that shape their behavior and to avoid testing them in a truly independent, objective fashion."

If you or your teammates approach the product process from a defensive position, you will learn less because you Check less. You're less likely to Check underlying assumptions that drive your decisions and analysis.

In contrast, move from defensive learning to collaborative learning. Collaborative learners don't think of themselves as owners of decisions and ideas. In contrast, they share control and ownership of ideas and decisions with the entire team. Rather than looking to "win" discussions or beat everyone else's ideas, collaborative learners focus on how the team can learn more, faster. Instead of trying to avoid negative feedback, collaborative learners trust their team's good intentions and don't take criticism as personal attacks (Table 21-3).

---

1 Argyris, Chris. "Teaching Smart People How to Learn." *Harvard Business Review*, May–June, 1991.

Instead of thinking about yourself, focus on the team. What ideas can the team Check? What can the team learn? What questions does the team need to answer?

TABLE 21-3. How defensive learners compare to collaborative learners

DEFENSIVE LEARNERS FOCUS ON "ME"	COLLABORATIVE LEARNERS FOCUS ON "WE"
Keep control	Share control with the team
Maximize "winning"	Focus on learning
Reduce negative feelings	Trust your team

SEPARATE YOURSELF FROM THE WORK

You are not your work. The feedback isn't about you. When you separate yourself from the work, you take the biggest step away from defensive learning and toward collaborative learning. If the work reflects you, then more negative feedback risks more embarrassment and rejection. If the work represents the team, then feedback helps you and the team learn, and the more feedback you generate, the more the team learns.

In many ways, when you move toward collaborative learning, you remove the risk of failure. Every hypothesis, idea, and design becomes one more test on the way to the perfect product. Don't fear being wrong or failing. As long as you learn, you've successfully tested the hypothesis.

IGNORE JERKS

Every once in a while, you meet someone who doesn't understand basic human decency. Maybe they missed breakfast. Maybe someone sucked out their soul and crushed their heart and kicked them in the shin. The reason doesn't really matter. They act like a jerk and there's no excuse.

First, don't cringe or flinch. When someone provides feedback in the rudest way possible, lean in. Remember, you are not the work, and this is about how much the team can learn. There's nothing to fear. The jerk leads with bluster. Ask questions to see what's behind the bluster.

If you disagree, ask why until you identify the root cause behind the feedback. If you disagree with the root cause, find some way to discuss that disagreement. If you agree with root cause, then find a solution you both agree on. When you agree, explicitly state you agree, clearly collect the feedback, and clarify how you'll make the change.

Most importantly, don't respond in kind. Jerks excel at hurting your feelings, even when you've separated yourself from the work. That's the definition of a jerk. Even though they hurt your feelings, stay calm, compose yourself, and lean into the bluster to find the learning that's hiding there.

Most people are so put off by jerks, they never learn anything. Imagine the moral victory when you help the team learn in even the worst circumstances.

Stick the Finish

So far in the Check, you've carefully framed the feedback you want, carefully discussed the feedback, and clearly collected the feedback. In the Finish, restate everything one more time. Summarize the Check and explain what happens next.

To summarize the Check, repeat what you reviewed, restate the question or questions you discussed, and reiterate the feedback the team collected. By quickly reviewing everything that just happened, you reinforce what everyone discussed, that everyone participated, and that everyone agreed to the feedback. The review makes the collaboration explicit, concrete, and real.

Second, if anyone disagrees with any of the feedback or your recollection of events, the finish provides one more opportunity for them to speak up and provide additional perspective.

After summarizing the Check, share what happens next. What will you do with the feedback? How will they know how you applied the feedback? Explain how you will use the feedback, and when and if they can see any outcomes, the next version, or what it turns into.

And to really stick the finish, type the review and the next steps and email everyone after the meeting. The follow-up email is the cherry on top.

Keep the Faith

In "The Emperor's New Clothes," a line manager hires two consultants to design a great new wearable product. When the manager demos the product to other managers in the organization, everyone laughs. Clearly, the consultants delivered vaporware and the engagement wasted time and money.

When you Check analysis, models, and ideas with your team, sometimes you're the emperor in the fancy new clothes, and sometimes you're the peasants laughing at them. The Check is the important step where you see if everyone else can see the same awesome that you can see. With my teams, I do what I call "crazy checks" where I show something rough and kind of out there to see if I'm onto something or if I'm crazy. Sometimes I'm onto something, and sometimes I'm crazy.

And sometimes, I'm one of those tailors sewing something awesome that no one else can see yet. Sometimes, your team, or the organization, or your customers just won't get it. Regardless of how much you try to explain the vision, sometimes you won't get any traction. When this happens, keep the faith.

Have faith in your idea and keep it around for another day when it might make more sense. Or keep the faith in the Check and abandon the idea that the team dismisses. Regardless of where you land, keep faith in Think-Make-Check. Every turn through the process turns the gears on the experience machine. Every turn reveals new opportunities to improve the product, your team's process, and how your organization delivers experiences. Turn by turn through Think-Make-Check, your organization will build better products, and you're going to help them do it.

[Index]

documentation
for formal checks, 366–367
for project goals and vision, 109–114
for user models, 199–224
drivers (strategy element)
about, 57
context that frames strategy, 61–62
explaining why to change, 58–59
duration of product use, 175

E

expectations
identifying, 161–163
setting, 42, 357–358
expected gains, 162–163
experience maps, 229, 255–258
explicit information, 355
exploration mode (projects), 65–66
extended users, 134, 142–145

F

facilitation stage (Frame-Facilitate-Finish model)
about, 39–40, 45
Analyze step, 46–47, 49–50
checks in, 368–372
Close step, 46–47, 51
Open step, 46–48
Synthesize step, 46–47, 49–51
Fairness (SCARF model), 35–36
features, discussing user goals/JTBD instead of, 124
feedback
capturing, 369–370
respecting, 34–35
transforming into gold, 372–375
fidelity
about, 11, 13
audience factor in. *See* audience (fidelity factor)
in communication, 17–21
controlling, 14–15
distance factor in, 13, 17, 20–21, 358
Frame-Facilitate-Finish model and, 53
interaction models, 23–24

interface models and, 23–24, 341–353
iteration and, 22–23, 350–351
reach factor in, 14, 17, 19, 358
shared understanding and, 27, 28
systems models and, 23–24
time factor in, 13, 17–18, 358
user models and, 23–24, 126–127
finish/outcome stage (Frame-Facilitate-Finish model)
checks in, 362–364
collaboration and, 39–40, 43–45
sticking to, 375
5 Why's technique, 154–156
formal collaboration, 52
form versus function, 284
4-corners method
about, 317–318
identifying interface content, 303–313
identifying interface functionality, 312–316
identifying interface user, 290–294
identifying next step, 297–300
identifying previous step, 300–303
identifying user's task, 294–297
making accessible, 333
mockups and, 316–317
prototypes and, 316–317
usage overview, 287–290
wireframes and, 316–317
framed sketching, 331
Frame-Facilitate-Finish model
checks in, 362–372
facilitation component in, 39–40, 45–51
finish/outcome component in, 39–40, 43–45
frame component in, 39–43
frame stage (Frame-Facilitate-Finish model), 39–43, 364–368
framing in future-state envisioning, 90
Fraser, Janice, 4
frequency of product use, 175
functional fidelity, 343–344, 348–350, 352–353
functionality
about, 279, 281–282
analyzing preferences, 177–178

About the Author

Austin Govella has helped the world's largest and smallest organizations build better products and services for over 20 years. Austin combines UX with agile and shares his experience at conferences like SXSW, Agile, Big Design, and others.

He leads Experience Design at Avanade's Houston studio, where he helps cross-functional teams design and develop websites, workplace tools, and mobile apps. His experience includes product teams, consulting, B2B, B2C, and the nonprofit sector. He cowrote *Information Architecture: Blueprints for the Web* and blogs at *https://agux.co.*

Colophon

The animals on the cover of *Collaborative Product Design* are white-handed gibbons (*Hylobates lar*), also called lar gibbons. These primates reside in the rainforests of Southeastern Asian countries such as Malaysia, Thailand, Indonesia, Laos, and Myanmar. They have extremely long arms and fingers, which help them move swiftly from branch to branch (known as brachiation)—most of their time is spent in the trees. When gibbons do come to the ground, they walk upright with their arms above their heads for balance.

White-handed gibbons have thick fur varying in color from black to light brown, with a ring of white hair around a dark face. As suggested by their name, the top of their hands is covered with white fur. The palms are hairless to provide a firm grip in the trees. This species grows to be 1.5–2 feet tall and weighs between 10–20 pounds. The gibbon's diet is largely made of up fruit and leaves, though it supplements this with insects, flowers, and eggs. In the wild, its lifespan is 25–30 years.

These animals live in mating pairs (along with juvenile offspring), and mark their family's territory by singing a duet every morning known as a "great call." Each gibbon subspecies uses a basic call of short hoots, which then moves into more complex and unique variations for each pair. These songs are also used to communicate the presence of predators.

White-handed gibbons are an endangered species. They are sometimes hunted for meat, but the largest threat they face is habitat loss as forest is cleared for new construction, logging, or agricultural use.

The cover image is a color illustration by Karen Montgomery, based on a black and white engraving from *Natural History of Animals*. The cover fonts are Gilroy Semibold and Guardian Sans. The text font is Scala; and the heading font is Gotham.